The North Side of Down

A True Story of Two Sisters

By Nancy J. Bailey and Amanda Bailey

The North Side of Down

By Nancy J. Bailey and Amanda Bailey

Copyright 2014 Nancy J. Bailey

Cover art by Nancy J. Bailey

Reviews

"What makes this memoir stand above all others is the unparalleled opportunity to read Amanda's wise and amazing journal entries, which introduce each chapter. Amanda, born with Down's Syndrome, cultivates a wit and genius that surprises and delights. Her wisdom places her at the heart and center of the Bailey clan, and her relationship with her sister Nancy glows from the pages."

-Sue Harrison, Author, "Mother Earth, Father Sky"

"I love this book! Nancy has a great writing style & ability to show the reader, not just tell. I loved the raw emotions... she's not afraid to show the negative sides of people, including herself. I also loved the parts Amanda wrote herself & was pleasantly surprised at how eloquent she is."

-Andrea Ott-Dahl, Delaney Ott-Dahl Foundation

"....Describes in unrelenting detail both the dissolution of a family and the bonding of sisters... Nancy's younger sister, Amanda, while intellectually disabled, comes to us in her sister's words as irrepressible, funny, and wise in her acute readings of others. But this is also a love story and a contemporary illustration of just how far loyalty and strength can carry two women."

-Mike Wall, "Every Good Morning"

"...Powerfully written from beginning to end and it was impossible to put down once I started reading it."

-Barb Scott

Acknowledgments

This book would never have been possible without the support of our brother Ted and sister-in-law Ruthie. Thank you guys. We love you.

Nancy needs to thank her friends who have stood by her through the most difficult years of my life. Claire, you have the enviable ability to make someone feel wanted – to always be there no matter what. You are the finest example of a friend.

Thank you Steve and Myrri for offering me a "home base", and for traveling all over the state and for stepping up to the plate at a moment's notice.

Thank you Kathleen Drzewiecki for taking in my horses in the middle of winter, for going out in the cold and giving them hay, for being there on the worst of days when your own world was collapsing around you.

Thank you Tabitha Rawson, and to my silly cousin John Lowe and his beautiful wife Esther for helping get Clifford and Trudy settled in.

Thank you Cindy Dunn for giving me a space and for a listening ear.

Thank you Jane Doty for your warmth and humanity and for sharing your home.

Thank you Paul and Janny for always being there.

Thank you Mike Wall for your heart, and your tremendous ability to offer comfort and inspiration from afar… And for performing the unenviable task of proof reading!

Thanks to Jo Hill for your kindness.

Thank you to all the citizens of DeTour Village and Drummond Island who saw what was happening and who always seemed to step in with a word of comfort when I most needed it: Most notably Desi, Cheryl, Jackie, Lisa, Candis, and Janet.

Thank you Annie Marie for always lending an ear and for years of supporting my artistic endeavors.

Thank you Linda for coming into my life at exactly the right time. What a gift you are.

Thank you to my poor dogs: Ms. Rip, Terrible Til, Este, Jack and Havoc, who endured an unsettled lifestyle, but were always happy anyway. Thank you gentle Trudy, for your wonderful steady ways and your patience. And thank you, thank you, dear Clifford, for grieving with me, for making me laugh, for making Dad laugh, for your endless stream of surprises and your willingness to participate in anything and everything. You have carried me farther than I ever imagined.

Chapter One

About Boyfriends – Amanda

I don't want to talk very much about my boyfriends. It is too personal.

How I could put this? Red was my schoolmate. He has red hair and a mustache. He is a few years older than me. He has Down's Syndrome. He asked Mom's permission to get engaged. He said, 'Elaine, I'd like to marry your daughter.' He followed up in school, in the classroom, when he got down on one knee and proposed. I said 'yes.' But I thought it was all a joke.

Then the whole engagement thing went out of control. I stayed the night at Red's house so we could travel to Special Olympics together. I stayed in his room but we were in bunk beds. He was like a roommate. Red's mother set us up with a special romantic breakfast. Actually I think they both did it. It was set up in their kitchen and we had Wheaties® by candlelight. Toast was included. We went to the Special Olympics after that, but I let the romance fizzle out. He was a great person but he was too old for me and too quiet.

Todd was five years younger than I was. He was a basketball star and more my type. His nickname was, 'Long Shot.' He would pass the ball to me, yelling, 'Here Manda!' and I caught it and shot it in. I couldn't run because of my bad knees, so I would stand under the basket, and Todd would get the ball to me. He moved down to St. Clair when we were still in school. He did come to my graduation, but I haven't seen him in years.

About Amanda - Nancy

"I hope they didn't go through my Drummond Island room," Amanda said. She was sipping her cola, looking up at me over the straw, her navy almond-shaped eyes snapping with intelligence.

"Yes. They did. But I saved all the stuff."

"You did? Like Mom and Dad's picture?"

"Yes."

"What about the map?"

"Yep."

"How about my bed I always sleep in?"

"Yes. Still have it."

"How about your big jacuzzi?"

"No."

"Oh." Her expression did not change. She was mulling it over. She had loved the Jacuzzi tub. She was little enough to actually swim in it, turning somersaults, her tiny feet waving in the air, her fat bottom rolling gracefully, her white bald head popping out of the water with a toothy beluga smile. Dad had taught her to swim in Lake Huron when she was small. She floated effortlessly, her skill extending to the pool at her high school, and from there on to Special Olympics.

Her social life had ended after graduation, when she was 26. With school over, she retreated to her upstairs nook in Mom and Dad's house with her TV, in the remote little town on the tip of the crooked peninsula. I knew she missed her friends. She'd had a lively love triangle with two suitors, Todd and Red. There was a third boy, Satch, tall and lumpy and perpetually adolescent. He grabbed the breasts and crotches of his female classmates. He was regarded by them with a sort of fascinated, disgusted awe. They loved to hate him.

Sex was a constant topic of discussion in school, but never at home. When Amanda was in her early twenties, Dad decided to have her tubes tied, as a precautionary measure. As far as we knew, she wasn't sexually active, but he was afraid something might happen. Having Amanda consent to the surgery required going before a judge. She had to assure him that this had been her decision.

"Kids are a pain!" she roared, and the gavel came down while the judge laughed.

She recovered almost effortlessly from the surgery. From time to time, whenever the subject of my own procreation came up, she would nudge me and whisper, "Get your tubes tied."

I was never sure if this meant I should just follow her example, like the time I drew lines on my knees with a magic marker, to match the scars left by her surgeries. But her intimation about my sterilization made me a little uncomfortable. Finally, I asked her. "Why? Why should I get my tubes tied? Don't you think I would be a good mother?"

"Yes," she said. "You're a great mother! To dogs and horses!"

"Shut up!" I roared.

"You shut up!" she said.

She was sitting now, facing me across the table, trying to read my expression. She watched me constantly. We would be driving and she'd be sitting in the passenger seat, and rather than looking out the window, she would be gazing over at me. It was almost as if she was studying my thoughts, examining each fragmented memory with a gentle sort of fascination. Her eyes were always soft and interested.

"I'm sorry about the jacuzzi tub," I said. "We will have another one someday. And I am sorry about your Drummond Island Room."

"Oh, it's okay."

It wasn't okay. .She had unquestioning faith in me, and I was not measuring up. For years I had provided Amanda with her summer home away from home, and now it was gone. I'd had to make the same apology to my two horses, who had lost their roomy stalls and grassy, rolling pastures. They were now languishing in a muddy, stump-studded space, overcrowded with ponies in Northern Michigan, taken in by the only friend who could make room for them.

I had handled the move with the same sort of vision I used on the divorce; a blank, flat opacity. I had lived on the farm for fifteen years. My trees were still young, stretching upward, nourished by the bones of various beloved dogs and cats, and a goat named Joe. The wild rose bush, that began as just a half dozen twigs my mother had given me, now flourished by the garage door. It spread there, covered in pink petals and humming bumble bees, perfuming the light wind. Perhaps in some sort of physical statement, my Achilles tendon had burst just weeks prior to the move. The resulting lameness, the foot flopping uselessly with no lift or power, made it impossible to carry anything heavy. Friends came with pickup trucks, sorting through the boxes, questioning what went where, lifting and stacking and hauling my life away. They joked and laughed, avoiding the inevitable, making light of the enormity of it. There was nothing else to do. I had taken the last load and driven down the hill away from my warm and sprawling home, forcing myself to not look back.

"Are you okay?" Amanda said. She still was sitting there with her bent straw, scrutinizing my expression.

"Yes. Vickie and Janny will be here soon. Let's get a pizza."

It was September 24, 2010, Amanda's fortieth birthday. We were celebrating with dinner and a movie. The closest movie theatre was in "the Soo", Sault Ste Marie, an hour away from Amanda's home.

"Tell me something about when I was a baby," Amanda coaxed.

I smiled. "I will never forget those days."

I thought of Dad's announcement to us all, on that day, forty years before. "Your new little sister is a Mongoloid."

His tone was somber and he watched us carefully for a reaction. He had sat us all down, all seven of us, so that we could

15

understand the depth of this new development. We lined up with our sun-tanned faces serious and all eyes in various shades of blue, widening with the new unknown responsibility. The baby, Dad explained, was going to show up with slanted eyes and a large, protruding, pointed tongue.

Our second oldest brother, Theil, already at 18 an ever-calming presence, nodded his head and said, "Dad, you and Mom will never have to worry about her. I'll take care of her."

At eight years old, I took this all very seriously. From Dad's description, the baby sounded like some sort of freak. But my heart immediately went out to her.

Then she arrived. She didn't look like a freak. She was a pink and golden infant with perfect skin and tiny, plump clenched fists. It had been five years since we'd had a baby in the house, and when this one opened her eyes, I saw they were navy blue, so dark that the pupils were indiscernible. I fell immediately, violently in love. I had never seen a baby more beautiful. I even loved her name: Amanda Christina Bowman Bailey. Maybe it was my age, or perhaps it was the fact that she was different from other babies, but my tender mothering instinct kicked in. This became my baby. I dressed her. I fed her. I changed her. I held and talked to her for hours. I sat by the crib and watched her sleep.

Well into her forties by that time, Mom hadn't wanted another baby. She had actually undergone surgery for a tubal ligation before getting pregnant for Amanda, but the doctor had tied off a blood vessel instead. It was an error that was ripe for a major lawsuit, but my parents never pursued it.

I was too young to understand depression. I just knew that Mom was sleeping an inordinate amount of the time, which gave me the freedom – as well as the responsibility - to mother the baby. Besides Amanda, I had three sisters. All of them had names beginning with the letter, "R". So I called them, "the R's." R1 was Raven, the oldest girl, an industrious sort with a strong mothering drive and a cleaning compulsion. She left for college by the time Amanda was 2 years old. R2 was Rose, a tomboy on the basketball team and always bicycling with her friends, and in general too busy to nurture a baby.

As Amanda grew, and eventually learned to stand, Dad would prop her upright on his legs and rock her, back and forward. The faster he rocked, the more she liked it. The chair creaked loudly in time and he sang to her in his booming voice while they rocked.

"Rock a bye and don't you cry, and we'll go up to Granny's,

Upon the hill, behind the mill, and see the little lambies."

The rocking made the baby strong, and she learned to hold her head up and walk and then run. She loved patty-cake, especially the "pick it" part. She loved the feel of scratching on her palm. When she would sit with one of us and watch TV, she would grab our fingers and force them against her palm. "Pick!" she ordered, and we would sit there scratching absently. Forty years later my brother Marcus and I both have the impulse to start scratching the palm of her hand if we hold it for any length of time.

In time I learned that Mongoloid was no longer the politically correct term for Amanda's genetic anomaly. It was called, "Down's syndrome," named after Dr. John Langdon Down, who fully described

17

the syndrome in 1866. Later, it became commonly called Down syndrome, dropping the apostrophe and "s". But I always preferred to spell it in the possessive form. To me, calling it "Down" could be misinterpreted as something negative: indicating that people with an extra chromosome were somehow lower or lesser than the rest of us. To say, "Down's" simply meant a syndrome had been discovered. The chromosome could be credited to someone. To me, that sounded much better, more like, "Nim's Island" or, "Hershey's Chocolate."

We lived in the far north, in a tiny, hardscrabble village perching on the rocky eastern tip of Michigan's Upper Peninsula, fondly known as the U.P., where gulls screamed overhead and freighters chugged their way along the narrow channel from Lake Huron to Lake Superior. It was called DeTour, so named, some said, because it was miles out of the way of anywhere else. Some claimed that the capital "T" was inserted into the name to thwart mail from being misdirected to Detroit. Others said that the name was derived from two French words, meaning, "The Turn." Ships heading southbound had to turn east to Detroit or west to the Straits of Mackinac. DeTour was a small village boasting one gas station and a single yellow blinking traffic light. The entire school, K through 12, took up one building and was filled by children of all ages from the nearest five communities. Many of the locals spoke with a thick "Yooper" accent, which had apparently descended from the Nordic dialect of early settlers from Finland and Sweden. "Yoo godda learn to talk da right way, eh?"

Questions were abbreviated with the word, "Eh?" My mother had insisted on the correct pronunciation of words, so our accent was softer, but we all carried the habitual, "Eh?" without realizing it.

By the time Amanda was four years old, our older four siblings had moved out. That left the youngest group of kids to grow up with Amanda: Me, brother Marcus, and then Rowena, the third R.

R3 seemed perpetually angry. She fought constantly with her siblings, especially Marcus. My childhood memories echo with the sounds of her screaming. During one altercation she bolted into the kitchen, grabbed a big butcher knife and ran up the stairs. "I'm going to kill myself!"

I was sitting with Amanda on the couch and just rolled my eyes. But her action, designed to get Marcus's attention, had worked. He paced back and forth. "What is she doing up there?" He started up the stairs.

"Don't do it," I said.

He came back down, but was popping his fist into the palm of his other hand. His eyes were wild. Finally, we heard a scream and then a thud. Marcus went shooting up the stairs. A minute later he came down with a sheepish look. "She was curled up in the fetal position on the floor, holding this against her stomach."

He held up his fist and unfurled a long red sock.

Amanda grew up in the midst of constant racket: a blaring TV, slamming doors and belligerent yelling. She took it all with aplomb, managing to maintain a happy serenity. I escaped by hiding in my room, drawing pictures of horses and writing hundreds of pages of stories about them on lined notebook paper. I would hear the familiar "thunk, thunk," of Amanda's hands and hard shoes climbing up the stairs, and her voice calling my name. "Ceecee!" She would climb up on my bed, content to just sit there with me while I worked on my current project. Eventually my parents decided that she shouldn't climb stairs because it was dangerous. They put a baby gate at the base of the stairs. It wasn't long before she learned how to work the latch and swing it open. One day the stairs had a fresh coat of white paint on the banister, and around the cheap brown vinyl tile on each step. Amanda decided to climb up and try to find me anyway. There were white hand and foot prints that told the story; three steps up and then a swipe on the fourth where someone had grabbed her. The prints stayed there until the house was sold some 15 years later.

Dad served on the school board and when Amanda was six years old, she was inducted into kindergarten with some fifteen other children her age. Every day, I walked her to school, holding her pudgy hand the entire mile. She would dawdle happily, chattering and asking questions. I was in high school by that time and I always had to go to the principal's office and ask for a late slip. Mr. Grey, the principal scared the crap out of me. He was a big round man with a puffing red face and an angry voice. He would stomp down the hallway amid the gauntlet of teenagers, yelling, "Git ta class!" The worst part about him was his fake hand. It was hidden inside a black leather glove, frozen into position like a mannequin's. I'd heard that he lost the hand when a grenade exploded in his fist during the war. No one knew what was really under the glove. It had become a trademark, like Darth Vader's mask. I would walk trembling into his office, edging around the corner and he would be sitting at his desk, with the Glove resting on top of some papers. He'd look up and say, "Late again?" I would nod my head. "Don't you have an alarm clock?" he said gruffly.

I understood that this was his attempt to tease me. He knew my dad and he knew Amanda. He would reach for a pad of paper with his good hand, and scrawl a few words on it and then hand it to me. I would take it, whisper "thanks", and flee.

Once past that daily meeting, being late for class didn't bother me. I was a terrible introvert, encumbered by crippling shyness, and I would do anything to avoid the crushing social obligation that was school. Besides, the first hour was gym. The only thing worse than ducking the onslaught of round, red, bouncing missiles in dodge ball, was the humiliation of being picked last for every team, every time.

Amanda and I took our time getting to school, and the morning walk became our own pleasant little ritual. In the afternoon I would rush straight home to watch Grizzly Adams reruns with her while our mother napped. We would sing the theme song and I would help her practice pronouncing her words. "Ceecee," she called me.

"Nannn-see," I would say, exaggerating my lip movements.

"Ceecee," she repeated dutifully.

Amanda's hair fell in golden ringlets around her pink face. Combined with her navy eyes, this gave her an exceptionally angelic look that belied her bouts of stubbornness. Once she made up her mind to sit down, we couldn't move her. She would turn to rubber. We would grab her rib cage and try to pick her up, and she would slide limply out of our hands like jelly. She threw a tantrum one afternoon when trying to follow me to the post office in her pajamas. "Ceecee! Wait!"

21

I was mortified. She was waddling down the street behind me in a sagging pink bunny suit, the slippered feet blackened and flopping as she shuffled along. "Amanda!" I shrieked. "You get home right now!"

Her face clouded. She folded her arms and plopped down on her behind, right in the middle of the street. I ran over to her. "Get up!" I grabbed her and she started screaming, arms flailing as she squirted from my grasp and slid backwards onto the asphalt.

To make the situation even more awful, Craig Fox was watching us from the front step of the grocery store. He was one of the coolest guys in school, as well as one of Marcus's best friends. I looked up and to my horror, he was approaching us. His gaze was empathetic behind his wire-rimmed lenses as he bent over the sobbing angel. "Aw, what's the matter, honey?" He offered his hand, and tearfully she accepted. She got up and waddled home with him while I glared at the back of her head.

Unfortunately, when it came to Amanda's tantrums, the kindergarten teacher exhibited even less patience than I did. Amanda came home with bruises on her arms where the teacher had pinched her black and blue. "She pulled my hair," Amanda said to Dad. There was a volatile school board meeting that evening. He nearly came to blows with the superintendent. After that, Amanda was withdrawn from the mainstream program and was bussed to a Special Education class in Rudyard some forty miles away.

When Amanda hit puberty, her voice deepened and she spoke in hills and valleys that were accompanied by a chortle or squeak, like a combination of Scooby-Doo and Yoda. She began to have physical problems, as is the way of many people with Down's syndrome. She developed alopecia, a condition that caused her hair to fall out and her toenails to thicken into little clubs. She took to wearing a wig that perched crookedly on her egg-white head, a disheveled mop above the bright, intelligent almond eyes. She had one kneecap that she could slide out and back in at will, with a confident "pop". Marcus and I used to make her do it, to freak out other kids in the neighborhood. As she grew, her knees became more and more wobbly and she would tumble and fall, usually landing with a soft grunt and an angry glare. She would get right back up again. "I'm fine. I'm fine," waving her chubby hands dismissively. She had surgery on both knees, the long scars remaining on her legs forever like fleshy rick-rack crosses. Her reluctance to move and her love for mayonnaise sandwiches, unfortunately indulged by all of us, caused her to pack on weight.

Like the rest of the sibs, I grew up and moved away, but I returned to Michigan in 1989. I was astonished by the way Mom catered to Amanda. Snickers bars were a staple for the two of them. They were eating buddies. Mom was in an eternal search for comfort, and it usually involved food. She had lost her second child, a son, to a horrible condition called hemorrhagic perphora, causing his blood vessels to become inflamed and then burst. He died on the way to the hospital. He had been two years old.

Mom had never quite recovered from the tragedy, even though it happened in the early 1950's and she had gone on to have seven more children. I didn't know if this was what had made her so angry. She was resistant to any physical activity. She would sit with her back to the refrigerator, and say, "Get me some ketchup!" Dad would jump up and get it. Or she would say, "Amanda, get me my glasses." Amanda would sigh, and scowl, but Dad would chime in with, "You do as your mother says, now!" Amanda would get up, swinging her wide hips through the narrow spaces in the cluttered house, looking for the glasses.

My ex-husband had described Mom as, "A two-year-old with power."

One autumn when Theil was visiting from Arizona, Mom had a tremendous fight with Dad. They screamed and yelled at each other, and Dad left and went to stay in his sanctuary, a trailer on the Island. Marcus and Theil and I took a trip over there to visit with him. He was a little down, but happy to see us. "Your mother is an intelligent woman," he said. He was sitting at the table in the camper, enjoying a grilled cheese sandwich with onions. He cracked open a beer. "She is a good woman."

When we got home later that evening, Mom was sitting at the kitchen table with an open bottle of wine. Mom didn't drink very much so it was a bit of visual shock, which I am sure she had intended. She looked up at the three of us. "Well, there they are, the two prodigal sons and the prodigal daughter! Well, what did the old son of a bitch have to say?"

From that point on, Theil and Marcus and I secretly referred to ourselves as, "The Prodigals." We laughed about it, but it cemented our bond for years afterward. We were P1, P2 and P3, in chronological birth order.

Living with Mom 24-7 was not ideal for Amanda. I managed to spirit her away every summer for several weeks, when she would come and stay at my house. We started an exercise regimen. We would take half hour walks every morning when she got up. There was an art to convincing her to go. It involved complaining along with her. "I know! I hate this! It sucks. My butt hurts. I want to go back to bed."

We would shuffle along the wooded gravel road near my house, both complaining the entire way. When she grew stronger, I would say, "Slow down!" and she would burst into a power walk, laughing hysterically while I lagged behind and yelled at her. "Wait! Wait up! You're so mean!"

She would pause, looking back with her dark eyes flashing. "How's your butt now?"

One day, we took R3 with us. That turned out to be a mistake. Her coaxing techniques were akin to a drill sergeant. "Come on, Amanda, move your fat ass!"

It didn't help matters when rain sprinkled down on us that day. "Oh great! Now it's raining! Come on Amanda get a move on!"

We never invited her after that.

Amanda still refers back to that walk in the rain. "She called me Fat Ass!" R3 herself was pushing the pounds, her rounded cheeks puffing with every verbal barrage she spouted. The hypocrisy wasn't lost on Amanda.

Amanda didn't take walks for cash. She took walks to earn the occasional cheeseburger and a cola. Each summer, during her weeks with me, the weight fell off, and we'd go shopping for new school clothes for her. When she went back home, she would gain it all back and resume her habits of TV and Snickers bars.

They were the trio, Mom, Dad and Amanda, maintaining our rickety home base and immersed in their own hilarity and dysfunction until Amanda was a forty-ish Buddha, and my parents both well into their eighties. Over the years, various people would ask us, "When your parents are gone, what will happen to Amanda?"

There was never an easy answer. Amanda was adept socially, but could not drive a car, count out correct change, or live by herself. We occasionally referred back to Theil's guardianship promise, but he was Arizona, which felt like another continent. The potential for disaster loomed as my parents aged and the inevitable closed in. Still, they refused to discuss it realistically, draw up documents or make any real plans. It's not that they didn't talk about death. Mom especially loved the topic. "I want to have two coffins, buried side by side, with a hole in each, so our hands will stick out and we can hold hands throughout eternity."

"Holes in the body box? Ugh, Mom." Amanda slapped her hand to her forehead and shook her bald head.

"What about you, Amanda?" I had asked.

"You can just prop me up beside the jukebox," she had said.

Amanda loved to make jokes like that. But my parents' disregard for the eventuality of their demise remained like a hole that was never filled; the proverbial white elephant in the room. The three of them agreed that Theil would be Amanda's guardian, and that seemed to be as far as the plan ever went.

There were many stories about Amanda's childhood. Her birthdays came and went, most of them just like this one, with me showing up to take her out for a movie, pizza and cake. She was still waiting patiently, looking at me from across the table.

I took a sip of my cola and then said, "You were a really bad singer."

She screeched with laughter. "Oh, come on! I wasn't that bad."

"Oh yes. Yes you were. It was painful to listen to you. And you sang loud. You used to sing along with the Lawrence Welk show."

She snorted. "I still do that. With the reruns. Mom and Dad do, too."

"I'm sorry."

She laughed.

Not long after that, my two friends Vickie and Janny arrived. The table filled up with cards and gift bags and bright, wrinkled tissue.

The four of us had just placed our order, when in marched my oldest sister, R1. She was wearing a crushed polyester business suit in a flat grey color. It made a dry swishing sound as she approached. A silver cross dangled crookedly over her pointed collar. A shard of hair poked out from over her glasses, bobbing as she moved, glinting and probing the air like an antennae on a preying mantis. She shoved herself into the booth beside me. Her eyes flicked briefly across my friends' faces. She turned to me.

27

"I just spent $60.00 on groceries for Mom and Dad."

"Sorry I can't chip in," I said. Her erect strand of hair was still waving and pointing at me. "You have a hair-"

"Well, it would be nice if someone could help out." She shifted in her seat and the silver cross flickered sadly in its askew position.

I sighed. "Raven, I just lost two major publishing deals that I had invested my entire retirement in. I lost my farm. I am losing my car. Everything is gone. I can't afford to pay my bills. There are no jobs. I would file bankruptcy if I could afford that. I can't feed myself right now let alone anyone else."

"There are other things you can do to help. I want to get in that crawl space upstairs but there is some heavy furniture in front of it. That all needs to be cleaned out."

"Yes, it sure does."

"Well, I'm going to tackle that pretty soon. Those things are going to require some heavy lifting that I can't do by myself."

"I can't lift anything. I told you I tore my Achilles tendon just three weeks ago. I can hardly even walk right now."

"Well, maybe there is something else you can do like sort through some of those boxes."

"Are Mom and Dad even aware that you are planning this?"

"Well, you know they will sit in the middle of that mess forever."

"Maybe that's how they like it."

Amanda was silent. My friends stared at us from across the booth. Their awkwardness rolled out from their expressions like a big sad cloud.

But R1 was oblivious to them. Her mind was on her mission. She was confident in her goals. She had acquired a master's degree in social work several years prior, forsaking her BS in anthropology. She and her husband were both devout Christians. In a statement about their faith, they had burned her school books about the studies of early man. This act had disgusted my father. An avid reader, he had deemed it, "Destruction of knowledge." Later, R1 had raised four kids on her own, after her husband had left them all when the youngest was barely out of diapers. As the kids grew, she had immersed herself in legal battles with her ex-husband to secure child support payments, and then she battled over custody of various grandchildren. She always acted as her own attorney, and often emerged victorious. Her life had been anything but easy. Looking at her, with her disheveled hair and limply professional demeanor, I softened.

"Ya know," I said. "I appreciate your concern. I really do. But this is Amanda's birthday. We're trying to have a little party here."

"Okay, well, I have a meeting with a friend about a job tonight anyway so I will be off."

"Why don't you stay and have some pizza and cake with us?"

"It's okay. You guys enjoy." She got up and left.

"I am glad she's gone," Amanda said immediately. "She makes me nervous."

"Ya think?" I looked at the others and we all were breathing a sigh of relief. We began to enjoy ourselves again. We were even served up a free cake with a candle on it. We sang and took pictures.

"What a great birthday party," Janny said as we stood up to leave.

"Oh, it's not over yet," Amanda said.

"It's not?"

"That's right," I agreed. "We have one more thing we need to do."

Lake Superior State University, my alma mater, stands on a hill overlooking the Soo Locks, where the freighters pass through on their route between Lakes Superior and Huron. Just behind the campus is a high hill with a sprawling view of the Locks, the bridge to Canada, and the lights of the Canadian Soo. We pulled up in the campus parking lot and stepped out, shivering, into the cold Lake Superior wind. We looked out over the roofs and treetops. Clouds of steam rolled up from the distant factories, turning into billowing purple columns in the fading light. Following our lead, the other women lined up on the soft grass. "You start," I said to Amanda. "These guys are amateurs."

With a powerful bellow, Amanda bent with the effort and her voice hurled the phrase far out over the city. "I'm FORTY!" she shouted. "I'm FORTY YEARS OLD!"

I followed suit, jumping up and down and waving my arms. "I'm FORTY-EIGHT! I'm FORTY-EIGHT! WOOHOO!"

Our friends stepped up, shouting and shrieking, yelping into the wind until their voices cracked. There we were, the four of us, braying at the top of our lungs, announcing our years on the planet, embracing the passage of time, letting our shouts carry far up into the wind and away.

Chapter 2

About Grizzly Adams – Amanda

I remember Nancy and I used to watch Grizzly Adams show. The show was about a guy living in the mountains and he had a friend named Tonto." She hesitated. "No, that's not it. The friend's name was Nakoma. They got a knife and they cut their hands and both put their hands together. They tied their hands and then cut the rope off, and became blood brothers. Nancy and I copied it. We just used pretend knives. But we became blood sisters.

She ignored me and continued talking about me in the third person. "We still sing the theme song. Nancy sang to me a lot. One time I asked Nancy, 'How do you like having a Down's Syndrome sister, Nancy?'

And she said, "I love it!"

That makes me happy.

About Mom - Nancy

Our birthday celebration ecstasy was short-lived. Some six weeks later, I came back for another visit and found Mom sitting in her easy chair, her once-luxurious silver hair now a thinning whisper, her wet blue eyes shrunken.

"Oh, Nancy's here." She looked up with a smile that was still wide and white. A bowl of red jello angled precariously on her lap. The spoon lay on the floor.

I knelt down next to her and picked it up. "You don't look so good, Mom."

"She wouldn't eat today," Dad said.

"Nothing all day?" I gently pinched the skin on her arm, pulling it up and watching it sag slowly back, like a soft peak of dough in a mixing bowl. "You're dehydrated. You are going to have to go up to the hospital in the morning."

She didn't say anything but her lips pursed together. I patted her arm. "It will be okay. They will get you fixed up." I stood up. "Are you ready, Amanda?"

"Yes!" She lurched to her feet, knocking her wig askew in the process. She lumbered toward the door where her coat was hanging. When she got out of sight around the corner, Dad nudged me, indicating Mom, sitting there in her easy chair. We exchanged a look, and I nodded my head. "Get some things packed up."

Amanda stepped back into the room with her coat on, collar folded crookedly under, her face flushed with anticipation. "Girl's Night Out!" she crowed.

DeTour was an hour from the nearest movie theatre, so our outings always required planning. It also gave us ample time to discuss everything on the way, from family gossip to politics.

"Mom is mad at Obama," Amanda said.

"I'm sure she is."

"She said it's too bad that John McCain didn't win."

"Still? That was ages ago."

"What do you think of Sarah Palin? Did you hear she has a Down's syndrome baby?"

"Yeah, that's nice for her. But would you want Mom to be president?"

"Vice president," she corrected me.

"Okay, well would you want Mom for vice president? She had a Down's syndrome baby. Does that qualify her?"

She paused for a moment. "I see your point."

We drove on in silence for a while, past the stubbled hayfields and rustling hardwoods of Chippewa County, where the weakening autumn sun flickered through the trees. Finally I said, "You do know that Mom is pretty sick, right?"

"Yes, I know." She said it with the tolerance of someone enduring a topic which has been beaten to death.

"Well, I'm not kidding. She will have to be admitted tomorrow when we take her up there. She'll be in the hospital. They will have to put her on fluids for dehydration."

She sat there looking out the window. Her expression was blank.

"Okay, I get it. Let's just try to have fun tonight." I turned on the CD player and the speakers blasted a Queen song, "Somebody to Love." It didn't take long before the pulsing music infected us. I was playing air guitar while driving with my knees. We both sang, our faces grimacing as we forced out the words, "Anybody find meeeee…"

When Amanda and I are traveling together, I often think it must look like a scene from, "Wayne's World". She kind of resembles Garth, her rumpled blonde wig bobbing as we rock and contort ourselves in time to the music. The wig had become her trademark. Around the house, she would become tired of wearing it and just leave it lying in random places. I might lift up a magazine or newspaper and there it would be, a shapeless mass of hair, like some sort of animal carcass. The visual ambush would usually cause me to jump and let out a yell, and she'd crack up laughing.

That night in the Soo turned out to be a different sort of night at the movies. Dad reported to us later that, after my comment about dehydration, he and Mom had gotten into an argument. Dad wanted to take her to the hospital on the spot. Mom refused to go.

"You want to die right here in this house!" Dad yelled at her. "And you want Amanda and me to witness that!"

He called the ambulance and they came to the house and loaded her up. She was admitted and immediately placed on an IV drip while they ran tests. All the family members who were in Michigan made the trip to come and hear the diagnosis. They included Marcus, R1 and R3.

"We don't know exactly what it is," the doctors said. "But it seems to be some form of ALS."

I turned to Marcus. "What is ALS?"

"It's Lou Gehrig's Disease," he said grimly.

"But doesn't that usually affect people who are younger?" I said. Mom was 86.

He just shook his head. None of us knew. If the doctors didn't know, we sure didn't. Mom certainly had the symptoms typical of ALS. She couldn't swallow. She couldn't get up out of a chair or even walk on her own anymore. We began discussing moving Mom to a larger facility.

Dad had ridden with Mom in the ambulance, thus leaving himself without wheels.

"Did you remember to pack her stuff?" I asked him.

"I didn't. She is going to go braless. It will be shocking." We both burst into helpless, nervous laughter.

Our family was scattered nationwide, so the email network buzzed. Theil sent a group message to family members, saying that R1 and R3 were, "Keeping abreast of the situation."

I replied, "Speaking of abreast, does anyone know Mom's bra size? We left her clothes at home."

The humor was not appreciated by the R's, who responded with a verbal flogging. "Jokes like that are not appropriate," R1 snipped.

My next update read: "Mom is still having tests done so can't be released yet, which might be okay because a) the car has no brakes and b) we forgot her clothes. So, here we are." I was tempted to add, "Mom didn't cotton to the MRI machine – she wanted to push up out of there. She really needs some support now." But I restrained myself.

Mom continued to refuse to stay in the MRI. She had to be tranquilized to endure it the next day. As soon as we had the results, Dad roared into the phone, "She has a brain!" Mom took it with good humor. Amanda did too. She was quietly observing everything, staying close and watchful.

Because the doctors suspected a neurological problem beyond what they could diagnose, they decided to move Mom to a larger facility in Petoskey, a whitewashed tourist town overlooking Lake Michigan's Little Traverse Bay.

Mom did not regain her ability to swallow. On November 16th, she was fitted with a stomach tube, and with the injection of nutrition, she immediately began looking better and showing more energy. She was released for rehabilitation to Lakeview Lutheran Manor, an assisted living center near Marcus's home in Cadillac. Since Marcus was maintaining a full time job, and I was working only sporadically training dogs, I moved into his house to help Dad and Amanda. With me, I brought my two dogs. Ms. Rip, a 5 year old Australian shepherd, and Til, a border collie puppy. Marcus's old Labrador, Sydney, seemed grateful for the company.

Mom had been pretty brave about her whole ordeal, and even maintained her sense of humor. On her first day at Lutheran Manor, a nurse asked her, "Where's the best place to take blood?" and she immediately pointed at Dad.

Each day, just as dawn was edging above the timber surrounding my brother's back yard, Dad would get up and head straight for the center. He spent his mornings playing cribbage with Mom and keeping her company, and taking calls for her from family members. Every day, the physical therapists had Mom working out in the gym, riding the bicycle for 20 minutes. The machine worked her arms and legs. Her color and energy levels were improving.

Amanda and I would arrive later, so Amanda could sleep in and have her cereal. She was a slow mover in the morning. Always scizing every opportunity to socialize my puppy, I brought Til with me to the center. He had a fuzzy white body and a silky black mask and ears, with a bright white blaze. He had soft, intelligent brown eyes. His tail wagged perpetually. I loved all dogs, but this one was special already because of his brilliance. He was learning a myriad of tricks and had a good sense of humor and fun. Like most puppies, he was irresistible and when the nurses saw me come in with him, they surrounded me. "There is a man in room 105 who would love to see this dog! He loves dogs. He has a dog picture on his wall and a dog on his bedspread."

A nurse led me to his door and I peeked in as she entered. She yelled, "Harvey, look at this!" Her voice boomed through the tiny room.

Harvey was resting back in his easy chair, an aged giant of a man. His head turned and his face did not change, but his eyes narrowed when he saw the puppy straining on the end of my leash.

"He does TRICKS!" the nurse brayed. She turned to me. "Show him the tricks."

I held up a finger and Til sat and waved one paw. I gestured and he turned one way, and then the other. He lay down and rolled over. I "shot" him and he fell dead, smacking his head on its side on the cold tile floor and lying there with his brown eye rolling up at me obligingly.

Harvey's face did not change. He said nothing, but he reached his hand down. Til got up and licked it happily, wagging until his whole body jerked with enthusiasm.

The next morning, I delivered Amanda to Mom's room and then I walked Til back up the hall, his delicate nails ticking across the tiled floor. I peeked into Harvey's room. There he sat, in his chair, just as before. He was looking at the TV but the volume was so low that I could barely hear it.

"Hello," I said. "I brought someone to see you."

His head swiveled and he looked at the dog, with that same sort of passive expression. But he put his hand down. Til ran to it and performed another wiggling greeting. Harvey had some toast on a plate on his TV stand and he took a piece, a half slice, and handed it to Til. The puppy accepted it and devoured it carefully.

Every day after that, Til went to visit Harvey and was rewarded with a stack of graham crackers, saved over from the previous day's lunch.

Routines were important at, "The Manor" as Amanda and I called it. Dad came day after day, sitting with Mom faithfully. Her official plan was to gain strength so that she could go home. She worked hard, and I continued to be surprised by her toughness. One day, she sat down and stood up on her own ten times, an exercise akin to doing squats. She was not a pleasant patient. She would complain, chiding the nurses and Dad, too. He suffered through most of it, though on occasion he would snap back at her. Amanda patiently stayed near her, sitting quietly writing letters and watching daytime TV. I tried to break up Amanda's days by taking her to movies and shopping. We picked up odds and ends for Mom. My Aussie, Ms. Rip was a nervous traveler, so she usually stayed home. But Til was resigned to life with his blanket and toys in the back seat of my car. Amanda was always willing to take a ride somewhere. The three of us logged many miles that winter.

One morning, when I was getting ready to go, Amanda was lolling around on the bed in sweats and a tank top.

"Is that what you're wearing to breakfast?" I asked.

'Yes. Let's go."

"Okay, but you're gonna be cold."

"Not really. I'm just trying to get your gloat."

"I'm aware. Although the phrase is, 'Get your goat.' It's 'goat.' Like, 'Baaa'. Not 'gloat.'"

"No it isn't."

"Yes it is." I was running a brush through my hair. I paused before the mirror, noticing my tired eyes. The nursing home vigil was taking its toll. "Do I look bad?"

"Yes," Amanda said.

I whirled to look at her. "I do? I look bad?"

"Yes, you do." An almost imperceptible grin flickered across her face.

I smiled.

"Ah." She pointed. "There it is. Good gloat."

As the weeks passed, days at the Manor stretched into monotony. My brother was busy with his financial planning business and squeezed in about an hour a day. We had no other relatives in Cadillac.

I was torn. I had two horses staying with friends, most of my things in storage, and barely any income to speak of. My car's trunk was packed with clothes and bedding and bags of dog food. I knew that I needed to be getting on with my life, but Marcus was living alone and he said, "You can stay here as long as you want."

I knew it meant that he wanted help with Dad and Amanda. Dad was beside himself with worry, Marcus was working long hours, and that left Amanda somewhere in between. Dad himself was in need of attention. It wasn't long before Marcus and I were immersed in that weird role-reversal that happens when children reach a certain age: We became the parents. Marcus would text me. "How's he doing today?"

"He's a little down. What time are you coming home?"

"I'll be there right away."

Marcus would drop everything on days like that, and to his great credit, he would come home and sit down with Dad and regale him with humor and cheerful stories.

Born just a year and a half apart, Marcus and I had the type of relationship where one look between us could speak volumes. Amidst the chronic narcissism of our mother and sisters, Marcus and I counted on each other for support. But we were very different from each other. I was an artistic introvert, preferring the company of animals over people. He liked the tavern and I loved the woods. Marcus was athletic, gregarious and popular. He was handsome and well-loved within our small community. When I was a teenager, I often joked that I was going to get a T-shirt that said, "Yes, I am Marcus's sister." But he still made time for a nerd like me. If there was anything I wanted to learn that required some type of physical ability, Marcus would teach me. He taught me to throw a baseball, shoot a basketball, ice skate and downhill ski. He taught me to ride a bike. He taught me to swing a golf club and throw a football. He helped me through some troubled times, and the reverse was true. As we both aged, he knew that I was always there for him. He would call me up in the wee hours. If the phone rang at 3 am, I would shoot upright in the bed, grab it and leave the room so I could talk without waking my then-husband. The calls continued even after my divorce. "I'm getting on my motorcycle," he would say. "I'm coming down."

"Listen to me," I would say. "Don't come here tonight. Go straight home. Come down tomorrow. Okay? Call me in the morning."

He did listen. During the years while he was raising his two boys through the throes of a troubled marriage, I worried about him constantly. I loved his sons and his wife, dearly. But the boys were grown and gone now. They had become what every parent dreams of; both sweet and well-educated young men, one a naval aviator and the other a therapist for children with autism. Marcus's wife had left. Now I worried about what the change was going to do to Marcus. Like most middle-aged men, he didn't want to live without a woman. His house, which had been his family home for close to twenty years, seemed colder and lonely now. I thought it was no surprise that he welcomed us and offered a place for Dad and Amanda, although it seemed the right thing to do. If I still had the farm, I would have done exactly the same.

Day after day, the hours at the assisted living center consisted of Mom and Dad and Amanda, little Til and me. Mom fretted about her possessions left at the house in DeTour, especially her jewelry. She had only a few pieces that were worth anything: a string of pearls left by her mother, a black Australian opal necklace my cousin Bill had given her, and an opal ring that I had given her one Christmas. And there was Amanda's favorite piece, a "Mother Ring," adorned with a string of birthstones; one for each child.

"I need my rings," Mom said. "Someone needs to bring me those rings."

The irony was that Mom had never worn any of them. They were treasures that she had squirreled away somewhere. I hadn't seen them in years.

Mom kept bringing up R1 and her cleaning fanaticism. "She called. She's up there going through my stuff."

Day after day it came up. Dad fretted, too. "They always do this when we aren't home."

I was trying to think of someone who had good rapport with the R's. I sent a note to Theil, far away in Arizona.

"Hi P1, Can you please talk to the R's about something for me? Dad has mentioned this again today. He is profoundly upset about them going into their home and rearranging things and taking stuff out of there. Mom is unhappy about it also. I realize that offspring have the need to feel useful at times like this, but both Mom and Dad feel violated and it is contributing significantly to their stress level. There's no harm in the house staying as is for now, especially when it's locked up and Postulas and Maxine and Frank are keeping an eye on things. If R & R want to help, the best thing they can do is send money (maybe help Marcus with expenses), visit and call Mom regularly and maybe buy Amanda some underwear!"

I don't know if Theil did anything about it. His physical distance was an effective shield and he tended to stay out of such disputes.

November edged into Thanksgiving. Mom wanted to go to Marcus's to be with the family. At that point, she was strong enough to get into the car with some help. It took two nurses to maneuver her. Marcus made a makeshift ramp up his front steps and we wheeled her into the house, where the big, warm family room wafted the aroma of turkey and yams and pumpkin pie.

"I can't have any turkey," Mom said to me softly. Something in my chest flew up into my throat. I realized then the irony we both faced. I could no longer walk long distances, or dance or skip or hop. Mom could not eat. We each were facing this Thanksgiving having been robbed, in my case temporarily, of our greatest joy.

I patted her arm. "I think I understand, just a little, how you must feel, Mom. We will try to get through this Thanksgiving by remembering its real purpose. Uhmm... What is that, anyway?"

To my relief, she did laugh.

We turned it into a rather informal Thanksgiving dinner. It was a quiet time with a gentle group. Marcus's two grown boys were there, and his girlfriend Gina, and Dad and Amanda and me. We had a buffet where each person helped himself, and we walked around with plates in our hands, while Mom sat in the living room with her oxygen tank. Amanda still insisted on saying grace. She always galloped through it, as if it needed to be finished as quickly as possible so we could get down to the business of dinner.

"God is great, God is good. And we thankhimforthisfood. Byhishandwemustbefed. Giveuslordourdailybread. Amen."

We made it through that day, but it gave us a heads-up about how much care Mom really needed. She didn't become any less insistent about going home after that. Every day she asked. Every day we explained to her that, until she could stand up and walk on her own, she had to stay here and keep working on her strength. The battle was taking its toll on Dad. Still he showed up faithfully, day after day. To me, it was just the right thing to do. I didn't realize how rare this was until the nurses started making comments to me. "Your dad is just wonderful. He's so loyal and patient."

"Yes," I would agree. "He is."

In many ways, I thought, he was too patient. He received a call from R3 one day when Christmas was looming. Til was playing on the floor of Mom's room, beating up a stuffed toy Abominable Snowman. "Terrible Til," Dad called him, watching as he slammed the Bumble against the floor.

"That's for messin' with Rudolph!" Amanda growled.

"Well, hello there!" Dad said. I looked up to see that he was sitting beside Mom, holding the cell phone by his ear. I watched as the joy quickly passed away from his face, like a scene change fade, as

R3's angry voice resounded through the electronic garble and bounced around the room.

"You need to tell Marcus that I am not spending Christmas with his girlfriend! I don't want to spend family time with some stranger!"

Amanda and I looked at each other. Mom's eyes drifted toward the ceiling. I could tell she too heard every word. Dad's hand went up to his face and he began rubbing his brow. "Okay. Okay."

Of course, Dad would never do any such thing. It was awful. To make matters worse, Mom was sure to report this episode to my hot-tempered brother Marcus.

In the days following, the inevitable happened. There was a string of emails with "Tucson" in the subject line. The first was from Theil.

"Hi. In the middle of things, I've been called for a second interview on December 7. Wish me luck!"

I replied, "Good luck, P1!"

R1 replied, "Wow! That's coming up!! Good luck....."

R2 responded from Colorado, "Hope it goes well, Theil!"

R3 wrote, "Marcus...."

Following were seven or eight paragraphs of venom spewed at Marcus, explaining how she was exposing his abusive behavior and his tantrums to his siblings, again saying how she was not interested in sharing family holiday time with his new girlfriend, and then she directed him to a website where he could get some help for his problem.

I responded. "What does this have to do with Tucson?!"

It was my way of defending Marcus. When R3 indulged her outbursts, the other siblings would clam up. But I would call her out on them.

R3 had no real vision into our struggles, even though I was posting daily journal entries in a Caringbridge site. My entries were incessantly positive, projecting the image of a happy and supportive family:

Written Dec 11, 2010 6:28pm

Mom ate jello today! YAY!

She needs to practice swallowing, to see if her muscles will "remember" how to work. The nurses were giving her thickened water daily, but she (understandably) had no interest in that. She had tried pudding without much luck. Amanda and I brought her a Frosty from Wendy's one day; no dice. So today, we tried Jello, and she managed to get several bites down.

One small step at a time...

Written Dec 12, 2010 1:51pm

We got dumped on! Our cars were mired in over a foot of snow, so Dad valiantly drove out with the Tahoe. Thank God for 4WD!

Anyway, it never did quit snowing.

Mom told me that she ate some coconut cream pie! I asked her if it was any good and she said, "It was all right." Of course, she is never hungry due to the stomach tube. But I am hoping this will reawaken her interest in tasting things.

Dad is celebrating because he beat her in 2 out of 3 games of cribbage. This is following a two week losing streak. He said, "I finally quit feeling sorry for her."

Through the online journal, Mom received comments and good wishes from friends and relatives who were keeping track of her progress. Most could not visit in person, but I would print out their comments every day and bring them in to read to Mom. She kept a pad of stationary by her chair, and she wrote letters in reply to them, which I would take and mail for her.

I brought watercolors in for us, and a calendar with bird photos. She loved to paint, and birds were her favorite subject. Amid all our differences, it was one thing that we were able to share and I treasured it. During the long days at the Manor, I would sit and make paintings, and show them to her, in an effort to inspire her to do some of her own. She never did pick up a brush, but she admired my work. "Oh, beautiful," she would say. I left the paints and pad on a table near her chair. She would take the pad and show it to nurses, "My daughter did this."

My relationship with Mom had always been rocky, but I kept trying to think of ways to reach her. "She loves you," Dad would offer up, almost every day. He would say it suddenly, with a little chuckle, and it was never prompted. I thought his efforts through this crisis were heroic, on every level. I kept trying to think of ways to do my part, to make the ordeal easier on everyone. I had never spent much time in an assisted living center. But I was getting a good dose now of what life in one was like, how closed-in the space was, how the hours sagged with heartbreaking monotony. I wondered how many people were here alone, without the benefit of family to sit with them or laugh with them, or even pick fights with them. I wondered how many were here merely waiting to die. I thought I should try to make a difference to them, at least while I was here every day.

The day of the big snowstorm, I had a meeting with the Manor's Entertainment Director. I took Amanda with me and sat down in her office.

"I have an idea for a Christmas treat for the residents."

Her face appeared just a little short of ecstatic. "Really? We are always looking for new ideas. What is it?"

"I have a horse who does tricks. He's house trained."

I had barely gotten the words out and she was making plans.

If I could count on one sanctuary in the stressful phase, it was in my horse, Clifford. He was a Morgan gelding with a cheerful temperament and a sense of humor. He was well into his teens by that time and I was in the middle of a farm store Christmas tour. I had written a book about him, called, "Clifford of Drummond Island," and he would go into the store and sign the books using watercolors and a sponge. He did a few tricks, and thanks to my dog training background, I had figured out how to house train him, using his horse trailer as a toilet. He understood that relieving himself indoors was a no-no, and he was good for about an hour. After that, he would begin shifting uncomfortably and lifting his tail, and that was my signal to get him to the trailer. He would climb in and immediately deposit a steaming load into the shavings awaiting him. When someone found out that I took my horse into libraries and farm stores and other public facilities, the inevitable question was something akin to, "Doesn't he crap everywhere?"

I was a little bit surprised that with the Manor, this didn't even really seem to be an issue. Maybe they were just too desperate for entertainment to worry about a little manure.

The entire residency was invited to our event, which was held in the chapel on December 20. They taped mats to the floor in a large area in the center of the room, forming an indoor arena space for him to perform, surrounded by elderly people in wheelchairs. Mom sat in the corner by the piano in her chair, with Dad and Amanda. Clifford marched in through the doors as if he had just arrived home, and proceeded to do all his tricks, rearing, "counting", dancing with me and playing fetch. He delivered a toy stuffed bear that said, "Get Well Soon", right into Mom's lap. TV 9 and 10 News was there, taping a live story with Clifford signing books while wearing his Santa Claus hat. He greeted each resident, one by one, gently snuffling their arms and hair. I watched as time and again, a gnarled hand reached up to caress his thick curtain of mane, and a weathered face leaned close to inhale his sharp scent. The expression was peaceful and reverent. Each individual seemed transported through their corridors of memory, perhaps to sun-touched fields of their past. This generation knew horses.

Mom was in her glory for days afterward. She was the center of attention throughout the entire facility. "Clifford the Horse's Grandmother," the other residents and staff called her. She and Dad and Amanda ate it up. Any time Dad wheeled her out for physical therapy, or to the cafeteria, they were bombarded with questions and smiles and comments about Clifford.

It was the best Christmas gift possible, for them and me.

Two days after Christmas, as Amanda and I were getting ready to follow Dad over to the Manor, he came around the corner from the kitchen hallway, looking pale.

"Are you okay?" I was standing on the other side of the bar.

He grabbed the wall and said, "No. I've never felt… So weak."

To my horror, he collapsed, face forward, hitting the floor with a crash. Amanda yelled, "Dad!"

We ran to him, where he lay face down with his head just a few inches from the dishwasher. He woke up almost immediately, but as he turned his head, I could see where his glasses had carved a line above his nose and he was bleeding.

"Dad," I said. "You are going to the hospital.

Chapter 3

About Talking with the Dead – Amanda

How I could put this? I don't want anyone to call me crazy. I don't think I am crazy, but I have a funny gut feeling. Grandma and Grandpa still talk to me. I just lie in bed at night and let them talk to me. They are together. Well, Grandpa said he bumps into Grandma now and then. He has a curly finger that points straight up and he pounded it on my bedroom window. He said, "Are you still being my Snicklefritz? And how's Jo Mo Fraw doing?"

He was talking about Nancy. He called her Jo Mo Fraw.

My cousin Frankie was a really funny person. He went to school and graduated with Nancy. He was a great basketball player. He had a family, a wife and five kids. He gave me hugs and kisses. He came over to fix a leaky pipe under our counter. When I said the faucet was still dripping he said, "Well gol darn it!"

Frankie did construction and he was working on a roof and he fell. Now he talks to me at night.

About Talking with the Dead - Nancy

When I walked into Mom's room in the Manor on the day Dad collapsed, Mom was sitting all alone in her corner chair. There was no TV, no book in her hand, no crochet project, nothing. She was just sitting there. It was after noon by that time, and she had to be wondering what had happened to us. She looked up when I came in.

"Mom, Dad's got the flu bug, really bad. He fainted in Marcus's kitchen. He's in the hospital."

"Oh, my God."

"He's going to be okay. He is awake and alert, and flirting with nurses. They are just keeping him under observation to make sure it isn't heart related. He is going to have to stay in there probably overnight."

"They said I am sick with that virus that's been going around."

"Oh, no, Mom. You too?"

Marcus had been in Cancun with Gina for the week. Amanda stayed at the hospital with Dad, and I sat alone with Mom. "I want to go home," she said.

"I know, Mom. I don't blame you."

"How would you like to sit here all day by yourself, every day?"

"Mom, Dad is here all the time."

"He is not here all the time. He goes out to lunch."

"Yes. Sometimes he does."

"I want to go home."

"I know you do."

"I am falling behind in my exercises."

"I know Mom, but you are sick. You have to rest. You will catch up again."

"I don't want to catch up! I am tired!"

"Mom, you are just saying that because you feel crappy right now. But you have been doing so well! You will catch up."

Her bottom lip crept out. "No. I won't."

"Mom! You can't quit!"

"I can quit! I am old!"

With those words, Mom sealed her fate. She was hospitalized that night, and almost immediately began having trouble breathing. Three days later, in the early morning on New Year's Eve, she insisted that they remove her breathing tube. The small group of family members were called in after they pulled the tube out. The nurse had a sense of urgency in her voice, "Okay, you can come in now!"

We knew it wouldn't be long. Mom was not conscious. Her machines bleeped haltingly. We gathered around her bed. Dad sat on the edge of it, holding her hand, weeping. I sat on the bed beside him, next to Mom's feet. Marcus stood silently behind me in the corner. R3, sobbing loudly, went to the other side of the bed and took Mom's left hand. Her teenaged son Josh stood at the foot of the bed, looking sad and a little scared. We all watched as Mom slowly faded away. Finally overcome with grief, Dad held Mom's hand out to me. He stood up and stepped away from the bed. I immediately took her hand and moved into the spot where he had been sitting.

"Go ahead, Mom," I said. "It's okay. We understand. We will look after Dad and Amanda."

Within minutes, she was gone. The nurse came in and switched off the machine, and said, "I'm so sorry."

I thought Dad might never stop crying. "Close her mouth," he said to the nurse. He turned to me. "You girls, take her rings off."

R3 began removing the jewelry from Mom's left hand. Mom had a couple of rings on her right hand, but her fingers were swollen. I tugged and twisted the rings. "They won't come off," I whispered.

Marcus leaned down and presented me with a gob of foamy soap from the dispenser on the wall. "Try this," he said softly.

It worked. Mom's rings slid off and I handed them to Dad. He turned to look at me, his eyes glimmering with tears. "Go get Amanda."

Amanda was sitting in the kitchen eating cereal when I walked in. She was illuminated by a thin shaft of light coming through the French doors. It caused her bare head to glow a little. She looked up.

"Hi," I said.

"Hello."

"Are you having breakfast?" I sat down by her.

"Yup."

I decided not to mince words. "Our Mom passed away."

She dropped her spoon and covered her ears with both hands. "No, no, no no no."

"Yes, she is gone. She didn't want that breathing tube any more. She asked them to remove it."

Amanda's eyes welled up. She reached for her glass of juice and took a big gulp.

"The family is coming," I told her.

"They are?"

"Yes. Theil and Rose and Jon will all be here tonight."

"Oh good. I can't wait to see my family."

She began to cry. I jumped up and grabbed her and held her tight. "Oh, Manda. I just want to thank you for all you did for our mother. You helped her out so much. You made her life so much better. You did great."

"I hope so," she wailed.

After that good cry, her grief became dignified. She would greet each person as they arrived, shed a few tears, and then laugh at stories of Mom. When Marcus came in, I turned to him. "Maybe we should go back to the nursing home and get the rest of Mom's stuff, and tell them she's not coming back there."

"I think Rowena is handling that."

I felt a sense of relief. It was, I thought, one less thing that I would have to take care of.

Marcus's house became flooded with people. Plates of food materialized. Noodle salad. Casseroles. Brownies. More noodle salad. Even though it was a somber event, the group was loud and bawdy. R2 arrived from Colorado. R1 and R3 came with an assortment of offspring, and a curly-headed tot I secretly and unkindly referred to as the Drug Baby. She was the result of an allegedly addicted parent, and I thought it showed in her wild, vacant expression. She had a dirty face from throwing up a little, and having it not thoroughly wiped off. Despite the fact that there was a crowd of her stewards to supervise, the baby kept running to the staircase by the front door and climbing up. Her actions were so jerky and erratic that I was afraid she would tumble down the stairs. I kept finding her, and three times I pulled her off of them and turned her loose in the living room. Finally, she and Til discovered each other, and as usually happens between creatures of corresponding ages, they both were completely intrigued. They played together on the floor with some of Til's rope toys, in a quiet corner by the dining room. It crossed my mind for the millionth time, how therapeutic and calming animals can be. It was the longest I had ever seen that baby sit still. Then, the child stood up and the puppy, smelling the regurgitated food on her face, hopped up to try to lick it off.

R1 happened to see it, and she grabbed the baby up. "That was a nip! That was a nip!"

I rolled my eyes. But soon, her whole clan was yelling about the vicious dog. "Hey, what is the deal with that dog?" "You know she is right at face level with him." "We can't have that." "Lock that dog up! If he hurts that kid I'm going to kill him!"

I didn't bother going into an explanation about what had really happened, or animal behavior or food begging in puppies. They were all buying into R1's panic and drama, and hadn't bothered to ask me. I knew there was no point in addressing it. I merely went to the closet and got my coat.

Poor Til, sensing the persecution, sought refuge under the kitchen table. I crawled in after him. "Come on out," I said in disgust. "You're not in trouble. Maybe next time you can use her for a squeaky toy. We'll see what they say THEN."

I carried him out to the car, and I drove off. I realized that all my dress clothes were in storage. I needed to get some funeral clothes, but of course, being New Year's Eve, there wasn't anything open. I went out to a restaurant where I sat by myself and had a late dinner salad. I thought about Mom and her unexpectedly brave last moments earlier that day, her choice to have the breathing tube removed, and poor Dad's grief. It grew later, and the restaurant was quiet. I knew that the next few days would be inundated with family, and it would bring more episodes like the one tonight. I wished I could drive the three hours back home. The farm would be coated in snow, the pines I had planted would be dripping with it. The owls would be calling tonight. The horses would be standing on the hillside, their dark shapes

59

blowing clouds of steamy breath into the night sky. But my farm was gone. My horses weren't there. It was a strange feeling, not to be able to just go home. It left a throbbing emptiness, deep in my stomach that needed a panacea. I decided to go see a movie.

"Happy New Year!" the ticket booth girl said. I managed a smile and wished her the same. Armed with a bucket of popcorn and a soda, I marched down the aisle to the front row and sat alone, the only person in the darkened theatre. I was transported away for two hours, munching my popcorn and immensely comforted in my temporary solitude. Meanwhile Til curled up in the back seat of the car, in a cozy ball with his fleece blanket. The snow was falling gently when I left the cinema. The night lights shone on the soft white street. I was starting to think maybe I should go find an open tavern, or maybe even a motel room. But then my phone chimed. It was a text message from Marcus. "R's are gone. It's safe to come back now."

When I returned to the house, R2 was still there, but at least that was whittling them down. Theil had come from Arizona. Our oldest brother Jon, the mountain man in his cowboy hat, was sitting with his arm around Amanda. He had flown in from Seattle that day. Now he was impressing Marcus's girlfriend Gina with his exaggerated stories. "I was attacked by a grizzly bear!"

"Really?"

"Yep. He came at me and when he got close enough I reached right down his throat and grabbed his tail, and turned him inside out and he ran the other way."

Amanda was glowing, relaxed and thriving in Jon's love and attention. She glanced knowingly over at Gina. "He's a rootin' tootin' boy, isn't he?" Then she turned her gaze on me. "Nancy had to go take a break. She has Middle Child Syndrome."

"Well, you have Down's syndrome!" I shot back.

"Middle child!" she taunted.

"Down's!"

"Middle child!"

"Down's!"

"You two get along," Dad said.

Amanda turned to Gina. "We're the Syndrome Sisters."

Amanda was taking refuge in her family, but I knew that soon enough, our siblings would all go back to their own lives and she would be left without her mother, and only Dad for company. I wondered how that would affect her. I would still go back home to take her to the movies, and out for pizza. I would be as available to her as I could. But her daily life would be forever altered. There would be no more shared soap operas, no gossip, fewer Snicker's bars. Though he adored Amanda, Dad didn't participate in the same way. His style was not sedentary like Mom's. He liked the outdoors and he liked to keep moving, two things that weren't Amanda's specialty. The gender difference alone was a significant one. The feminine bond was deep and profound in so many ways.

Amanda was a stoic character who rarely cried in front of anyone, and never complained about her physical ailments. I wondered what her grief would be like.

One of her greatest idiosyncrasies was that for years, she had spoken of conversations with the dead. She claimed that she was contacted by dead relatives when she went to bed at night. She admitted that sometimes these encounters scared her. Our parents found these stories amusing, but didn't question them. Our siblings ignored them. They were categorized as a write-off, part of life with a family member who had a disability. But I took an interest in them. I asked her about them from time to time, and she would tell me little snippets of what dead people said to her. Usually they were greetings. "Grandpa Bailey said to tell you hello." I didn't know if it was Amanda's imagination working overtime, or perhaps she was dreaming. But I wanted Amanda to feel accepted, and know someone was hearing her. So I would ask her about the dead relatives. "Have you talked with Grandma lately? How is she doing?"

I never knew what the answer would be. It could be, "Yes, I heard from her last night." Or, "No, I haven't heard from her."

I would respond, "Well, if you do talk to her, tell her I said hi."

Whether it was Amanda's imagination, or a dream, it was okay with me. We addressed these conversations as casually as if she was talking to people on the phone. As far as I knew, I was the only one in the family who asked her regularly about these encounters. In mixed company, she generally didn't bring them up. She was aware it wasn't considered normal. She was very sensitive to the fact that she was different, and she didn't go out of her way to accentuate it. In public she was generally quiet unless she was in a familiar setting. I teased her, "You're calling me crazy? You're the one who talks to the dead!"

"I don't talk to them. They talk to me," she corrected me.

When I asked her about these conversations, it was always when the two of us were alone. She usually spoke of relatives. Occasionally she mentioned ancestors she hadn't met, such as our mother's father. A few times, she mentioned my friend Linda, whom I had known in Arizona when in my twenties. Amanda had never met Linda. She was a dear friend to me and had been killed during a camping accident, when she fell out of a jeep and struck her head. Once, Amanda gave a little laugh and said, "Linda keeps talking about Clifford. Linda really likes Clifford."

This struck me as a little odd. When I knew Linda, she had owned two horses. She was an accomplished rider and loved her horses, but I had never mentioned this to Amanda. Linda had a tremendous sense of humor and fun, and of all my friends, would probably have appreciated Clifford's quirky traits the most.

At that point, I began taking Amanda's contacts from beyond a little more seriously. After all, there were certainly things in the universe that couldn't be explained. I decided to do a test. It involved another friend of mine named Kimmy, who had been like a sister to me. Kimmy had died in 2003 of complications due to alcoholism. Amanda had known Kimmy, and claimed to talk with her frequently at night.

"Hey, next time you hear from Kimmy, I want you to ask her something for me."

"Okay," she said.

"When she was a kid, she had a dog named Cookie. Ask her why she named her dog that."

"Okay."

I repeated the information, just so she had it right. "If you think of it, be sure to ask. Now I never met the dog, but Kimmy talked about her a lot. Her name was Cookie. Ask her why."

Weeks passed, and I let it slip my mind. Finally, it occurred to me to check with Amanda. "Hey, have you heard from Kimmy lately?"

She inhaled sharply, as someone does when suddenly remembering a forgotten detail. "Oh, yes, I have."

"Did you ask her the question? About why they called her dog Cookie?"

"Yes, I did." She rolled her eyes upward, as someone does when trying to recall a conversation, and not fully remembering the details. There were a thousand answers one could imagine. They called the dog Cookie because she was sweet. They called her Cookie because she loved biscuits. They called her Cookie because they had adopted her from a girl scout.

"She said it is because the dog is round and brown."

I felt a tingling along my hairline that shivered down across my shoulder blades. Amanda had hit upon the answer. Kimmy had named the dog, a white collie, Cookie because she had a round brown spot on her side. To Amanda, this translated to, "The dog was round and brown."

From that day on, I never teased Amanda again about these conversations. And I didn't ask her any more test questions. There were things about Amanda that were deeply spiritual, that set her apart from the rest of us, beyond merely having an extra chromosome. Now I was hoping that this quality, this weird connection or ability, or whatever it was, would help her through the loss of our mother.

She sat under the shield of Jon's arm, looking around at us all serenely, comforted by the temporary closeness that the loss had created. At the stroke of midnight, Dad and the remaining group of us raised our glasses in a toast to Mom. "Happy New Year," we murmured. With the softness of the lamplight, the smell of cinnamon candles burning, and the heat of champagne warming my insides, I remember thinking, "This is how families are supposed to be. Why isn't it always like this?"

Chapter 4

About Clifford – Amanda

Clifford is named after our uncle. He plays tricks on Dad. I rode him in the 4th of July parade one year, and my cousin Brandon walked with me and helped me. Dad rode him in another 4th of July parade. Marcus rode him and fell off. Clifford is very good with kids. He touches their hearts. Their eyes light up. The library tour is amazing! I love doing that kind of stuff. With all the years together, Clifford and Trudy will always be family.

About Clifford - Nancy

When my farm foreclosed, people kept telling me I should sell my horses. Selling them would have made life easier for me, even though, as horses go, they weren't terribly expensive to maintain. They both were sound and healthy, with good, hard feet that never needed shoes. Clifford and Trudy were "easy keepers". They would live and grow fat happily on summer pasture. The problem was finding someone with an available summer pasture. They weren't spring chickens anymore, either. Trudy was eighteen and Clifford was twenty. That year, the Michigan economy was tanking and people were getting out from under their recreational luxuries. As a result, the market was glutted with motor homes, boats, SUVs, and horses. Horse rescues were overflowing. People were giving them away. I had no desire to part with either of mine. I'd had them since they were two and three years old. Sending them to auction was out of the question as they would be prime candidates for slaughter. This was aside from the fact they were both as precious to me as any other loved one. So, I kept them and endured the constant urging by the uninformed to sell them. They had wintered on the pine-studded pony farm in Northern Michigan, none the worse for wear, although both significantly thinner. Clifford has gouged his eyelid somehow; I thought probably on one of the sharp pine limbs. It healed, but the hair grew back in as a white visible scar. I was grateful to my friend for taking them in, but I planned to move them out of there as soon as I could.

In spring, Dad and Amanda and I returned to our stony, moss-covered Drummond Island. The woods were brilliant green and dripping with cedars, and smelled of mud and balsam. Sharp bird calls echoed through the timber as we performed our spring ritual of opening, "The Lodge," which Marcus had dubbed the long beaten trailer sprawling like a boat at the top of a little slope in the campsite. Dad started the furnace and the water heater, and I cleaned the cupboards of mouse droppings while Amanda vacuumed. My old corral, with its weathered cedar poles and green grass sprouting up among a litter of fallen poplar leaves, stood waiting for the annual arrival of my horses. My canoe lay next to their shelter like a long red beacon begging for adventure.

There was a pervading sadness, a loneliness that hung over Dad like a cloud. But as he walked into the woods, I watched the years fall away. There was buoyancy to him that had been missing. He was home. The camp had belonged to his father, and before him, his father's father. There was great comfort in returning to a place where generations before us had known the same trees, the same sky. The corral was located over Grandpa's old potato patch, a good flat spot with dark rich earth where I had planted timothy and clover twenty years prior. The horses of course devoured every sprig of it, trampling and churning the manure and earth, along with shavings deposited for them every summer by Uncle Bob from the sawmill. The corral dirt was deep and fertile and rich, and each year the grass grew back. It came with a flourish of clover and daisies, only to be devoured again as soon as it reached about a foot high when the horses returned in mid-May. There had been enough seed for me to plant the whole lot around camp, and the lawn now grew thick and lush. Dad's white picket fence stood guard over the group of rose bushes I had given Mom over the years: One rose a year, every year, for Mother's Day. Every spring and fall we mulched them, cutting into the soil around them and filling the spaces with scoops of nourishing black earth from the corral. Dad had carefully fashioned each white picket of the fence by hand, lining them up side by side with the precision of a seasoned military parade. "You are crazy to do that," I had once told him as I watched him cut and tediously measure each piece.

He had laughed good-naturedly. "I know. The things I will do for that woman."

But when looking at the fence, I understood the appeal of something handmade, and how it seemed to unify us with the place. It was the same with the horse corral. Every log, every post, we had hauled out of the woods, cut and stripped and positioned. We had built a gazebo for Mom the same year; a hulking monstrosity that stood over the stone fire pit. I had financed the hardware and roofing; it had green shingles that matched those on the horse's shelter. I pounded nails and fetched measuring tape and saws and screw guns for Uncle Bob and Dad while they climbed around on the scaffolding. Our camp was littered with Dad's unfinished projects; stacks of wood covered with tarps, a big pile of cement blocks, a broken-down jeep. His dream was to build a log cabin on the site. My dream was to fulfill it for him.

Now Amanda and Dad and I shared a sense of self-conscious busy-ness. We were uncomfortable with how things would work with the glaring absence of Mom. I couldn't imagine what it must be like to lose a partner of 62 years. Dad had to feel lost. He was accustomed to her managing his time from her sedentary indoor post. He used to escape her in the long afternoons. He would go sit out on the deck, reaching under the side panel of the camper to his hidden flask, and get pleasantly inebriated. I would take him a sandwich, and then we would watch the sun dip below the treetops while we talked. We talked about

Thomas Jefferson and the Lewis and Clark expedition. We talked about birds. We talked about Dad's childhood when he had run and played in these woods with his brother Bob and his cousins. But now, he had beers in the fridge and there was no need to hide them anymore. He didn't have to get up in the morning and go to the sterile assisted living center, and sit there all day thinking of ways to entertain and encourage her. The long winter was over. We were home.

My lifestyle as a struggling artist and writer had afforded me much time here in summer over the years. Since the collapse of my book deal with a major publisher, and my subsequent foreclosure, the pressure to survive was greatly magnified. Now that Mom was gone, I was going to have to return to work, and work extra hard to recover. I planned to go back on the road once I got Dad and Amanda settled. But for now, I had to make sure they were okay. Amanda was having her moments of hilarity, but in general was quieter than I had ever seen her.

On this, our first day back, Amanda was settled on the couch with her ever-present notebook, writing thoughtfully, and I was drinking water from out of the faucet. The water came from a well Dad had drilled years prior, and it was deep and cold and clean-tasting. Dad stepped in through the squeaky door and said, "Would you girls like to go out for a sandreech? I'll treat."

Amanda and I looked at each other. "Way!" I yelled. "Pizza at Pins!"

We high fived.

Pins was a bowling alley located near the golf course, deep in the hardwoods of the island by the posh, Frank-Lloyd-Wright type resort that Tom Monaghan had built years prior. Monaghan was the owner of Domino's Pizza and the Detroit Tigers. He had put Drummond on the map before vacating it in the mid-90's. He wasn't popular with the Islanders, but had undoubtedly increased the tourist trade there, just by raising awareness of its existence.

We sat in the restaurant that day, seeing people we knew and acknowledging the many greetings and condolences offered by the locals. Amanda and Dad sat side by side, facing the door so they could check out everyone in the place. Amanda sat with her cola and looked at me, raising her eyebrows. "I told you about Elizabeth Taylor, right?"

Amanda liked to keep up with celebrity news.

"I heard," I said.

"She's going to be buried right smack dab next to Michael Jackson. At Neverland Ranch."

"Michael Jackson is buried at Neverland Ranch?"

"Yes. They have a cemetery there."

"They do?"

"Yes."

"Who else is buried there?"

"Elizabeth Taylor!"

I smacked my hand to my forehead. Dad laughed. Just then the pizza arrived, steaming on its pan. "I'm so sorry about your mom," the waitress said.

"Thank you," Amanda replied.

"Good to see you, Amanda," the waitress said.

"Good to see you too."

The waitress walked away. I looked at Dad. "Padre, are we invisible, or what?"

"I guess so." He laughed again. I grabbed the spatula and started scooping out pizza slices.

"Hey, there's Michelle!" Amanda said. "I better go speak to her."

She got up and waddled across the room, with a sort of hitch in her limping step that resembled a skip. I didn't know the young couple she was approaching. She stood for a long few minutes, deep in conversation with them.

"She knows everyone," Dad said.

"I know. Do I tell you we went to a movie last winter in Cadillac, and there was a lady at the theatre who knew her?"

"No!"

"Yes, she was like, 'It's Amanda! Hi Amanda!' And of course Amanda introduced her but I can't remember her name. She was from the Special Olympics years ago."

"I'll be damned," he was chuckling.

We left the restaurant that night and I drove back to camp with Amanda beside me and Dad, always the gentleman, sitting in the back seat.

"Were you jealous that I was talking to that good looking guy?" Amanda said.

"Flirting," I corrected.

"I wasn't flirting. Just talking."

"Flirting."

"Talking."

"Flirting."

"Talk!"

"Flirt!"

Amanda grabbed a chunk of my hair and gave it a tug. "Would you pipe down?" She turned her head to address Dad. "I had to get violent with her, Dad. That's what Mom told me to do with her. Be violent."

"I don't think she said to be violent," I said. "I think she said, 'Be silent.'"

"No," Amanda said. "It was violent."

"Silent."

"Violent!"

"Silent!"

"She's so mean, Dad." Amanda said. "Why did you raise her that way?"

"You two get along," Dad said.

Moments like this seemed comfortable and almost normal. I missed the sound of Mom's laugh. I didn't realize it until after she was gone, but she had usually been first to laugh at my jokes. "Nancy!" she would say, and I'd look over and her white smile would flash, her belly jiggling as she guffawed appreciatively.

As the days lengthened, I continued traveling to dog shows. Til was performing his Frisbee routine for an audience, and Ms. Rip was an accomplished high jumper. It didn't pay much, but it was better than nothing. The search for any substantial job was useless. Unemployment was at a record high. Gasoline prices soared. A new governor canceled our state film incentive, putting an end to many part-time jobs for people like me who worked on movie projects. Michigan was at the low point of its economic collapse. Potential employers were so swamped with applicants that they didn't even bother acknowledging query letters anymore. But I continued to hear from libraries interested in hiring Clifford for their summer reading programs. We were able to schedule a tour throughout northern Michigan. I brought Cliffy and Trudy back to the island where they resumed their grazing on the current year's crop of corral grass.

I was hauling my trailer with Dad's Tahoe. We watched the Drummond Islander III chug toward the dock, with the sun bouncing off its square cabin windows. I said, "Whew, whaddaya think it's gonna cost me to get this rig on the ferry?"

"I don't know what the senior citizen's ticket is," Amanda said.

"Will you shut up!" I yelled, while Dad burst into guffaws.

"You shut up!" Amanda said.

"You two get along!" Dad said.

We pulled into camp and I released the horses. Their hoofs beat a quick tempo as they trotted around camp in a big circle, then marched single file into their corral. "Everyone has been asking about those horses," Dad said. "It's good to have them back. And they are happy to be here."

It was true. Drummond had long been a summer home for all of us. It was comforting to get back to some sort of normalcy. Every day, I rode one horse down to the shore while the other followed along. It was Clifford's turn to run free and I'd saddled Trudy up. We enjoyed a lively trot down the road. Til the border collie was now just under a year old, with beautiful white feathered legs and a plumy tail. He had taken it upon himself to do some sort of ad-lib herding. It consisted of blasting ahead at top speed, coming back and circling behind both horses. Ms. Rip stayed in position next to Trudy as I rode. Clifford was lagging behind to eat grass and then periodically galloping to catch up. On one trip back, Til saw him coming and hit the brakes. Most horses would slow down upon seeing a dog directly in their path. Clifford sped up. He came flying past Trudy, straight at the little dog. My heart was in my throat, but I said nothing. Clifford, though a tremendous practical joker, was never mean-spirited. Til did a quick double back and ran for his life with Clifford pounding along behind him. Cliffy was leaping into the air and flinging his back feet high. He was clearly ecstatic that he had produced the desired effect. Til ran off up the road and Clifford stopped, looking after him, and let out a huge snort. "Take that!" Then he looked back at me, as if to make sure I'd caught the whole thing.

We rode out to the shore and I dismounted there, so the horses could drink lake water, lick the rocks and eat some of the harsh tufted shore grass. Clifford had expressed no interest in dogs since his friend, my German shepherd Reva, had died in 2001. But I could see that Til was not the least bit afraid of either horse and they seemed to have some sort of arrangement. On the way back, it was the same, with the dog circling and racing and Cliffy nibbling grass. Then Clifford trotted past us with his tail up, and I started yelling. "Git him, Clifford! Get that bad dog!"

More than happy to oblige, Clifford took off, chasing the white dog madly up the road, shooting out his front legs and arching his neck and shaking his head. He had that same old suspension, floating above ground like he did when he was two years old. It was all a game, and the whole group of us, Trudy, Ms. Rip, Cliffy and Til and me, whooped and hollered and ran and rode like mad, all the way back to camp.

I took the saddle off Trudy and was brushing her down. I took a few minutes to rub her head, talking to her softly and petting and hugging her. Amanda came out the door then, smiling, carrying her camera. She had seen us through the window. "You quit mushin' on that horse!"

Most people might glance through the window, but she had to get closer. She was attracted to love, I realized. She was drawn to love and gestures of love. There was something simple and pure about her expression of it. Somewhere, I had heard a story about how one five-year-old child defined love. She said, "When someone loves you, you know your name is safe in their mouth."

To me, this was brilliant. It reminded me of something Amanda might say. In many ways, Amanda was just as sophisticated as any adult I knew. But when it came to love, she was refreshingly uncomplicated.

She stood snapping photos while I posed obligingly with Trudy. Finally, I said, "Hey, Amanda. Do you want to go on the road with Clifford and me for a couple of days?" I was getting ready to leave for Paradise, Michigan, and then travel to Manistique the next day. "We can have a cheeseburger in Paradise!"

"That sounds great!" she said, and took another picture.

The Paradise Library had arranged a room for us in a quaint hotel that was right on the shore of Lake Superior. It was across the street from a little tavern. I nodded to it when we pulled in. "I bet that's where we can have our cheeseburger."

After we got Clifford all settled in the trailer with some hay for the night, we carried our bags in and made ourselves at home. I selected clothes to wear to the library the next day. Amanda had brought a little hardbound journal with a striped cover, and she sat on the bed, writing in it. She looked up. "Why aren't you wearing the new blouse I picked out for you?"

It was a sleeveless purple nylon top with tiger stripes. "It's not warm enough," I said. "I'll freeze in that."

"Well just tear my heart out, and stomp on it!"

"Sorry! What are you working on, there?"

She looked down at her journal. "Oh, I am just writing my thoughts."

"What are you thinking about?"

"I'm thinking about our mother."

"Oh. I have been, too. Gosh, I miss her."

"Me too."

She sat with her head down, carefully shaping the letters with her pen.

"Would you mind sharing with me? I mean, you don't have to, but I would like to hear it."

"Sure. I don't mind." She lay the pen down and carefully held the notebook up. Haltingly, she read, "I do the sad moments just for me, but you can do happiness for yourself. I don't want to be sad. How can I sleep that way? How am I supposed to enjoy myself? Tell me how to be happy and proud."

She lay the journal down and looked at me. I stood up and went to her and sat down on the bed next to her, and put my arm around her. "How are you supposed to enjoy yourself? Oh, honey, that's the dilemma of anyone who has lost somebody close to them."

"It is?"

"Oh yes. That's the big question!"

"I see."

"But you know, it is really good that you are asking that."

"Why?"

"Because you are getting right to the heart of the matter. It means you are dealing with things. I think you are doing really well."

She huffed then, a sort of half-laugh. "I'm not so sure about that."

"I know it feels that way right now. I feel that way too. About a lot of things, not just Mom. But you just wait. Things will get better. You'll see."

"I hope so."

"Anyway, I need you to help me pick out a song," I said. "I want to play a song at the end of our program when the kids come up to pet Cliffy."

"I know the right song," she said softly.

"What is it?"

"There's a better world. A better place," she said.

She was talking about a song called, "Heal the World."

"Michael Jackson! Amanda, that is perfect!"

It worked beautifully. Amanda and I trundled our gear into the library the next day while Clifford waited outside, tied to the trailer. Amanda settled at her station, near a table with the CD player, while I ran back outside. I plopped a medium-sized suitcase on the ground. Knowing our routine, Til obligingly climbed in, curled up and lowered his head. I zipped him up, leaving a small air hole by where his nose was, and left it parked outside the library door. I walked in to find Amanda sitting quietly and a whole roomful of children and parents watching me. Children lined up on the floor behind a strip of masking tape, which I had encouraged the staff to put down as a visual barrier. With a horse in the building, we wanted to ensure that no one would get stepped on.

"Hi everybody!" I said. "Welcome to our program, 'Horse Tales from Around the World.' Thank you for coming. I'm Nancy Bailey. I'd like to introduce my sound technician, Amanda Bailey." I gestured to Amanda, and the room erupted with applause while she waved.

"Is everyone ready to meet Clifford?" I said.

"YEAHHH!" the kids screamed.

"Great! Okay then, all we need is – wait a minute. Are we forgetting something?"

I started looking around the table among the watercolors and sponges, and underneath in the box among our other props.

"You forgot the books!" Amanda roared, right on cue.

I slapped a hand to my head. "The books! The books! Oh my gosh. We need those! This is, after all, a library. Where are they?"

"They're in the suitcase!" Amanda said.

"Oh yeah! They're in the suitcase! I almost forgot. I'm sorry! I'll be back in a sec."

I galloped to the door, ran outside and then came back in pulling the suitcase by its handle, at top speed. I laid it down on the floor in front of the audience. "Here are the books!" I unzipped the suitcase, and out burst a very enthused, wiggling border collie.

The kids screamed in delight. They loved it.

"Til!" I shouted. "I told you you had to stay home!"

Til ran down the row of kids, greeting them, wagging excitedly while I put my hands on my hips and shook my head. "Looks like we have a stow-away. Oh well. You guys want to see some dog tricks?"

Of course, the kids yelled, "Yeah!"

"Okay," I said. I nodded to Amanda. "Bad dog, Til. Very bad. Hit it, Manda."

She punched a button on the CD player and the Michael Jackson song, "Bad," blared forth.

"Come on, Til," I said. He ran to me, following my signal, circling around between my legs and standing up on his hind legs with his back against my stomach. We danced backward, together. We were moonwalking, Michael Jackson style. The kids screamed. Til weaved a figure eight shape through my legs, lay down and rolled over, crawled, sat up and begged, and did flips, a flash of white with his enthused doggy grin. The kids were ecstatic. Amanda sat in her chair and took pictures.

When the music ended, I "shot" Til with my finger, and he fell down "dead," a dramatic ending to his high energy performance. The kids were screaming and laughing. I took a leash from beneath the table and clipped it on his collar, handing the end of it to Amanda. She took it and spoke softly to the dog.

"Whew," I said to the kids, fanning myself with both hands. "He wears me out. And now it's time to bring Clifford in. You should see THAT suitcase!"

The kids shrieked with laughter as I walked out the door. Clifford was waiting expectantly by his horse trailer. He had his ears perked and was looking toward the school. He knew what was up.

"Here we go," I untied him and led him through the doors and down the hall. His hoofs clip-clopped, and he skidded a little bit on the newly waxed floor. He was the picture of alert fearlessness, with his ears forward, his stride purposeful. When we came through the door, the kids screamed like he was a rock star. I led him slowly and carefully down the front row of kids. His head was down and he greeted each child. If that child shrank away, he moved politely on to the next one. Kids crowded forward from behind the front row, stretching out to touch his face, but they stayed behind the tape. When we completed our pass, Clifford stood beside me, looking over them like a benevolent uncle.

"Now. How many of you have a horse?" I asked. A number of hands shot up. "Okay. How many of you think an animal can feel happy or sad, or disappointed?"

And so it went. I had begun the summer with a large laminated book on an easel, to talk about how horses had changed the world, with centuries of service to mankind and artistic inspiration. But the program had evolved into a question and answer session about horses and other animals. My focus was on empathy and consideration for other living things. I had a bag full of spongy, brightly-colored balls that I tossed to each child who answered a question. I realized that many of the kids might not remember exactly what we talked about, but I knew they would never forget the day a horse came into their library. I had given a lot of thought on how to make the best use of this lasting impact. I had decided that, if I had ever had children of my own, I would have most wanted them to learn how to empathize. People agree that money is the root of all evil. But I think the root of all evil stems from lack of empathy.

Amanda's love for Michael Jackson, and her selection of his song, "Heal the World," prompted me to finish the program by asking the children a new question. "How do you think you can make the world a better place?"

"Recycle," one girl said. I tossed her a ball.

"Pick up trash," another girl said.

"Picking up trash is good!" I said, and tossed her a ball.

Most of the answers were about recycling or cleaning up. But the answers I liked to hear the most were something like, "Be kind to another person. Pay it forward."

At the end of the program, I said, "Wow, you guys have been just awesome. I am so impressed with your group. Some of you have answered more than one question, and you have earned more than one ball. So now, if you want to, feel free to share the extras with someone who doesn't have one."

I was a little surprised by the generosity of the children. They immediately turned and started handing out their prizes. Throughout the room, good will prevailed.

"Who wants to come up and pet Clifford?" I asked.

More hands shot into the air. I pointed at the end of the first row, and said, "Okay, you, and you and you, come on up."

Some kids approached happily. Some were tentative. It didn't matter; Clifford loved kids and didn't spook at their sudden movements. I nodded to Amanda and she put the song on. The kids and their parents petted and talked to Clifford while the lilting music filled the room.

"Heal the world,
"Make it a better place…"

Clifford stood, completely relaxed, with one back foot cocked, as horses do when napping. He accepted all the attention happily. He would single out the smallest children in the group, blowing softly and nuzzling their hair. It was very touching, and in fact with the music playing, it was difficult for me to watch without getting choked up. I realized what a brilliant choice the song was. I knew she had been thinking of Mom. I looked at Amanda and gave her the "thumbs up" sign.

The next morning, while we were packing up, I looked out the window at the sandy beach. "Gosh I wish we had time to go walking down there," I said.

"I know!" Amanda said.

We bumped the horse trailer down the driveway and headed south. As the road curved out ahead of us through the cattails and budding hardwoods of the Upper Peninsula, I said, "Did you have fun yesterday?"

"Yes. Did you?"

"Yes," I said. "I always have fun with you. What was your favorite part?"

"The speech you gave at the library."

"Really?"

"Yes. I could tell what those people were thinking."

"What was that?"

"They were thinking you were crazy."

"Very funny!"

She laughed, an evil chortle.

"How many books do you think we will sell in Manistique?" I said.

"I hope a lot," she said. Then she added, "They should write a book about you, Nancy!"

"Aw, thanks! What should they write about?"

"About how I put up with you."

"Ha, ha, ha. You're so funny, I forgot to laugh! You know, I still want to write a screenplay starring you and me as bank robbers."

Amanda rolled her eyes. "Oh, please."

"Oh come on, it will be great. I will drive the getaway car, because you don't have a driver's license. You have to go into the bank and be the holdup guy. Can you handle a gun?"

She snorted. "Get real."

"No, seriously. Once you get the money, you won't be able to run, because of your knee. But it's okay. You can tell them to count to a hundred and then just fire off a couple of warning shots."

"Who's gonna watch the door for me?" Amanda asked.

I hesitated. "I don't know."

"Well, I guess we're not gonna be bank robbers then, are we!" She folded her arms in satisfaction and looked out the window. It was clearly the end of the discussion.

Chapter 5

About Mom – Amanda

How I could put this? Mom is trying to find herself. She has nine families, plus nine of us kids. She said her dad was a captain of a ship. He is there with her. He said, "Oh you're here!" when she arrived. He was surprised because he thought she would live longer. Mom is visiting with her family. She told me I did a good job taking care of her. She said we have to take care of ourselves now. She said, "You keep track of your dad for me." She is sad that she can't be here, but she's eating crackers and wine. She loves the music there.

Without Mom - Nancy

I had told everyone that I had run off and joined the dog circus. The Cosmic K9 Show was a broken-down traveling dog sport arena that had been touring the eastern part of the United States for some twenty years. Since I had a background in theatre and loved teaching tricks to animals, I was a shoo-in. The show's producer, Bud was a broken-down relic as well, bright but short-tempered, slugging down a six-pack every evening, a veritable poster child for wasted potential. We had started out in a dating relationship, but the romance died quickly once I realized how mean-spirited and negative he was. His rage bordered on absurd. If anything inconvenient happened, such as our crowd barrier getting tangled during setup, he would scream, "I hate life! I can't wait to get off this god-forsaken planet."

We had local teams that came out at each city and performed, but I was the only trainer that traveled with the show. Til and Ms. Rip were the ringers on the team. Til opened the show with his Frisbee routine. I pulled him out in the suitcase under the pretense of setting up. Bud would say, "Nancy always starts out her frisbee routine with a few props. What you got in there?" and I would open the side zipper pocket and pull out some discs, and wave them around.

"Oh, Frisbees, of course," Bud would say. "What else have you got?" I would unzip the main compartment just as Bud started the music, and Til would come bursting out of the suitcase to the opening riff of Kenny Loggins' "Footloose". He would spin around and around in tight circles while the audience screamed, and then I'd fling the Frisbee and he would shoot after it like a rocket. He almost never missed. His performance was unfailingly energetic. He would roll over, weave around my legs, dance on his hind feet, and twirl and flip and jump. He could catch almost anything I threw. He never tired of it. When he would fall "dead" at my signal, on the song's last note, the audience would leap to their feet, screaming. He loved performing, and I loved performing with him.

He didn't stop there. He would compete in the speed race too, circling the course of low jumps. He would run it by himself while I waited near the finish, tapping my wrist as if I had a watch on. He usually had the fastest time. Ms. Rip ran it too, but she was much slower, and I always ran Til last. However, Ms. Rip excelled at high jumping. On a good day, she could clear 54 inches. At some shows, we had dogs who could go higher, but we always counted on her to clear a child's head. Bud would pull a kid from the audience and set them in front of the jump. "Are you nervous?" Bud would say. Then, "I'm not talking to you, I'm talking to Ms. Rip! She's over there praying for a good jump!"

I would have Ms. Rip praying, with her paws up on the podium and her head buried in them. I would be praying next to her. The audience loved it. Ms Rip seemed to know when she had to leap over a child, and she would lift her feet extra high. We always ended the show with high jumping. When we were short on team, I would put Til in high jumping too, but I never asked him to go higher than 36 inches, just because he was working so hard in all the other events.

We trundled all over the Midwest, from Michigan to New York, from Florida to New Jersey. The dogs loved the show, and the schedule was erratic but the pay was decent; when Bud decided to pay me. Putting up with him was a chore. Aside from his drinking, he was surly, insulting and ungrateful. He would cover the microphone and scream at me or other team members during performances. "You idiots! Get over there! What the fuck are you doing?"

By the time Mom got sick, I had been with the show for nearly a year. But after she died, the tour provided a good excuse for avoidance on my part. Dad's pain was palpable. At Marcus's house, my bedroom had been next to Dad's. In the early mornings I could hear him groaning, "No!" and beginning to sob, as he came back to consciousness and realized Mom was no more. It was making me weep too. Each morning at daybreak, I lay awake, waiting and dreading the moment he woke up. I had no idea how to help him. I thought I couldn't bear it any more.

I was staying away for long stretches. Then I came home after one road trip and opened the refrigerator, and found it crammed full with the same things I had left there the week prior. Nothing had been touched. I opened a carton of cottage cheese to find a dark green mass covering it. I dropped it into the trash and looked at Amanda.

"What the heck have you guys been eating?"

"Bologna sandwiches. I make them for Dad," she said.

I sighed. I dragged the trash can over to the refrigerator and began the process of cleaning it out. "We are starting over, here," I told Amanda. "Grab a pen and paper. We are going shopping."

My other siblings generally didn't appear, and in fact they didn't even call very often. They had gone back to their own lives, leaving Dad and Amanda to putter around and fend for themselves.

Mom had been gone about five months by that time. Our cousins Frank and Maxine would stop by to check in on them, but Maxine was suffering serious health issues. My closest siblings, R1 and Marcus, were each three hours away: R1 in Escanaba area, and Marcus in Cadillac. I felt no resentment toward either of them; just a sad resignation.

"I have to quit being such a wimp," I told Amanda as we left the house that day.

"Oh, come on now. You're fine. Gotta love you for who you are," she said.

Cooking wasn't my forte, and since I had been living alone for ten years, it hadn't been much of a necessity. But I realized that I was going to have to make some changes. Dad and Amanda had to eat. The house was a mess. Every flat surface was covered in papers. Mom had made a hobby of ordering magazine subscriptions. Magazines were considered a thing of value. They were never thrown away. They were stacked everywhere. "Outdoor Life," "Men's Health," "Birder's World" and Amanda's "People" magazines filled every imaginable space. Amanda and Dad both seemed addicted to tissues. Their pockets were filled with them. If I forgot to empty their pockets before doing the laundry, I found bits of tissue spread inside the washing machine and all over the clean clothes. Tissues were stuffed between the couch cushions and into every cranny in the car. I was no clean freak, but it drove me nuts. Still, I would have to pick things up furtively and not make extreme changes to the house in any noticeable way. They would resent the intrusion. They had never been tidy, but they were worse now, languishing in their grief. I knew that, since I was the one with no spouse and no kids, and the flexible schedule, it was going to fall on me to help them.

"You know that old saying," I said. "If you want something done right –"

"Don't do anything at all," Amanda said.

We hit the grocery store. Amanda was leaning comfortably on the cart, pushing it around while I marched up and down the aisles searching for staples on our list: Hamburger. Cream of mushroom soup. Spaghetti sauce. The all-important breakfast cereal, Wheaties®. Orange juice. Bananas. I picked out some of Dad's favorite treats: Dry-roasted peanuts and dried apricots.

The kitchen was another matter. The counters were cluttered with mail, old broken dishes glued together, cups full of pens that didn't write. I wondered how anyone could function in this mess, much less create the culinary masterpieces Mom used to make. Amanda sat watching while I opened one cupboard after another. "Where is the lid to that skillet?"

"Other cupboard," she said. "Bottom shelf."

"Oh great. I guess I gotta get down there and dig for it." I squeezed behind her, absently carrying a ladle in my hand.

"Please don't spoon me," she said.

"Hardy har. You're so funny." I got down on my hands and knees, grunting with effort as I searched and clattered through the stack of pans and lids.

Behind me, I heard Amanda whisper. "Say bow-wow."

"SHUT UP!" I roared.

"YOU shut up!"

Dad's voice floated in from the living room. "You two get along!"

There were moments like that when Dad was his old self, but his melancholy remained. He seemed to be feeling okay physically. He was diabetic and his diet had certain requirements. He was diligent about testing his blood sugar regularly. He had a pacemaker and his cardiologist was a young, beautiful German woman named Dr. Underwood. She had dark, curly hair, a thick accent and a delicious smile. "Your dad is the same age as my dad," she had once told me. "So I try to treat him as I would want someone to treat my dad."

This endeared her to me forever. Her main office was in Petoskey, which was about an hour and a half drive from DeTour. It required crossing the Mackinac Bridge, a five-mile suspension cable monstrosity that spanned the watery gap between Michigan's Upper and Lower Peninsulas.

I thought it was the bridge that provided some type of psychological boundary to people. Those in the U.P. seemed loathe to cross it. Dad was no exception. He always hated traveling downstate, although he loved Dr. Underwood. Because he was 85 years old, she required him to come down for bi-annual checkups. That spring, she had asked to see him. Since it was a morning appointment, Amanda stayed in bed and Dad and I went. He was unusually quiet as we drove.

We crossed the bridge, driving past the miles of steel and cable, humming over the steel grate on the road suspended beneath the two shining towers. The wrinkled blue Straits of Mackinac shimmered far below us. The sky arched above Lake Michigan to our right, and to our left, the sprawling, island-studded Lake Huron. As the hilly road of the southern peninsula curved out before us, Dad said, "I know I am not supposed to say this. But I really don't think I want to go on without your mother."

"You can say whatever you want," I said. "And I think I knew that you felt that way. And it is your decision. Whatever you decide, I will back you up. But there are lots of people who want you here."

I knew that when people had been married for as long as a half century, if one partner dies, very often the other will give up and go shortly thereafter. My dad's own mother had passed away just six months after her husband. I was afraid Dad might make that choice. It was a little bit funny, I thought, because for years, I had viewed him as virtually indestructible. After all, he had survived some remarkable traumas. He had flourished after a five-way bypass. On his way down the hill to the Drummond ferry dock, the brakes had failed on his old pickup. Rather than go sailing off the end of the dock into the St. Mary's River, he had swerved and smacked into the metal guard rail. The truck was totaled, but Dad walked away from it. He had fallen through the ice at least four times in his life. And he had a knack for setting himself on fire. The last time he had ignited himself was when I had given him a large electric space heater for Christmas. He had been working in his shop and had backed into it, without noticing that his nylon snowsuit was starting to heat up. Finally he smelled something, and realized he was ablaze. Fortunately, there was plenty of snow to roll in.

After Mom's death, I felt there wasn't too much I could do for Dad's morale, but I could see that by staying away, I wasn't helping him. I had to come back and participate in his life. I decided to spend more time with him on the Island, to re-create my normal routine of walking the dogs and riding the horses, and meanwhile bone up on duties like the cooking. Making ends meet was going to be tough, but I no longer had my farm to worry about. I could sell art, and continue to do the dog shows to make the bills. My true financial recovery would have to wait.

I contemplated how best to cheer him up, without being too pushy about it. I wanted his recovery to come naturally. I had read somewhere that, if your body begins to do things, then your mind will follow. In essence, your body can train your mind. I thought if I smiled more, Dad would smile back. If he was smiling, he might be able to "trick" himself into some happy moments.

Anyway, it was worth a try.

Cribbage brought him back to life. I didn't know if it was the competition, or the nostalgia of all those mornings with Mom, but during a game he would light up. He got that old glint in his steel-blue eyes and start yelling, "Fifteen two, fifteen four, fifteen six and a pair are eight! I'm in the hole." He would slap down the cards, his knobby fingers moving the toothpicks we used as pegs, from one hole to the next in the knotty old board. I would count out my own points and he would say, "Are you sure? Look again." He would tap me gently, pointing to my cards with his crooked forefinger, and sure enough I would have missed something.

Another highlight in Dad's life was driving down the road ahead of us one day, past the old Drummond Cemetery and the airport that doubled as a golf course. Out of the passenger side of the car in front of us emerged a thin arm, waving us on in a circular motion, beckoning us to follow.

"I think that's Maxine," I could recognize Frank's shorn orange head bent behind the steering wheel.

We pulled up behind them right in front of the mechanic's shop, and Maxine got out and came to the window. She was thin, ravished with illness, but beaming. "I have a pie for you," she said. "Come on over."

Besides being relatives, Maxine and Frank had been longtime friends to Dad and Mom. They had supplied them with furniture, food, endless emotional support, and good company throughout their lives. Their eldest son Frankie, who was just my age, had been killed while doing construction on a roof several years prior. The loss was terribly hard on everyone, but especially Amanda. She had talked of Frankie constantly over the years.

Finally, Maxine's time came. I was hosing Clifford off by the picket fence, squirting a cold stream of water over his back, and Dad came trundling up in the Tahoe. Amanda got out and immediately hobbled up the ramp into the trailer. I looked over at Dad and he said, "Maxine died."

I put the hose down, went over and turned off the water, leaving Clifford to graze.

"That's a hard loss," I said. "How did you find out?"

"Sue just told me."

I walked up the long ramp into the Lodge and found Amanda sitting by herself on the couch. She looked up at me through red-rimmed eyes. "Did you hear about Maxine?" she said.

"Yes," I said. "Dad just told me. I'm so sorry."

"We have to let the family know."

"Yes. We will." I sat down and put my arm around her. "Do you think she and Mom are together now? She and Frankie?"

"Oh yes," she said confidently.

"Well, I guess that is a good thing. She will watch over our mother."

Amanda was quiet. Damn it, I thought. Damn the luck. Maxine was barely into her seventies. She was such a treasure for these two. It was the worst possible timing; a tremendous double whammy. I struggled for words that might comfort Amanda. Finally, I said, "Well, that does it, then. We have had enough loss. Enough death. I hate death!"

"Me too," she said.

"We need some solace. We need some comfort. We need a solution." I was allowing myself to get pissed off, letting it show.

"That's right," Amanda was looking up now, watching me intently.

"We need a Girl's Day Out!" I roared.

She smiled. "You're crazy."

"Hey! I'm just trying to help out, here!"

She laughed a little. We both knew there was no use in fighting the inevitable wave of grief that would engulf us all. But we knew there would always be Girl's Day Out. Pizza and a movie was our old reliable consommé, our sanctuary, our consolation prize. No matter how bad things got, we always had an escape.

Helping Dad through it was another story. The only thing I could do was be present for him. I thought if I helped Amanda feel better, that might be of some comfort to him. He also had the unenviable ability to commiserate with Frank, although I was sure neither of them would prefer it that way. There was nothing left to do but let the long days take us away from the shock of another loss, while the hard rain beat the rocks clean, and the sun dried the scented balsam needles, and the loons cried out from the inland lakes. This was our comfort; Drummond Island with its ancient cedars and the soft, sweet earth where our ancestors had tread. We carried on. The horses nickered softly, munching their mix of grass and alfalfa, enjoying the slanted sun on their withers while the border collie wore a path around their corral. Every afternoon I walked over flat rock in the warm yellow light, with the wind tumbling over the poplars and a host of dragonflies flitting and hovering around me.

Then the Fourth of July arrived with all its crackling fanfare, and a host of tourists and relatives came from all parts of Michigan. They crawled all over the Island in jeeps and SUVs, mowing down small saplings and creating deep ruts in the back roads. The uproarious R's and their offspring showed up, yelling, hurling insults, laughing too hard. They filled the refrigerator with enormous tubs of egg salad and cold soda and beer. They had chips and cookies and jam and hardened sweet rolls with cellophane adhering to them. The lower shelf of the fridge was crammed with a cake that had blue icing reading, "Congratulations on Your Engagement".

The Cosmic K9s were doing a dog show at the ball field that year. I had orchestrated it in part as an excuse to get away from the relatives. I rode Clifford in the parade. After all these years, I thought I could probably just turn Clifford loose and he could do the parade by himself. Dad and Amanda sat and watched us go by from Aunt Sue's front yard. I waved to them. "Hi Clifford!" Amanda roared.

The parade ended at the ball field, which was convenient because I could tie Clifford to the trailer there so he could enjoy some grass while we got ready for the show. I had recruited some local handlers with dogs to come and run the course.

Amanda was entranced with the idea of the show being in her hometown. She and Dad sat backstage under the tent to watch. She had supplied Bud with her Michael Jackson CD, and so Clifford performed his tricks to the song from Free Willy, "Will You Be There". She was dressed in a red, white and blue T shirt and holding a small flag that she waved enthusiastically.

"Nancy," she said. "Find out if Bud will let us sing into the microphone."

"Sing what?" I asked.

"A patriotic song. To celebrate our country. How about, 'God Bless America'?"

"I'm sure he will," I said. "But we will have to do it a capella. No music."

"I can handle that," she said.

When the show ended, I said to Bud, "You have to give us a proper introduction."

He just shook his head and handed me the microphone.

"Fine, I'll do it myself!" I switched the microphone on. "Now, coming to you live from Drummond Island Michigan, a patriotic statement from the Hot Blood Sisters, Amanda and Nancy Bailey."

Amanda leaned into the mic and shouted, "This is for our mother! Elaine Bailey!'

She immediately began to sing. Her low, raspy voice boomed from the speakers. "God Bless America."

People stopped in their tracks. Mothers and little kids, old fishermen and bent old ladies craned their heads to see where the guttural voice was coming from. Many of them were relatives whom, upon hearing Amanda, beamed broadly and nudged each other and pointed. Amanda glared at me while she sang. I took a deep breath and joined in. "Land that I love, stand beside her, and guide her, through the night with a light from above."

There we stood, face to face, singing to the entire community on the little baseball field now littered with crepe paper streamers. With no music, it was worse than the worst karaoke ever. Amanda belted the lyrics in a flat alto that had no resemblance to the original song and in my higher pitch, I was nearly as bad. It was an onslaught to the senses.

"From the mountains, to the prairies, to the oceans, white with foam..."

Amanda had not taken her eyes from mine. She was in full-throated concentration.

"God bless America..." At this point I felt it would be appropriate to salute. I snapped a quick salute to her, and she reciprocated. But she still had the flag in her hand, and as a result she slapped it across her forehead. She never lost her serious expression, holding the stick firmly while the stars and stripes unfurled over one eye. When I started laughing, she scowled and said, "No! Keep going!"

I sobered quickly. "My home sweet home..."

Perhaps mercifully, we were drowned out by the crowd that had been subjected to our performance. The applause was uproarious. They hooted and yelled, "Nice job Amanda! God bless America!"

She beamed, leaning into the microphone, "Thank you! Happy Independence Day!"

101

Clifford stood by his trailer and grazed while we packed up the agility equipment. When the truck was loaded, I hauled him back to camp and saddled up for my annual ride to the rocky shore. The family was still in town, and I soaked up the quiet hours with Clifford and Trudy, brushing them both and squirting them with fly spray. I rode Clifford at a gallop down the road and Trudy and the dogs took off after us.

When I got back to camp, I went in for a cold drink and noticed the remains of the cake on the bottom shelf of the fridge. The blue letters now spelled out, "Engage."

Chapter 6

About Being Home – Amanda

How I could put this? At first it was sad. I was picturing Mom sitting in her spot at the table, next to Dad. Dad was lonely and sad, very quiet. I went into Mom's room and her dresser and I picked out her shirts. I started wearing some of them to be close to her. My favorite was the white one with flowers embroidered on the front. It still smelled like her a little. After some time I started sitting in her chair at the table. I don't know why. It's awkward for me to try to explain it. But I think it helped Dad that I started sitting there. I make sure he takes his medication at every meal. That's what Mom used to do. I make sure he doesn't work too hard. I ride with him in the truck and I go everywhere he does. I stick to him like glue.

About Being Home - Nancy

Dad and Amanda had Direct TV installed and began a nostalgic review of old episodes of, "The Waltons" and, "Dr. Quinn, Medicine Woman." Amanda loved TV. I scorned it for the most part, although hearing Dad laughing at, "The Big Bang Theory" caught my attention. "This is a good show," he said.

I began watching reruns with them every evening while I made dinner. It helped that the theme song was performed by one of my favorite groups, Barenaked Ladies. I learned all the words to it and would sing along. Amanda would finish it off with a squealy, "Bang!" at the end. Even though we did this each night, Dad laughed every single time.

Physical activity was demanding for Amanda. She didn't want to take walks with me. I figured if I weighed over 200 pounds, with bad knees and tiny, flat feet, I wouldn't want to walk, either. But she could swim. Our cousin Denny had a pool at his hotel, and so as summer heated up, that became our ritual. Best of all, on days when she went swimming, I didn't make her take a shower. If the chlorine was heavy, she could just hose off at the pool. She didn't have any hair to wash. I did insist that she shave her armpits. When I wasn't around, she had a tendency to let the hair grow. That was easy enough for me to fix. If she happened to lift her arm for any reason, exposing armpit hair, I would make the motion of pulling the cord on a lawn mower.

"Rrrrummm… Rummm rum rum rum!" I would grab the invisible handle and jounce like I was pushing it.

She glared at me. "Knock it off!"

But it always worked. She would shave her armpits.

She hated the whole shower effort. "It's always the same old thing."

On our first swim day, she came out of the bathroom wearing her shorts and tank top over a leopard print one-piece.

"I had to wrestle my swimming suit to get it on," she said, sitting down and reaching for her shoes.

"Okay, I'll be ready in a sec." I went in the bathroom and glanced into the bathtub. On the curve of rusty porcelain near the drain there was a creature about the size of a quarter, with eight tentacles. I believe the scientific name for it is Lupus Arachnis Horribilis. Being an animal lover, I had no fear of spiders, regardless of their size, but this was a good opportunity to stir things up with Amanda.

"Amanda!" I screeched. "You've got to see this!"

She must have known what I was yelling about, because she came hobbling in armed with a fly swatter. "I'm gonna swoosh him."

I jumped up and down screaming while she swooshed and Lupus ran down the drain. She turned on the faucet. "It's okay Nancy. He's gone. Pull yourself together."

As we got in the car, I said, "Jeesh, after all that I am gonna need a cola. Let's head over to the Northwood. You can tell Celia's mom about your conquest."

"Celia's mother doesn't own the restaurant anymore," Amanda said.

"She doesn't?"

"No. She said she misses working there."

"Who owns it now?"

"The other owner."

We drove on down through the woods to Pins restaurant, turning down the cracked ribbon of pavement to the resort area where the big wooden fence surrounded Denny's pool. Til was panting in the back seat. He jumped out when I opened the door and ran into the woods with his nose down, his plumy white tail waving. "Hurry up!" I yelled. "Go potty! Hurry up!"

"Jeesh. Pressure, Nancy. Pressure!" Amanda said.

"Well, you don't want any accidents in the pool, do you?"

"Don't be gross!"

Til performed his duty and came blasting back, and we walked up to the big, creaky gate and stepped inside. As I had expected, we were the only ones there. As Amanda rolled and played in the water, tossing a ball for the elated dog, I watched from the poolside.

"Here," I took a couple of quarters from my pocket and dropped them in, watching as they glinted and flipped to the bottom. "See if you can find these!"

She dove, slippery as a seal, her little flat feet pointing and waving up at the wrinkled water's surface, her hand patting the pool floor all around the quarters. She was so buoyant that it was taking hard scissor kicks to keep her inverted. I was thinking I could probably get some muscle tone on her just by dropping things into the pool a few days a week.

Finally, she came up gasping for breath.

"You missed!" I shouted.

"I know," she said.

"Can't you open your eyes?"

"I don't like getting them in the chlorine. I don't have my goggles. Hey, you should come in with me!"

"Not gonna happen. You know I don't swim."

"Chicken. Bawk, bawk buk buk."

"That's right. And if the ferry ever sinks, you're under contract to save my sorry cement block ass."

"It's a deal." She dove again, patting the bottom and this time I saw her fist close over a quarter. She surfaced. "I got it!"

"Waytago!"

She swam to the poolside, putting the quarter up by my foot. "Here's your change, Nancy."

As I bent over to pick it up, I was hit in the side of the face and head with a blast of cold water. "Hey!"

I looked up and caught a glimpse of the squirt gun she was aiming at me, just before another shot of water hit me right between the eyes. "You're gonna get wet, one way or the other, you rat!" She was roaring laughter, dousing me with rapid bursts of cold spray as I screamed and ducked away.

"How did you…" I shouted, and then choked as she caught me with another shot square in the mouth. I had never heard her laugh so hard.

"Let me introduce my secret weapon, Nancy!" she shouted. She was floating upright, bobbing gently in the water like a buoy, her bald head gleaming in the bright sun, pointing the lime green plastic gun at me.

"Nice!" I said.

"I got you good! I can't wait to tell Dad."

At that point, anything that could make Dad laugh was welcome. He was putting forth a good effort to be cheerful, but I knew he was missing Mom terribly. One cool afternoon, when I was feeding the horses a scoop of grain, he came out and stood by the fence and I stopped to talk with him. He held up a sheet of paper. "I am leaving you this property."

He showed me a penciled map of the Lodge area, with the thirteen acres sectioned off, except for the largest parcel which included the Lodge, the corral and gazebo, on which he had written, "Nancy".

"This is for you to share with Amanda," he said. "I am going to leave you the tractor and my shotgun, too."

"Your shotgun?" I started to laugh.

He shrugged. "Well, you're going to need to protect yourself!"

I was amused at the thought of him picturing Amanda and me, living out our lives back here like a couple of bootleggers. "Okay," I said. "Thank you. That is nice of you to think of me. Come on in, and I will make you some dinner."

I fixed Dad and Amanda what I called my Cowboy Dinner: Pork chops and applesauce, Santa Fe style brown rice with black beans, and biscuits. They cleaned up every scrap and then enjoyed some fresh baked chocolate chip cookies. Dad was diabetic but he was faithful about checking his blood sugar every day. As long as his numbers were good, he could have cookies. I would bake the cookies until they were nearly black on the bottom. It made Amanda angry, but Dad and I liked them that way. "You're outnumbered two to one on the cookies," I said.

"Well, how about you make up a special batch for me?" she said. "Don't leave mine in so long!"

"Oh, okay," I would sigh. I usually did.

I was glad to see Dad enjoying his meals. After all my years with animals, I knew a hearty appetite was a good sign of health and well-being. If an animal still wanted to eat, then it still had the will to live. I knew that thoughts of his own demise were inevitable, and that planning was a necessity, but I still hoped that Dad wouldn't give up. He had a few health challenges, but he was at good weight and very strong and fit for his age.

Dr. Underwood had let us know that he was going to need a stent put into one of his arteries. As the summer lengthened into August, we scheduled the surgery. I took him back across the bridge to Petoskey and we checked in at the heart and vascular center, where we were greeted by the pretty German surgeon. It was only a couple of hours later that she came out to where I sat in the waiting room. She looked rather like she'd just awakened from a nap, with her fresh complexion and the signature rumpled white cap on her head. She sat down next to me companionably. "Your Dad is the Miracle Man. Everything looks good. He should start having more energy after this."

"Thank you. That is wonderful. I appreciate you taking such good care of him."

When I got up the next morning he was eating Wheaties®. "Another day of sitting around doing nothing," he grumbled.

"There he goes again. 'Blaine Complain'," Amanda said.

"He has a few more days to take it easy," I said. "That incision has to heal."

A message chimed in on my Blackberry, a little signature, "bling" sound.

"That phone is calling you, Dad!" Amanda said, "It's saying, 'Blaine! Blaine! Blaine!'"

.   We laughed. I thought Dad's impatience was a good sign. Dr. Underwood turned out to be right. As the season extended into a long and colorful Indian summer, Dad's spirit prevailed and he began to rally. We had to travel back to see Dr. Underwood for his recheck. As we drove along the beautiful hilly shores of Grand Traverse Bay, admiring the blazing maples, Dad said, "You didn't have children."

"No primates," I said.

"Why not?"

"No worthy donors."

"I think you should."

"Good grief!" I said, "What's happening in six weeks?"

"What?"

"I'll be fifty!"

"You'd have good ones."

I snorted. "Not now. They'd be maladjusted and deformed, borne of a pre-menopausal bohemian and sired by some addict. Or worse, a relative."

He laughed. "Nuthin' wrong with that!"

"Besides, you have enough grandchildren."

"I'd like yours."

I shook my head. "Wasn't this argument supposed to take place like 20 years ago? Yet I'm flattered. In a twisted sort of way."

He laughed again. When we met with Dr. Underwood and he told her, "I'm single now, you know," I knew he was coming back from wherever he had been.

Dad financed most of his road trips, and our dinners out. He always made sure Amanda had a little spending money, which she used to help with our Girls' Day Out. But other than that, the rest of it fell to me. I ended up covering most of the groceries. I was cooking for them faithfully, creating meals I thought would be nutritious without over-indulging their love for junk food. One night it was chili the way Mom had taught me to make it. The next, New York strip with mushrooms, sweet potatoes, baked beans, and biscuits hot out of the oven. I was constantly baking chocolate chip cookies for us, thanks to the convenience of the modern refrigerated dough rolls. The three of us laughed together, watching reruns of Big Bang Theory. Dad walked through the cedars, his stride as light as a young man, calling out to Clifford with his speech slurring, but his voice still deep and powerful. The Indian summer days were growing shorter on the Island, but still in the seventies and sunny. I was wading up to my knees in Lake Huron, playing with dogs while the sun touched my shoulders and face, and looking at the trees tinged with shades of crimson and burnt yellow.

"I've never seen a fall like this," Dad said.

All of Michigan was warmer than usual that year, and the colorful hardwoods lined I-75 all the way south of Grayling. I continued doing the dog shows, hauling Ms Rip and Til all over the state and even to the east coast; New York, Pennsylvania and New Jersey. On the way back one day, I was sitting in the car on the ferry as it chugged toward the island, and my cell phone rang. It said, "R1." I answered it.

"Hello from the middle of the Saint Mary's River," I said cheerfully. "Your timing is impeccable."

It was one of the few places in the area where one could get a clear signal. Once I drove onto the island, it quickly became a dead zone.

"Hi Nan, what are you up to?" R1 said.

"I'm heading over to cook dinner for Dad and Amanda," I said. "I am just getting back from downstate."

"Oh, good. Hey I was wondering when your next trip down is. I might need you to transport a kid and some boxes for me."

I hesitated. "Well, my next show is in two weeks, but I am not sure how much room I will have for passengers and the like. My back seat is crammed with dogs. My trunk is crammed with show equipment and stuff."

"You're not going back sooner?"

"Nope. I'll be here for awhile."

She sighed. "Well, maybe I can finagle something where you can meet them downstate and be a ride back up."

"I'd love to help you out – but you should see my car!" I started laughing. "It's loaded. There's barely room for me in here. I am thinking of teaching Til to just drive himself to these things."

"Are you sure? I could really use the help."

"I wish I could. Sorry."

She sighed in exasperation. "You are worthless."

I was stunned into a brief silence, but I realized that dead air might be giving her the effect she wanted. So, I agreed with her. "Yep, that's me! You called it. I'm worthless. And now I am taking my worthless ass to Drummond Island to feed your dad and sister!"

I hung up.

The boat groaned in to the dock and I bumped over the lowered ramp in disgust, thinking that it was exactly like the scenario at Amanda's birthday party: R1 looking to satisfy her own agenda, without seeing what was really going on around her. She had not visited, or contacted me to ask what we may need, or find out if she could do anything for Dad.

I pulled over in the parking lot by the ferry dock and got out of the car and walked around, breathing the clear, cedar-laden air. The evening sun was dappling the river with spangles, and I stood there watching the rest of the cars unload, listening to the crash and thump as they came off the ramp. Looking at the bright sky, I felt myself grow calmer. I was in the right place, I decided. I was doing the right thing. Whether others deemed me worthless was irrelevant.

When I was on the road, I had to make sure I had enough gas money to get back to the Upper Peninsula. It generally added an additional five hours onto any trip. Ferry tickets were expensive, too. As a regular passenger, you could get a coupon for ten trips for $54.00, which worked out okay as long as you weren't driving something with more than two axles. In that case, it cost more. If I was hauling Clifford, I had to be prepared. I wasn't saving a penny, but I told myself that it was a phase. My priority was just to make sure I was available to Dad and Amanda. But I wasn't above complaining about how broke I was.

On Amanda's birthday, I was driving her to the Soo, bemoaning the cost of gas and ferry rates while sucking down a can of mocha double shot.

"You and your Starbucks," Amanda said.

"Hey. I know quality."

"I think THAT'S where all your money goes."

"Who asked you?"

"I guess I'd better shut up now."

"Like that's gonna happen!" I smirked. "Anyway. I didn't sleep all that great last night. It was like – hey. Have you ever fallen asleep with your eyes open?"

"No."

"How do you know?"

"What?"

"If you fall asleep, how do you know if your eyes are open?"

She scowled and shook her head. "You're driving me crazy."

"Gotta love me for who I am," I laughed and turned on the music. Michael Jackson's "Beat It" riffed through the speakers. "Happy Birthday, Girl!"

"Thank you!"

We settled into our usual seat at Ang-gio's restaurant, and the waitress delivered our colas without us having to ask.

"It's my birthday," Amanda announced.

"Happy Birthday!" the waitress said.

"Thank you."

"Did they make you a cake?" the waitress asked.

"No. I can't trust anybody."

The waitress laughed. "What can I get you?"

"Well, if it's all right with Nancy, I would like a glass of wine." Amanda looked at me slyly.

"Sure," I looked at the waitress. "White zin?"

"Yes, for both of you?"

"No, I'll just have my cola," I said.

I wasn't a big wine drinker, but Amanda loved it. She was astute enough to realize it was for special occasions. It was always just one glass. I would let her order it if she wanted to, although the unspoken agreement between us was that Dad must never know. He would certainly disapprove. Mom had loved telling the story about them coming home to Amanda washing dishes. "I wish you guys hadn't come back so early," Amanda said as she rinsed a wine glass and laid it gently in the dish rack.

Whenever Mom told the story, she would crow, "We busted her! She was drinking from a bottle of cooking sherry!"

The first time Amanda asked for wine at a restaurant, it was shortly after Mom was admitted into the nursing home. I thought maybe she would like to relax. When the wine came, she picked up the glass and took a big swallow.

"You're supposed to savor it, not gulp it," I took the glass from her. "Inhale the bouquet first, see?" I dipped my nose in past the rim and sniffed deeply. "Ahhh. Then, swirl it, and hold it up to the light, and look at the color. Then you sip it. Wine isn't just a drink. It's an art."

She watched me intently, and then followed my instructions to the letter. Now every time she had a glass of wine, she would sniff it, then swirl it, and then slowly taste it. She enjoyed every minute of it. On occasion, I would have a glass with her. But usually I just let her imbibe, and watched with some amusement. I loved the way she appreciated it.

Today, she drank until the glass was not quite empty, and said, "I left you some, Nancy. You can have the last sip."

She pushed the glass across the table toward me.

I didn't really want any, but I realized this was her small sacrifice, a gift for me. "Oh, thank you." I took it, and swirled it while she watched. Then I downed it. "Ahhh. Great way to celebrate your birthday."

She did earn a free cake at the restaurant that night. After a boisterous dinner, we celebrated on our bluff, the high hill overlooking the International Bridge. The first stars were poking through the darkening sky. We stood for a moment just breathing the cool air, smelling the great space of the deepest inland sea. What a year it had been, I thought. It seemed like hardly any time had passed since we were last standing here, with me on my damaged foot and Amanda marking another decade. The last time we stood here, it had been our mother's final days at home. Now she was gone.

"Hey Mother!" Amanda yelled. "I'm forty-one! I'm forty-one years old!"

"Woo hoo!' We're here Mom!" I shouted. "I'm forty-nine! I'm forty-nine! We're still here!"

"Yeah! Mother! I'm here!" Amanda flung her arms upward and raised her voice to the sky.

Chapter 7

About Brothers - Amanda

Marcus wanted a little brother. He told Mom, "Please don't have another girl!" and then I showed up!

And Theil said, "Don't worry about it, Mom. I'll take care of Manda."

Jon is the oldest and he was in the Navy. Nancy and I got him a t-shirt that said, 'Old Navy.' We laughed about it. Jon is a mountain man. He's a rootin' tootin' boy. He can't take care of me because of his health. His lungs gave out. He almost died. It was scary. I sat by his hospital bed and sang to him. "Oh Jonny, Oh Jonny, what have you done? Oh Jonny, oh Jonny, show them your big guns."

He woke up and walked out of there and drove himself home.

About Family - Nancy

"My back hurts," Dad said. His wrinkled face was deeply furrowed and he wriggled from side to side to emphasize his point. "Jon took me to the doctor and then Rose took me to the doctor."

I turned away from the sink with a water glass in my hand. "What did they say?"

"They said it was inconclusive."

This bothered me. I began firing more questions.

"What kind of doctor was it?"

"A VA doctor."

"Where does it hurt?"

"Right over my shoulder blade." He jerked a thumb back toward his left.

I set the glass down. He was 86 years old, a heart patient with diabetes. Back pain was nothing to mess with. "I want to take you to the ER. Will you go?"

He sighed. "I guess so."

It was April 2012. Dad and Amanda had just returned from spending the winter in Washington State with my brother Jon. They had stopped in Colorado on the way back, to spend a few days with R2, the second oldest sister, and then hopped a plane for home. I was recovering from surgery on my Achilles tendon. I had had the surgery in Lansing and stayed on the couch for two months afterward in the home of my friend Cindy, who was a medical professional. The foot was still weak and basically useless even though the cast was off. While still in the cast, as soon as I was able to move around, I had gone back to running my dogs in the show. I couldn't run with them. But I had taught Til to run the course by himself, and adding hopping over my crutches to his Frisbee routine. It was not as dynamic, because I couldn't dance around with him, but the audience loved it. Ms. Rip didn't need my help to high jump. I would just send her, and she would run out, go over the jump, and come right back. I could do that with crutches.

But now I was out of the cast and home, welcoming Amanda and Dad back from their long absence, hoping for a summer that was better than the prior one.

Dad appreciated time with his kids, but he missed being home. "This winter I want to go to Arizona, Colorado and Washington," he said. "But only for six weeks. This time away was too long."

"Just don't make it for September," Amanda said. "I'd have to clear my calendar."

Over the winter I had added two more dogs to the family. Both were tiny, given to me by friends, to perform in the show. One was Estephar, a plucky six pound Chihuahua female the color of sand. The other was Jack Johnson, a black and white spotted fluffy male, ten pounds, with a propensity to be timid. I was playing with them, having them spin and jump for bits of chicken.

"Do they sit up and beg?" Amanda said.

"They don't know that one yet. Til can do that one."

"Oh I know Til can do that one. Til is a top-notch dog!"

I smiled. Amanda was not what I considered to be a real animal lover, but she had always honored my love for animals. She embraced mine as members of my family. She had even taken to adding them to cards and letters she sent to me. She meant to address things to, "Nancy Bailey, Dogs and Horses." Her phonetic spelling combined with her dyslexia, and it always came out reading, "Nancy Bailey, Gods and Hores." Mom and I had laughed and laughed over that one. It had been emblazoned forever in my signature. On the keyboard of Mom's organ there perched a card, a small yellow rectangle left over from my last bouquet of flowers to her. "Happy Mother's Day, with love from Nancy, Gods and Hores."

Unfortunately, Dad's back pain continued to plague him with no medical solution. Within a week, I had him back to the doctor trying to get him some help. They determined that it was not heart related or life threatening. Due to lack of "urgency" they scheduled him for a visit in two weeks. They suggested he take Motrin in the meantime.

This was unacceptable to me. Dad was suffering. He still tried to do his normal routine but he would catch himself, bent with pain and resigned to sitting in Mom's recliner with the back of the chair straight up, the only place he seemed to find any relief. I scheduled an appointment with his heart doctor just to be sure it wasn't related to his pacemaker.

Finally in early May, we visited his VA doctor, an old Native American who had the habit of calling him, "Dad."

"Lift your arm up for me, Dad," he said softly, as he ran his hands across Dad's rib cage. I found the way he was addressing Dad to be annoying and unprofessional, but Dad didn't seem to mind it.

Dad winced in pain.

"There?" the doctor asked.

"Yes," Dad grunted.

"You have a broken rib."

I sighed with relief. Finally, an answer.

"How could that happen?" I said. "Did you fall?"

Dad shook his head. "I don't think so."

The old doctor looked at me. "At his age, that can be caused by just a cough or a sneeze. He's going to have to take it easy. Those take awhile to heal."

Dad grumbled, but at that point I was ecstatic. The end of his ordeal was in sight. We could go back to Drummond Island and he could resume whatever project he had left off last fall. Things were looking up for all of us. I had decided that Amanda would benefit from some activity to get her out of the house on a regular basis, other than socializing with me. I scheduled a meeting with a counselor at Hiawatha Behavioral Health, a community organization in Sault Ste Marie.

We met with counselor Tom West in early May. Tom was a soft-spoken, thoughtful sort with a frame of white hair around his gentle face. "Amanda, we need to write up a health history on you. That okay?"

In her usual state of caution when dealing with someone new, Amanda rolled her eyes to the side and said, "That's fine."

"Do you have any history of heart disease? Thyroid? Cancer?"

"Our mother has thyroid," Amanda immediately looked over at Dad.

"Her mother died last year," Dad said. Suddenly, tears began flowing down his face. He was sitting there in the office chair at Tom's desk, wrenched with his perpetual back pain, crying silently.

"Oh, I'm sorry!" Tom pushed his chair back away from the desk and folded his hands. Then he reached down in his desk drawer and pulled out a box of tissue. I looked over at Amanda and saw her eyes were welling up, too. I shot a look back at Tom. Dear God. The poor man. This was supposed to be a routine visit to just collect information.

I tried to think of something helpful. "Dad and Amanda just returned from a trip to Washington State. They spent the winter with my brother."

He graciously accepted my offering. "Oh really! Out in the Pacific Northwest. It's very beautiful out there."

He handed Dad the tissue and Dad took it. "Thank you." Dad blew his nose with an unceremonious honk. Amanda had managed to hold herself together. She patted Dad's shoulder.

"Yes," I said. "It is beautiful. Jon lives in the high desert. He runs the irrigation systems for the farms out there. He gets winters off, so he had lots of time to spend with Dad and Amanda. Jon is a good egg. He hunts elk."

Amanda and Dad said nothing. Tom nodded and said, "Is he your only brother?"

That was all it took. Amanda piped up. "I have three brothers."

Tom nodded again. "I see. Are they all out west?"

"No," Dad said, wiping his nose. "Marcus is downstate. Theil is in Arizona."

"With Katherine," Amanda added.

"Yes, his wife Katherine," Dad said.

"And Jon has Judy," Amanda said.

"So you have three brothers, and Nancy, here," Tom said.

"Yes and three other girls," Dad said.

"Wow!" Tom chuckled. "Are you guys Catholic?"

"Episcopalian," Dad replied. But he was smiling.

125

Good job, Tom, I was thinking. Way to pull this one out of the hat. I felt an immediate admiration for his kindness. I looked at his left hand and noticed a wedding band. Of course. I sighed. We chatted with Tom for a good hour, and near the end of the meeting, I said, "I saw where you sometimes arrange work for people with disabilities."

"Yes, we do that," Tom said.

"I think Amanda needs a job," I said.

"Oh please!" Amanda said.

"She needs to get out of the house. Her only social life is me. I think it would be good for her to have her own activities," I said.

"I had a job," Amanda said. "I worked for the laundry."

"It was a laundry service Dad started, a nonprofit to employ disabled people in the area," I explained.

"Really? That's wonderful." He looked at Dad, smiling, clearly impressed.

"We serviced the resorts in the area. It went under about ten years ago," Dad said.

"That's too bad. It sounds like a good effort. Well, Amanda, we may have an opening at the Goodwill. That is sorting and hanging clothes. It's a little like laundry, but not exactly. Is that something you would be interested in?" Tom looked over at her.

"Well, I don't want to be rude, but…" Amanda said.

"Oh come on!" I said. "At least give it a try. Trial basis."

"Yes," Dad agreed.

"How about just a couple of days a week to start out with?" Tom said.

"Maybe one day," Amanda said.

"I know," I said. "You could work Mondays. Since Tuesday is our regular movie day, that will give you something to look forward to, after the work day."

"Oh, sure," Amanda snorted.

So when Dad called Amanda to get up at 6 AM on her first day of work, she shuffled past me with her slippers in hand. I opened one eye and she growled, "Thanks a lot!" and hit me with the slipper.

Dad's X ray had revealed no broken rib. We had scheduled a CAT scan and were trying some new medications. I had decided to be vigilant in my search for answers. But it required constant visits with doctors and specialists, and due to our remote location, it always meant a road trip of two hours or more, twice a week or more. The CAT scan revealed bone spurs in his neck, twanging on his nerves as if they were guitar strings. "You're going to have trouble finding a neurologist willing to do surgery on those bone spurs," one pain doctor told him. "You're too high risk. They won't touch you with a ten-foot pole."

The doctor was testing the charge on an electrical current that he planned to run through Dad's arm to check circulation. "Don't worry," he said. "I won't get too shocking."

127

"Good!" Dad said. "If anyone here gets shocking, I hope it's the nurses!"

Despite his good humor, his pain was incessant and he was having trouble sleeping. Eventually Vicodin would have the reverse effect and make him want to sleep all the time. I would get up in the morning and come downstairs, and he would be sitting upright in the recliner, wrapped in the flowered comforter that I had given Mom and him for Christmas years prior. They had deemed it too heavy, and had hardly used it. But he was sitting with it every morning now, dozing, sleeping to avoid the pain in the only position that allowed him any semblance of rest. Still, when I came down, he would look up at me brightly and say, "Hi!"

He would have always eaten cereal, but I'd go to the kitchen and see what else I could tempt him with. Often I made him strawberry shortcake, his favorite dessert. He never refused it. It was probably more for my sake than his own. It was a terrible feeling to watch him suffer, unable to participate in his usual activities. He would sit and watch inane daytime TV, with the volume turned up to a deafening pitch. I would sit and watch with him, although it was completely out of character for me. The summer days were washing past. My horses were boarded nearly an hour away and I was missing them and our island terribly. I could only imagine how Dad felt. Every afternoon I allowed myself an escape, and I would take all the dogs to the beach for an hour. The dogs delighted in running on the clean sand and swimming in the hefty waves that Huron flung up. The sun beat down on us, shining on the tossing water. I knew I had to get out of the stifling house, but there was no escape from the worry and shared pain that Dad's problem was causing. If anything I felt guilty that, even with my still-lame foot, I could move and run.

Amanda as always was accepting of her circumstance, but she was able to inject constant humor into our days. The dogs helped too. One evening Dad was watching Este the Chihuahua drink from my water glass. "They lick their butt before drinking the water, you know."

"See how smart she is?" I crowed. "It doesn't make sense to clean her tongue in the water first. She has to lick her butt first."

"I don't understand you," Dad said.

Amanda said, "It's better not to, Dad."

Between the shows and the daily beach routine while at home, the dogs were having a great summer. But they met their nemesis upon the arrival of R1. She showed up in her long black car, puffy in her stretch polyester, lugging a zippered suitcase in a bland corduroy print. She had made no formal announcement to me. Dad hadn't either, perhaps wishing to avoid any explanation. She had taken a job at the Sault penitentiary, counseling prisoners. She was opting to keeping her Gladstone home, a large two-story house in town, instead of putting it on the market, despite the fact that it was three hours away from the new job. She was wearing the same grey business suits, except that she now sported a large opal ring on her right hand. I had noticed it immediately after Mom's death. The stone was hard to miss with its flashing rosy glint.

"What a beautiful opal!" I said. "Where did you get it?"

I was hoping she was going to say she had a new boyfriend. I thought, of anyone I knew, she had the most desperate need to get laid.

"I bought it for myself," she sniffed.

"Well, it's very pretty." It seemed out of character for her to spend money, when she didn't have much, on a ring like that. I thought it would be more typical of her to spend it on car repairs, or new bedding or shoes. But I didn't say any more about it.

However, as time passed, the items that had been in Mom's room in the Manor never surfaced: The hoodie I had given her for Christmas. The stuffed bear Clifford had presented her with, during our news broadcast. Mom's jewelry box, and the treasures that she had stashed: The black Australian opal, the gemstone mother ring that Amanda had cherished, and the opal ring I had given her. No one seemed to know where these items were. The more I thought about it, the more I thought it no coincidence that R1 suddenly had a new opal ring. But I had never known R1 to be a thief. So I said nothing.

R1 made herself a bed on Dad's couch, where she would sit and look at the dogs with an expression of bemused superiority. The dogs wagged their greetings, each approaching her politely with a tentative sniff. Her hand would remain at her side like a dead thing. After awhile the dogs gave up.

Our other siblings, even the ones in Michigan, didn't take much time to visit Dad. Marcus would text me, saying he had rented a cabin on the island with his new girlfriend, and they might stop in on their way over. Or maybe I could come over and join them for a drink. I looked forward to some social time with peers. But it never happened. He would decide he wanted to catch the boat and then I wouldn't hear from him again until Sunday. At that point he might stop briefly on his way back downstate.

R3 didn't ever visit, but that was probably for the best.

Cooking for Dad and Amanda was one thing. They were grateful to have any departure from their bologna sandwich diet of the prior year. Cooking for R1 was another matter. "It's not too bad," she would sniff, poking at the chicken or some other offering with her fork.

Amanda always attempted a recovery. "It's wonderful, Nancy. Really." She didn't always appreciate R1's interference in our comfortable trio. "I hope she's not going to sabotage your chicken like she did your burritos!"

"How did she sabotage my burritos?"

"She put veggies in them!"

I was at first happy for the distraction R1 provided. Though she worked long hours, Dad would look up when she came home. His expression was always glad and he would say, "Well, hello, Raven! Come in here and tell me about your day!"

She would go sit with him and talk about some prisoner who was, "making progress in coping with his narcissism." She talked about people who didn't understand where they had gone wrong, and others who were finding the Lord. She said there were some homosexual prisoners and, "The problem with gays is all they think about is sex."

I laughed about that, picturing the reaction of my gay friends. I especially thought of Matt, a hematologist who was a brilliant comic and had starred in one of my plays. He would be the one most likely to make a joke. "Well, what else IS there?" he would shriek.

I found some of R1's comments to be so offensive that they didn't even deserve a retort. I would roll my eyes, stirring a pot of beef stew, or chicken soup while I overheard her tales. But Dad was always entranced. I was grateful for that. I suspect that like me, he craved a little change from our routine.

Amanda was less grateful. As I came back after weekends on the road, she would grab my sleeve and whisper fiercely. "She's going through my stuff! I don't want her going through my stuff."

"That's just how she is!" I would whisper back. "Just try to play along!"

In time R1 developed a cough. It was a shallow little, "uh-uh". "Oh," she would say, "I'm allergic to dogs."

Amanda and I would slide sideways looks at each other. Before long she was waking up in the morning making the "uh-uh" coughing sound. Dad stopped giving Este treats and would say, "Get down!" whenever she hopped up on the couch.

Since R1 worked all the time, she was no help with any of the chores and she claimed she always was, "too short on cash" to pay for groceries. I found myself with another mouth to feed. And it was an expensive mouth, since like Dad and Amanda, she demanded three meals a day, including a sack lunch. Amanda would roll her eyes, but she followed my advice and tried to stay out of the way.

My weekends on the road with the dog show were exhausting. The producer, Bud, insisted on one hotel room to save costs. He was a smoker, and while supposing himself considerate enough to do it outside, he would slam the door with every trip he made until 3 am. He would guzzle at least a six-pack of beer every evening. It was as if he was deliberately unpleasant company. He was loud and argumentative about everything. I would lie awake with my phone and complain via text message to my friend Claire. She replied, "Light up a smoke and stay up another hour, and you could be his dream woman!"

Rest was impossible. I was running all four dogs in every show, four times a day, sometimes for three days straight. Upon returning to Michigan, I would stay with Claire at her house, or any other friend who offered me a couch, before beginning the long trip north. I had begun the habit of taking a favorite pillow and blanket everywhere I went, in a desperate search for rest that never really came. I was starting to understand how Dad felt. It was as if I was fighting a low-grade infection all the time, a nagging sort of pain that inhibited any real movement. About halfway through the summer, I developed a cough. But mine would come in unexpected attacks that suddenly bent me over with the effort. It went on for months and I couldn't seem to shake it. It was dry and unproductive, a nagging side effect that I was certain was a psychosomatic expression of Dad's torturous days.

I would come home from these trips, armed with a schedule for the week's doctor visits, to find the tension in the house almost palpable. R1 had taken some of their clothes to her Gladstone home, three hours away, to launder over the weekend. She had a basket full of folded laundry and she pointed at it when I walked in.

"Amanda is trashing her underwear," she said. "There are blood stains all over everything." She stormed into the living room where Dad and Amanda sat watching TV.

"Amanda," she roared. "Did you get your period?"

I found myself feeling grateful that we weren't sitting in the restaurant this time.

Amanda was mortified. Her face deepened to an almost purple hue.

"No!" she said.

"Well, you need to tell us when you have it. Your underwear is trashed. There's blood all over it and I couldn't get the stains out!" R1 turned to poor Dad. "Dad, is she regular?"

Dad put his hands up in a helpless gesture. "I don't know."

I sighed. I got up and tapped R1 on the shoulder. "Come with me."

She followed me into the kitchen. I said, "There are ways to address this without causing embarrassment. Amanda has the world's largest collection of Maxi-pads. Mom should have bought stock in them."

"Well, I am not buying her new underwear just to have her trash it!" R1 snarled.

"She responds well to visual guidelines. Maybe we can help her out by giving her a calendar and having her mark her day on it."

"Oh, that might work," R1 conceded. That seemed to satisfy her and she dropped it.

"Amanda," I said. "Let's go take a little ride."

As soon as she was in the car, and we were a safe distance from the house, I brayed, "Amanda! Did you get your PERIOD?"

"Oh please!" Amanda said.

"No, no, really. Inquiring minds want to know!"

"Stop!" Amanda was not amused.

"Sorry. All you have to do is change your pads. A lot. Like every time you go to the bathroom. Oh, wait. That won't work. You never go to the bathroom!"

It was true. The girl had a bladder of iron.

"Cut me a break!" Amanda said.

"Okay, well, let's put it this way. Make sure you use a lot of pads, otherwise, you are setting yourself up for more humiliation. You have now seen how that works."

"I see your point," she said.

Despite my efforts, things did not improve between them. I returned from another long weekend on the road, and Amanda said, "She unplugged my TV."

"What? Why?"

"She said I'm not helping out around here enough."

I sighed and shook my head. "Let me take a look at it."

I went upstairs and found the entire cable disconnected, effectively yanked from the socket and coiled up in a plastic trash can. I picked it up and looked it over but was stumped on how it had come apart. As I surveyed the back of Amanda's television, realizing I was going to have to call the cable company to hook her back up, I felt a surge of anger. Amanda had very few ways in which to occupy her time. She couldn't read well enough to find books entertaining. She had virtually no social life, especially now that Dad was grounded. To take her TV was heartless. R1 was working ten and twelve hours a day and she had no real concept of what life in this household was like.

"She tried to snatch my writing tablet," Amanda said.

I looked up. "She got physical with you?"

"Yes, she went to grab it but I pulled it behind my back like this," she demonstrated.

"Good for you," I said. "Amanda, has she ever hit you or threatened to hit you?"

Amanda shook her head.

"Well, you be sure to tell me right away if anything like that happens, okay?"

"I will." She was quiet for a minute, and I looked up to see her eyes welling up.

"Good grief!" I went to her and put my arms around her.

"I just wish Mom was here," she sobbed.

"Oh I know, honey."

"She would never let Raven do those things."

"You got that right. Whew. Can you imagine Raven getting away with that if Mom was here?" I started to laugh. "Oh my God! Mom would nail her head to the floor!"

Amanda started laughing then too. I sat down by her.

"So how are you guys doing? How has Dad been feeling?"

"Terrible. He and Raven been yelling."

"She's fighting with him too?"

"Yes."

"About what?"

"You."

"Oh, that's just great," I was becoming furious. "Not like he doesn't have enough to deal with. What's that about?"

"She says you should not be doing those shows and driving all over."

"She may be right about that." I wasn't saving any money. It was all going into the gas tank, and board for the two horses, and groceries for four people. And lots of tissue. I had decided that it was just a phase and that I would keep on juggling the lifestyle until Dad was feeling better.

"She said that the dogs are making Dad sick."

"Oh the dogs are causing it? Okay. Because they are causing her allergies so it must be doing the same to him?"

"That cough is fake," Amanda said to me.

"How do you know?" I asked.

"I just know."

"You don't think she's allergic to dogs?"

"Uhm, not."

"Well, I know how we can find out."

We were alone in the living room on a rare day when Dad had opted to try to sleep in his bed. R1's bedding was still on the couch, folded up neatly on one end. On the top of the little stack lay her pillow, fluffed up like a big dollop of whipped topping on a layer cake. I grabbed it.

"What you gonna do with that?" Amanda said.

"You'll see." I held the pillow up and shook it, so it fell out of the case. I whistled for Este the Chihuahua. "This is what we call a fool proof allergy test."

Este wagged obligingly around my feet and I picked her up, stuffing her into the pillowcase like a potato going into a sack. Amanda shrieked with laughter.

"Nancy, you are evil!"

I swung the pillow through the air and then shook it gently. I reached inside and gave the passenger a big scratch. Then I laid it on the floor, letting little dog run out. "No person with a dog allergy would be able to sleep two minutes on this pillow tonight. We'll just see what she does."

We waited eagerly for R1 to go to sleep that night. Sure enough, Amanda had been correct in her assessment. R1 snored happily all night with her face planted firmly in the "Estified" pillow. It gave us a couple of good high-five opportunities, but the bad behavior continued to escalate. The next time I came home from a weekend away, it was a late Sunday night and R1 was sitting at the table. "We've been having some issues," R1 said.

"About what?"

"She refused to bring down her dirty clothes. That's all I asked her to do."

"Where is she?"

"She's upstairs."

As I walked past Dad in his easy chair, he reached for my hand. "Go talk to her."

I went up the stairs and Amanda was sitting at her desk. Her eyes were red-rimmed from crying. I sat down on the bed and said nothing. I just looked at her.

"She threatened me."

"Threatened you? How?"

"She said they are going to put me in a foster home."

I sat there for a minute, deciding that counting to ten would be my best option. But I couldn't keep my fists from balling up. Amanda saw them. Amanda saw everything.

"Why?"

"She said, 'If you aren't going to live by our rules, under our roof, then you can't live here!'"

"Whose rules? Whose roof?"

"Hers and Dad's."

"Oh, so this is her house now. Cool. Good to know. Her name's on the deed, then?"

"I don't think so."

"What did she want you to do?"

She pointed to a basket on the floor. "She wanted me to carry that downstairs. I told her I would get around to it."

"Jesus, why didn't you just do it to shut her up?"

"She wants everything right now."

"I know. She needs to learn diplomacy, and you need to learn cooperation. Can't you guys compromise?"

She shook her head. "I don't think so."

"Well, what did Dad say?"

"He just told me to do as she asked. He got mad and was yelling at me."

"Oh well, that is just great."

"I think I want to see a counselor," she said.

I paused, wondering where this had come from. "Wow. Well, that's a really good idea."

"It is?"

"Sure. Lots of people who have experienced a loss will go on to seek counseling. I think you would be smart to do it."

"Okay."

"I will hook you up."

I had decided that it was a job for our new friend, Tom West. He had found Amanda a job. Surely he could help find her a counselor.

The thought of this resolution calmed me, like a warm soft hand running along my spine. I stood up. "I'll go talk to Raven. You stay up here for a few."

I went downstairs and said to Dad, "She is missing Mom."

He nodded. I went into the kitchen, reaching for a cold glass and turning the tap on, keeping my body strategically positioned at an angle from where R1 was sitting, as to be non-confrontational, where she could not see how straight and angry my back was.

She spoke up. "Did she tell you Dad threatened her with a foster home?"

I looked up as she spoke. Her hand was riffling through her hair. I saw the brilliant glittering flash of the opal ring again.

"She did say something about a foster home, yes," I said.

R1 shook her head. "I hate when he talks to her like that."

"Yes," I said. "That kind of threat can be very damaging."

At that minute I was beginning to despise R1. I knew that Dad would never say such a thing to Amanda. I thought about what a coward this woman was, to first abuse Amanda and then lie about it and place blame on a helpless, suffering old man. I thought about what kind of person would move into a situation and take advantage of it the way she was doing. I thought I would like to take this water glass and fling it right in her face.

But Dad would not understand that, and it wouldn't help Amanda. "Deep breaths," I told myself. "Take deep breaths."

I drained the water glass and filled it up again. I carried it in and gave it to Dad. I patted him on the shoulder and gave him a smile. "Thank you," he said.

I took comfort in knowing our situation was about to improve. Our travels had a turn of optimism now, with the hope of relief once the bone spurs were gone. Neurosurgeon Dr. Blaine Williams came with good karma, I thought. First of all, his first name was the same as

Dad's. Secondly, he had horses, and one of them was a Morgan! This had to be a good sign. "We love our Morgan," he told Dad.

"We love ours, too," Dad said.

I beamed. Ours. Clifford was, "ours."

"He paints pictures and visits libraries," Dad said. "She writes books about him."

He pointed a knobby finger at me, but I could tell that Dr. Williams wasn't following what he was saying. Dad's speech was slurred, and Dr. Williams was busy flipping through his file. "Well, you are high risk, that's for sure. But the bone spurs are very pronounced and if your cardiologist doesn't have a problem with me taking those out, then I don't."

A wave of relief washed over me. Finally. Finally there would be an end to this suffering, an end to this endless stream of doctor visits and sterile hospitals and tubes and blinking machines. Finally we were getting back to the woods. Summer was waning.

As my relief was gently kindled, Amanda's frustration was growing. She made four visits to Tom over the next several weeks, always insisting that I stay with her. Tom was trying to schedule her with a regular counselor, but Amanda waffled. I understood. She was shy and more comfortable just talking with him. She wanted him for her counselor. He was patient and sat with her through each visit, asking her interested questions and, I could tell, trying to assess how best to help her. When words about the situation failed her, she would say, "I will let Nancy explain it to you."

143

I would interpret her thoughts as best I could. "She might think Raven is trying to take Mom's place. Is that right?"

"Yes. She is not my mother! She threatened me with a foster home."

"Raven told me Dad said that," I said.

"No. Not Dad," she corrected me. "Raven. Raven said she was going to put me in a foster home."

She was firm. Facts were facts.

Death was one of our primary topics. Amanda missed her mother. She went on and on about little things that Mom and said and done. R1 was upsetting whatever tentative balance we had created since her passing. I realized that Amanda needed to accept the changes that were inevitable. We were driving home one evening and I said, "Everyone has to die. Most people want to die warm in their bed, as mentioned in the Titanic movie."

"Oh."

"How do you want to die?" I asked.

"I don't know. How about a pillow over my face?"

I looked over at her. "What? Why?"

She shrugged. "It will probably be a family member."

Finally, in late summer, R1 found a modular home in the Raber woods, a half hour drive from DeTour. It was closer to her work. We were, all three, visibly relieved when she moved out. Amanda especially acted happier and immediately said she thought she no longer needed counseling. Dad continued to suffer with his back pain. It was all-consuming. He went through the pacemaker replacement as he had the stent the year before, with flying colors, even managing to maintain his sense of humor. While in Petoskey at the cardiologist's office, the nurse was printing his records. The printer, evidently an older model, began to cough and squeal. Dad gasped at the sound. "Is that my heart?"

The day after his surgery, I had to go to Detroit for a show with the dogs. I called R1. "Are you home this weekend? I really need you to come and stay with Dad. He can't be left alone right now. His new pacemaker is working out just fine, but Dr. Underwood says he needs to be kept quiet. So there is nothing special to do for him other than to make sure he doesn't try to do too much. His pain isn't any better, so there's probably not much chance of that anyway. But really, there should be someone here. Can you come?"

"Yeah, sure," she said.

When I returned two days later, I pulled into the driveway and noticed the Tahoe looking like it had been in a mud bogging contest. It was covered with splatters all over the doors, even up to the windows. The tires looked like they were made of wet cement.

I went into the house where I was greeted by R1, who was just leaving. "What's happened to the truck?" I asked.

"Oh, Rowena and the kids came up and we took it four-wheeling." She started to brush by me. She had her suitcase and was heading out the door.

"Wait. Wait a minute."

She stopped. "Yes?"

"Where was Dad while you were doing this?"

"Oh, we brought him with us. He was going to show us how to get out to Marblehead, but the roads have all changed and he couldn't remember the way."

I felt my mouth drop open. I clamped it shut, feeling something near my temple snap. "You mean, you took him four wheeling on the back roads of Drummond Island, two days after heart surgery?"

"Well, it wouldn't have been so bad, except we got lost."

I was having images of the Tahoe rocking and splashing through mud holes, up over rocks, following the little two-track that wove through the jagged terrain that was backwoods Drummond. Worse, there was no cell phone signal out there. If anything had gone wrong, they were literally hours from any kind of help.

"Yes," I screeched, "It would have been so bad! Do you even have a clue where Marblehead is? Well, it's a long fucking way! And it is a helluvva rough ride! It's all rock! It will take a jeep hours just to get there!"

"Well, we know that now!"

I was yelling. I couldn't stop myself. "Are you crazy? What was the one thing I told you before I left here? The one thing!"

"Well, it wasn't my idea. It was Rowena's. I was just going along with it, and I had that baby to think about."

"You had your dad to think about! I am holding you responsible for this, Raven! Not Rowena! You! You told me you would look after him! Why is it that every time I leave you in charge here, I come home to some kind of a crisis? Are you a nine year old? Do you need constant supervision too, or what? My god!"

I stormed through the house where Dad was sitting in the corner, wrapped in his comforter. He looked up at me.

"Dad, are you feeling alright?"

"No," he said. "But it's the usual."

I sat down next to him. "What were you thinking, trying to go to Marblehead two days after heart surgery?"

"Well, those kids didn't know the way out there."

"That's no excuse. You know you aren't supposed to be jouncing around like that right now. Once your bone spurs are removed, and you recover, then we can go up to Marblehead and we'll jeep out to Bailey's Lake again and we'll go canoe the river. Until then, you have to sit still."

"I could feel the pacemaker moving," he admitted.

I could feel my blood percolating. There was a slamming feeling inside my head. I understood how people had medical issues from stress. I looked up, but R1 had left. That was for the best, I thought.

The doctor's visits went on through the rest of the summer. Things kept cropping up to delay Dad's surgery. His blood levels weren't right. He needed more tests. He hadn't stopped taking his blood thinner for enough days. His sugar was off. I couldn't blame them for wanting everything to be just right with a high risk patient like him, but it was turning into a long stretch of one painful week after another. My frustration wasn't lost on him. During one long wait in an exam room, he said, "You don't have children."

"No primates," I said.

"Who's going to do this for you, when you get to be my age?"

I snorted. "Are you kidding? You're gonna outlive me. I'll be dead from the stress of taking care of you."

He laughed.

I still suffered with my psychosomatic cough, my "empathicough," I called it. Finally one day Amanda plunked a bottle of cough syrup in front of me. "I don't want this," I said. "I want ice cream."

"You can have ice cream after you take it," Amanda said.

"I think this has to be the last thing you take." I read the label. "It says it loosens phlegm. It actually says that. Isn't that a weird word? Phlegm. You say it."

"Phlegm," Amanda said.

"I don't want phlegm," I said, pushing the bottle toward her.

"If you take it," she said. "I'll sing 'Soft Kitty' to ya."

Dad was sitting up in his corner, wrapped in his comforter, dozing when I went to bed. When I got up the next morning, he was sitting out by the front door, with it wide open, letting the cold air blow in.

"I can't get air," he said.

"You can't breathe? Do you feel faint? Are you going to throw up?"

"No, I just can't get a deep breath."

"Can you get yourself dressed? I am taking you to ER."

He made no argument this time. His eyes were wide, frightened. I forced myself to remain composed and I put my hand on his shoulder. "We'll get this figured out, Dad. I will go see if Amanda wants to go with us."

He nodded.

I went upstairs to find Amanda in bed with her head covered. I sat down on the edge of her bed. "Hey."

A soft grunt came from beneath the covers. It told me that she was awake, but would rather not be.

"This is totally up to you. No pressure. But do you want to get up and come with us? I have to take Dad to the hospital. He is having some trouble getting air. You can stay home if you want, and I will just call you later."

She sat up immediately, but did not seem alarmed. "I guess I better get myself around, here."

"Okay, but make it quick. We won't have time for breakfast. We have to fly."

"Okay," she said.

Our trip to the Soo was quiet. Amanda snored softly in the back seat. I didn't talk too much, just letting Dad concentrate on breathing and staying calm. I thought about a conversation I had had with him a few days prior. "Don't take this wrong," I said. "But do you have any ideas about who you want to be Amanda's guardian?"

"You," he replied. "If you'll have her."

"Of course. Would you mind putting that in writing? It just seems like there should be documentation somewhere."

"There is."

"What does it say?"

"It names Theil as her guardian."

"Where is it?"

"Brandon has it."

He meant Brandon Farley, an attorney who also happened to be his sister Sue's son. Brandon lived on Drummond and his practice was in the Soo. I was greatly relieved to hear that Amanda would be protected. I didn't pursue the matter further.

When we arrived at the hospital, the medics immediately put Dad into a wheelchair, while Amanda supervised. I parked the car while they admitted him. I had sent R1 a text message giving her the news, but I got no reply. That was just as well, I thought. As I walked into the hospital, I posted on Facebook, "In ER with Dad. He is having a little trouble breathing. Don't know anything yet."

We waited for hours while the nurses flashed in and out of the room. They had put Dad on oxygen and he was immediately feeling better. "We're going to keep him under observation here, tonight," one of the nurses whispered. She had a bad case of laryngitis, which caused her to lean close so I could hear her. Unfortunately this was combined with a bad case of coffee breath.

"We think he either has pneumonia or CHF."

"What?" I thought I must be hearing her wrong.

"It could be congestive heart failure," she wheezed.

"How can it be his heart? He just got a new pacemaker."

She shrugged. For some reason, I was finding this nurse particularly off-putting. I didn't know if it was the whispering, or the

151

foul breath, or her aggressively cavalier manner. It was like talking to a de-barked Pomeranian with bad teeth.

"When can I talk to the doctor?" I said politely.

"He's gone home for the evening. He'll be in tomorrow."

"Didn't he know that I was waiting to talk with him?"

She shrugged again. I was starting to wish I had a choke collar.

I walked over to Dad, who was lying in the thin white hospital bed, looking exhausted. "Hey Dad, I am going to take Amanda out to dinner and then home. I am hoping you will get some good rest tonight. I will be back tomorrow to talk with the doctor."

He nodded. I kissed him and Amanda followed me out the door.

As I was leaving town, I got a call from Marcus. I figured he had seen my Facebook post, so I decided to sound upbeat as not to alarm him. "Hi!"

"Nancy, what is going on?"

"Dad's in ER but we don't know anything. He was having trouble breathing."

"Do you want to explain to me why in the hell you didn't call me?"

I sighed. Why did it always have to be this way? There was never any encouragement. Never any offer of help. Conversations with him had all degraded to some kind of verbal flogging. What was it about this family that made it so difficult for people to be kind to each other?

"I was going to call you when I got home tonight," I said. "Unfortunately there is nothing to tell. They know nothing."

"Well what are his symptoms?"

"Trouble breathing. He is on oxygen and will probably have to bring it home. Blood levels are normal for him. They said maybe pneumonia or CHF but I am not satisfied with what they are telling me. Then the doctor never even stopped to talk to me."

"Are you staying there?"

"No. I am taking Amanda home."

"Okay, well, try to keep me informed. I don't like hearing things secondhand through Facebook."

"Yeah, well, sorry about that. But I've been using Facebook to post his updates for months now. Today, it just seemed like the easiest way to spread the word when there is really no information beyond that. Besides, I would have called you tonight when I had a chance to really talk. But for now this is all I know."

"You should have called earlier."

"I know, sorry. Dad is resting, but he can talk just fine. You might call the hospital and see if he's awake and you can talk to him. Can you let the rest of the family know? I am about to drive into the dead zone."

"Yes, sure. I will spread the word."

We hung up. I felt a sense of relief that he was handling the communication end of things. No more verbal floggings tonight. I emailed Claire when I got home. "Yes, he is on oxygen now. I don't get why they give the big ol' lunkin tank to the more active people. Because his oxygen levels weren't too bad when he is at rest, he didn't qualify for a mobile tank. Well, DUH! When he's moving, oxygen levels drop, THAT'S when he needs the tank, so he should have the portable one! That's backwards, in my opinion. I plan to talk to doc about this tomorrow."

They released Dad the next day. The nurses showed me how to connect the oxygen and turn it on for him. I never did get to talk to the doctor. The Pomeranian told me that they had ruled out pneumonia, so the official diagnosis was congestive heart failure.

This didn't sound right to me.

"Dad," I said. "You need to see your cardiologist. I am going to make you an appointment with her. I want to get her opinion about this."

He sighed, but he agreed with me.

It was two weeks before Doctor Underwood could see him. During that time, Dad struggled with life attached to a tank. He hated it. I did, too. On occasion he would disconnect the tube by accident, and then fight to get enough air. He would end up yelling my name. I patiently showed him, time and again, how to reconnect the tubes and check to make sure the machine was working. But he would forget details in his ensuing panic as he grew short of breath. At night, I would lie awake in the dark, listening to hear if he was moving around the house or calling me because he had disconnected the tank again. He could breathe on his own, but it was a struggle especially if he was anxious. I knew that I could no longer leave him alone for more than a couple of hours at a time. It was clear that after the mud bogging episode, I could not rely on R1, even for a day or two. It had finally happened: His care was going to be on me, full-time, from then on. Without the pittance I was earning from the dog shows, I didn't know how I was going to afford to care for Amanda and him. Jobs in the community were next to nonexistent. I had gotten a food card, which had helped get us through summer, but it didn't cover everything. I knew Dad worried about that too. Right after Mom had died, he had named me as his co-signor on his credit union account. I had never so much as looked at the balance. He had me write checks to pay his bills, and he signed them. He was very conscientious about his bills. He didn't have much money. I saw in his checkbook where R1 had written checks to herself, and he had signed them. I knew she was having trouble and I assumed he was helping her out, but I didn't ask him about them. It was none of my business. The bigger worry was about his health; the question about what was really wrong with him, and why there was never an answer. I felt like I was running across a long flat desert, with the promise of water, but finding every creek dried up. To the south just on the horizon, there was an ugly black column. I didn't dare look at it, because if I looked, I would see it was a storm. I could sense it there. I thought if I just kept running for water,

155

it might blow away. Still it remained, as clouds do. But I just kept running.

When the morning finally arrived for our trip back to Petoskey, I loaded Dad up in the car with his oxygen tank and we left Amanda sleeping.   Dad and I had the tank system down to a science by that time. He had a small cart for the portable tank that I stashed in the back seat. I put his tank on the floor just behind his seat, draping the hose over the seat. It would be ready for him when he climbed in. I always brought along two extra tanks. When we arrived I parked by the door of the hospital, and took the cart out first, setting it up before disconnecting Dad so that he could get out of the car unencumbered. I immediately hooked him up again. He grabbed the handle of the cart and away he went, wheeling it along behind him and giving me a wave as he walked off. "I'll see you inside."

When Dr. Underwood came into the exam room, she wasn't beaming as usual. I could tell that she hadn't been expecting this, and she wasn't enjoying the surprise.

"There is no way you can be in heart failure," she said. "You have a new pacemaker. It's not your heart. It's something with your lungs. You need to see a pulmonologist. You need the electrician. I'm the plumber."

We were at Petoskey Heart and Vascular, in the wing of the hospital that sat like a great bird overlooking the choppy Grand Traverse Bay. Dad smiled at her joke, but despite her calm demeanor, I could see that Dr. Underwood was agitated. She said, "You will need to schedule a visit with one. Do you want to do it here? Or up in the Soo?"

"I will go back to the Soo," Dad said.

"No," I said. "Dad, you are staying here until you see the lung doctor."

Dr. Underwood turned to me. "You want me to have him admitted?"

"Yes," I said. "Please do. Thank you."

Dad looked at me as if I had just pulled the plug on the lifeboat. His steel blue eyes were striking flint.

"I'm so sorry, Dad. It's just that they have already misdiagnosed you up there. We can't go back and keep running in circles. There is something really wrong here if you can't breathe, and this is the best place to figure it out."

"Okay, I will set it up," Dr. Underwood said. She got up and marched out of the room.

I looked at Dad. He looked at me. We both shook our heads. "Let's just get to the bottom of this, once and for all," I said. "There is something going on here that nobody has figured out yet. Let's find out what it is."

The black storm grumbled darkly on my horizon, but I looked away.

I stood up. "I will go call Raven and have her pick up Amanda after work. I can head down to Saginaw for a show tomorrow, and Amanda can stay with me. I can pick up some extra bucks that way. Meanwhile you just try to get some rest here and I will see you Sunday."

He nodded.

Walking out of the room, I sent R1 a quick text. "In Petoskey. Having Dad admitted for tests."

Her reply came back. "What seems to be the problem?"

"WHAT SEEMS to be the PROBLEM?" I shrieked out loud. I wanted to type, "What planet are you on? Where have you been for the past six months?"

But instead I simply said he needed tests, and asked if she could come pack some of Amanda's things and bring her down, as I had to leave for the night.

R1 arrived later that day with Amanda. There had been no word from the pulmonologist. Amanda and I kissed and hugged Dad and then we left Petoskey.

The show was at a cold and windy fairgrounds in Shields, a small town just west of Saginaw. Bud had picked the date and location this time, in an attempt to promote his own festival, and it was a bad choice. It was the end of October, and nobody came. We were scheduled to have two performances. After he canceled the first one, some of the team members left. We had no audience. Amanda sat backstage, huddled under a blanket. About midday, I had a text from R1. "Talked with pulm, results inconcl frm CAT scan, waiting for biopsy."

I immediately called her. "What does this mean?"

"Well," she sniffed importantly. "The CAT scan showed a shadow on his lung. It didn't show up in the X rays because the pacemaker was in front of it."

At that moment, the black storm in my mind's eye came swirling around me, blowing debris and shrapnel in waves. There was no more desert, only wind. It howled around my head, banging through my eardrums.

"Shit," I said. "I knew it."

"Well, now, we don't know," R1 cautioned. "We're waiting for the biopsy."

"Raven," I sighed. "That's what they tell you because they are not allowed to say it. Tell Dad that Amanda and I will be back tonight. Thank you for the information."

I hung up and looked over to where Amanda was sitting backstage. She was completely wrapped in a big quilt one of my friends had given her. Her feet were sticking out the bottom, but her head was covered.

I walked away from the staging area, out past some of the outbuildings. I couldn't believe that six months of seeking the answer had culminated in this. With our visits to all the doctors, all the medical facilities, all the tests and procedures and running here and there all over northern Michigan, nobody had found this thing until just now. I felt suddenly exhausted. I felt a tightening in my chest and it was getting hard to swallow. I sat down on the ground and began sobbing uncontrollably.

"Nancy, oh my God! What is happening?" My friend Jennifer was a big, beautiful woman with long blonde ringlets. She stood by me, towering above me awkwardly while I sobbed and hiccupped. She was holding a brindle-striped puppy in her arms.

I knew I had to say the words now. "My dad has cancer."

"Oh, no. I'm so sorry," she said. "Here, get up. Come with me. Come and sit in the truck where it's warm."

I stood up. She handed me the puppy. "Here. This is for you. He's yours."

I took the puppy and buried my nose into his soft warmth. Jennifer led me over to her truck. It was packed with a bunch of wagging, sniffing border collies. I climbed in and sat next to her. The puppy squirmed and wagged and climbed out of my arms to join them.

"Did you eat? Do you want a sandwich?" She reached around into the back seat and flipped open a huge cooler. The dogs immediately swarmed it. "No!" she shouted. "Get back!"

She pulled out a sandwich and handed it to me. "It's tuna. And I brought you some of those Starbucks drinks you like, see?"

"Aw. Hey, thanks." I had tamped down my rising panic, forcing it down until it lay like a cold piece of granite in the pit of my stomach.

"Was that your sister on the phone?"

"Yeah – she said they are doing a biopsy."

I sat holding the sandwich, staring out the window at the flat, grey landscape.

"When are they doing it?"

"I don't know. I forgot to ask. I don't know how I am going to tell Amanda."

"Oh, I know you will find a way."

"Yes. She's actually not the one that worries me. It's the others."

"Why?"

"I have three other sisters. There's no way to describe them. They're just awful. Every one of them."

She sighed and looked out the window thoughtfully.

"I don't know how I am going to deal with them. And dealing with them will be inevitable."

She nodded. Then she looked at me. "Get a cold heart."

I was fiddling with the plastic wrap on the sandwich. I looked up at her. "What do you mean?"

"That's what I do with people who are like that. Nothing they say matters. I don't care about anything they do. I get a cold heart."

I nodded. I sniffed, and looked at her and nodded again. Then I unwrapped the sandwich and took a bite.

Chapter 8

About My Dreams - Amanda

Here is my Bucket List.

- Hot Air Balloon Ride

- Motorbike Ride

- Visit to Yellowstone Park

- Sky diving. Why not?

- Meet famous people, especially Harrison Ford, Jon Bon Jovi, Janet Jackson, Michael J. Fox, and the whole cast of, "Friends." I would like to have lunch with them. I don't know what they eat. They are probably all vegetarians, except Courteney Cox. She probably eats meat.

I think everybody should have a bucket list, because it's their life. Life is about special moments.

About Cancer - Nancy

Dr. Aikens walked softly, and spoke more softly. He had been Dad's family doctor on Drummond Island for decades, and Dad trusted him implicitly. He would tiptoe into the exam room and sit down next to Dad, leaning earnestly toward him as he spoke. Even though he almost whispered, Dad never had any trouble hearing him. They sat side by side, passing information softly, looking earnestly into each other's eyes. They looked like lovers, I thought. I would have teased Dad about it later, had the subject not been so grim.

"Blaine," the doctor said. "I have your biopsy results right here, and what you have is called moderately differentiated squamous cell carcinoma."

Dad nodded, absorbing this.

"The tumor is sitting on top of your lobe like a swimmer's cap," Dr. Aikens said. "It is interfering with two ribs, and that's where your pain is coming from."

Despite his age and months of inactivity due to his pain, Dad's prognosis was relatively good. Dr. Aikens explained that the ribs were fractured, but would start to heal following the treatment. I had a fleeting thought back to the Soo VA doctor, and how he hadn't been entirely wrong, after all, though the rib wasn't broken in the way he probably visualized.

"There's a crackling sound in your lungs. We've talked about that before," Dr. Aikens said. "It could be asbestos poisoning. Unfortunately this sometimes leads to lung cancer. Did you work around coal?"

"Yes, I worked at the coal dock. But that was forty years ago."

"That's how long it takes."

Dad looked down. I felt the familiar stab of pain at his sadness. But Dr. Aikens made a kind offering. "You should be able to travel to Arizona after your treatment ends. In fact, the warmer climate would be very good for your lungs."

At this, Dad brightened visibly.

Dad's diagnosis had led to an abrupt surge of interest in his well-being. I was suddenly flooded with emails from siblings. Theil and Katherine still wanted Amanda and him, and me too, to come out to Phoenix for the winter. R3 decided to offer her home near Detroit as a base for Dad, so he could have treatment at University of Michigan Hospital. Marcus again offered his home in Cadillac should Dad prefer to go back there, where he could attend Spectrum Health System in Grand Rapids.

I thought it was a stroke of sheer luck that Marcus's son Justin was dating an oncological nurse. Katrina was someone who, with her good looks, probably didn't have to be as smart as she was. She towered above me, reedy and leggy like a colt, and with her long, pale mane, she bore an uncanny resemblance to Taylor Swift. She had worked at Spectrum, and couldn't recommend it highly enough. "He's going to need rest and quiet during the radiation," she told me. "It pretty much kicks your butt."

I understood the concept of the immune system being compromised during treatments, and I didn't like the idea of the Drug

Baby and others running in and out of R3's house during Dad's stay there. Kids were generally acknowledged as germ factories. I thought we couldn't afford Dad to get a virus on top of his cancer. I knew I wouldn't be welcome at R3's. I desperately wanted Dad to have treatment at Spectrum. That way, I thought, I could continue to help with his care. Among all of us, I was the one most familiar with his medical history.

During the meeting with Dr. Aikens, he called both U of M and Spectrum. He said, "Blaine, U of M has a waiting list and the first appointment isn't for a couple of weeks. Spectrum can get you started next week."

Dad looked at me. I nodded.

"Spectrum," Dad said.

Dad napped as we drove onto the ferry later that afternoon. He was exhausted, I thought. I wanted to get him home. I decided that once I got his oxygen hooked up, I would take the dogs to the beach and let him nap. It was a grey October day, but we still loved to walk on the beach and watch the waves roll up on the cold sand, and the wind whip the whitecaps until they crashed up on the distant point of rocks.

After I got Dad settled in his chair with his quilt, and Amanda upstairs with her writing tablet, the dogs and I escaped. The beach offered little relief. Cancer was a specter that loomed over the clouds, the trees, the distant DeTour Reef Light. There was no escaping from it. I wished that I had thought to ask for a CAT scan on Dad's lungs sooner. I wish that we had not lost all those months just looking for an answer. As the dogs ran and gamboled in the sand, I grappled with the idea of other things I could have done for Dad. After all those trips to doctors and hospitals and specialists and surgeons, and all those weeks praying for an answer to his pain issue, we finally had the answer but there was no relief in it. It was stacking more worry onto an already towering pile of stress.

Upon our return from the beach, I walked into the house to find R1 sitting in the living room with Dad.

"Oh, hi!" I was glad to have someone to commiserate with. "Did Dad tell you about his doctor visit today?"

But when R1 replied, her tone was ugly. "Yes, and I don't appreciate you railroading him into going to Spectrum instead of Ann Arbor."

"It was my choice," Dad said.

R1 had picked the wrong day to complain. I snapped back at her. "You don't appreciate? You don't appreciate? You've got that right. You don't appreciate anything!"

"Calm down," Dad said.

But I didn't calm down. "You had free room and board here for months while I worked my ass off trying make ends meet and get to the bottom of this health issue. You have never thanked me for any of it! Now here's something I don't appreciate. I don't appreciate you coming in this house and terrorizing Amanda and terrorizing Dad and telling everyone what to do! I don't appreciate you coming in here with an attitude when you haven't the slightest concept of what's really going on!"

"Rowena is very hurt. She feels left out," R1 said.

I stifled an incredulous laugh. "Tough shit! This isn't about Rowena's feelings! This is about health! This is about survival, you idiot!"

R1 reached up with her hand and rubbed her eye. I noticed the opal ring, flashing on her finger, virtually flipping me off.

"Where did you get that ring?" I screeched.

"I bought it for myself!" As if anticipating my next question, she added, "And I still have the receipt!"

"I'll bet you do," I turned around and walked into the kitchen. I turned on the tap and started slamming dishes into the sink. I took the bottle of dishwashing soap and squeezed it, squirting a line of green that churned and foamed in the shooting hot water. So far, I thought, I wasn't achieving the, "get a cold heart" goal. In fact, I was failing miserably. It wasn't hard for the R's to get things stirred up under the circumstances. I knew I had to get my emotions under control, or I would be rewarding their bad behavior. Dad was right. I had to calm down.

I thought about how I was breaking the rules of fair fighting that I had learned in marriage counseling: No name calling. Don't change the subject. Don't use sarcasm. I hadn't followed them back in those days very well, either, I mused, feeling around for the first plate.

R1 came out and got her coat. I dried my hands and made myself hug her. I didn't feel like hugging her, but I made myself do it. She didn't hug back.

"Look," I said. "This is hard for all of us. Let's just keep his needs as our priority, okay? We all want the same thing here. Spectrum came highly recommended by Katrina. She used to work there. I mean, how lucky are we, of all times, to now have an oncology nurse in the family?"

"She's not family." She turned and marched out, and silence settled into the room like a blanket. I went back to the dishes. I had told R1 we all wanted the same thing, but I wasn't convinced of that. But I did know cancer was scary to everyone. The thought of it had terrified Dad at first. We went to the Soo a few days later, in order to follow up with a bone scan. Not surprisingly, he was very quiet during most of the trip. Finally, he said, "Everyone has to die, and I am no exception."

"Are you sure about that, Padre?" I said. "Who knows? You've always been a little odd."

He smiled. As we drove past the farm fields, and the wet street gradually narrowed to the first traffic light, he said, "Let's stop in and see Polly."

Polly was Dad's red-headed niece, and one of his life's greatest darlings. She had a perpetual smile that squeezed her eyes into happy slits. Her hair was a mass of tight curls and she kept it barely contained by pinning it up over her ears. Her home had always been open to Mom and Dad and Amanda. Nearly every trip to the Soo, whether it was for groceries, or doctor visits, or any type of business, involved a stop for coffee at Polly's. We parked in the alley behind her house and a walked through the yard to her back door, into the homey kitchen peppered with photos of grandchildren. She greeted us with a big grin, and hugs all around. "How are you, Amanda? You want some coffee?"

"I'm fine!" Amanda said. "Yes please!"

Dad sat down and stammered, "I've been to – to the doctor."

"Yes, what did you find out?" Polly was turning away from the counter with a steaming mug, and she set it down in front of Dad.

"They said I have lung cancer." It was the first time I had heard him say the words, and he gasped, a sharp breath after they came out. Tears suddenly began streaming down his face. I felt a cold, stabbing pain go through me; an awful helplessness.

"Oh, I'm so sorry." Polly's eyes immediately flooded. She came over and quickly embraced him. "Well, we don't have to talk about it if you don't want to."

Dad took a napkin from her little ceramic holder on the table, and mopped at his face. He looked calmer, I thought. As I sat down at her table, I marveled at this woman's ability to say just the right thing, to offer so much comfort in so few words.

She turned again, with a cup for Amanda, and I saw that her face was reddened, but she was maintaining an anguished smile. Amanda was steadfast as usual, but her eyes leapt from face to face, assessing every reaction.

169

Polly cradled her mug, sat down and talked about her grandchildren, and how everyone was spending the fall, and how the little ones were doing in school. She talked about how Frank would stop in now and then with her favorite donuts from Cedarville. "They're just the best." She nodded to Amanda. "They have that crispy little edge, eh? I can't get enough of 'em. It's a good thing they make 'em a half hour away or I'd weigh 300 pounds!"

Dad and Amanda laughed. While I watched, they both relaxed visibly as Polly chatted on about how lawn mowing was over for the season, and how Frank's grandson was doing in basketball, and how she had seen a late flock of geese flying south, finally, and wasn't it strange that fall had been so late in coming, this year and last. She talked about her childhood days on Lime Island with her sisters Bonnie and Maxine, and Dad absorbed this like one who has waited all day for a drink of water.

When we left there and I loaded Dad's oxygen tank back into the car, I reflected on the gifts of a person who asks for nothing, who has no agenda, who merely offers companionship through small anecdotes. This, I thought, was heroism in its simplest form. I thought that anyone should be able to do this. I thought Polly had the right idea. There was so much comfort in little things; in normalcy. It was a good example for me to follow. Driving past the brown fields and naked trees, we were all feeling grim. I knew attitude could make all the difference and I was firm in my resolution to meet this head-on. With this in mind, Amanda and I continued our bickering.

"Way to slop up the coffee, there, Java Sucker," I said.

Dad laughed.

"You should tell Nancy to stop teasing me, Dad," Amanda said.

"You should give Amanda a spanking, Dad," I said.

"You should pull her hair, Dad," Amanda said.

"You should pop out her eyeballs, Dad."

"You should run over her with the car, Dad," Amanda said.

Dad had his customary smile and delivered his line, right on cue. "You two get along."

Perhaps as a result of our determination to maintain some semblance of normalcy, Dad was able to recover his sense of humor. He was trying hard, I thought. I remembered when he had his biopsy, we had waited an excruciating four hours in radiology pre-op. I thought we might never get out of that room. Eventually, we noticed a Black and Decker power drill sitting on a desk in the corner. Dad nudged me, nodding toward it. "I hope they're not gonna operate on me with that!"

He had been, to that point, an exemplary patient: Always polite, so longsuffering and so courageous. I heaved a big sigh, knowing that his ordeal was about to continue in a magnified fashion.

His treatment regimen was to begin in November. We spent the last weeks at home with his pain boiling over the household, seeping into the cracks in the ceiling and dripping down the walls. He would get calls from my siblings, holding the phone in his shaky hand for a few moments. "I'm suffering," he would say. His words would cut through me, and I wanted to cover my ears. I wanted to run out of the house every time he took a phone call, so I wouldn't have to hear his slurring, wavering speech about how awful it was. I swallowed my own pain, every day, forcing myself to keep smiling. I cooked meals for him, but his appetite waned, so I brought him ice cream, the ever-reliable strawberry shortcake, or anything that he was willing to eat. If he drifted off to sleep, it was always a relief for both of us. Amanda seemed to be taking it all in stride, although I knew the stress was taking its toll. We were both so grateful to not have to deal with our older sister on top of it all. After our argument, R1 had stopped coming around so frequently. I knew Dad missed her, but I thought it was just as well that she stay away for now. She was a huge stress factor for all of us.

Every day I escaped to the beach. When the days got too long, and Dad drifted into an uncomfortable doze in his chair, I would take evening walks too. One warm, damp evening, I took all four dogs for a walk up the short hill by Dad's house. I loved hearing the freighters in the soft rain.

I did a head count. Til and Miss Rip had ranged ahead, trotting and sniffing up the road. I looked over and saw Este and Jack in the neighbor's yard. Jack's fluffy black and white shape was illuminated by the porch light. I called, and Este turned toward me, followed closely by -- not Jack. I looked down and Jack was at my feet. I started yelling at the dogs to come. The Not Jack had his tail up at full mast, a proud black-and-white banner, and was trotting right on Este's heels.

"COME ON!" I screamed. Este obediently broke into a run, and the Not Jack ran, too. Now we all were running, and the Not Jack was in hot pursuit. I flung the door open and looked back. Past my knees ran three dogs. Til and the Not Jack were nowhere in sight.

"Til!" I screamed. He came trotting, head down, and then it followed: the suffocating, wretched hallmark of the Not Jack. Til slunk into the front shed and lay down. Miss Rip walked over to the corner rug and lay down with her nose pressed against the screen door, facing deliberately away from him.

I walked into the house. Dad looked up. "I smell skunk."

I sighed. "Yes, you do. Guess who got it."

He paused for a moment. "Terrible Til!"

I nodded. He burst out laughing, and then we both were laughing. Amanda's voice sailed down from upstairs. "Hoo wee, that stinks!"

"That skunk was stalking us! First I thought he was Jack. He followed Este from Carper's yard. I think he has a crush on her! It was just like that cartoon where the skunk tries to romance the cats! Then we tried running away from him, but he was running too! He chased us back to the house!"

I had never been chased by a skunk. The whole scenario was so odd. Dad was roaring at the imagery. It was good to see him laughing. Meanwhile, I began to investigate more about his disease. I had an acquaintance who was an oncology nurse, and I sent her an email asking what to expect. She said, "Just make sure they make him comfortable, and reach for two more years with him. It is very obtainable. What you need now is comfort not a cure. I am sorry."

With comfort being the priority, I made what I called my, "Morphine Pizza Run." The pharmacy was in Cedarville, a half hour from us. Luckily for Amanda, the pizza was available there too.

"I don't want morphine," Dad had insisted. "I might get addicted to it."

"Just try a little bit for pain," I said. "Once your tumor is gone and ribs heal, we will think about weaning you off it."

That night, I thanked God for good drugs. It was Dad's first real sleep in a long time.

As we advanced into that realm where Cancer becomes the headline, and life happens incidentally, I helped Dad pack his things to go to Marcus's. Marcus arrived with his new girlfriend, an art teacher named Lily. They had been together only a few months by then. He had brought her to the house a couple of times, during trips to stay on the Island. They sat for a brief hour on the couch. They were staunch Republicans and ranting about President Obama. Marcus kept his hand on her knee and called her, "Baby."

Lily was a tall blonde with a firm handshake. "You look like me," I had blurted on our first meeting.

"That's what my brother said, too," Lily assured me.

"She doesn't look like you," Marcus said.

But she did look like me, I thought: A taller, more glamorous version of me, with better teeth and bigger boobs and a smaller butt. She looked, I thought, like me as an Action Figure. She looked like me in my wildest fantasies.

Perhaps realizing that this type of comparison was always the sincerest compliment, Lily granted me the kindness of pointing out to my brother that, "Nancy is sacrificing her life to take care of your father."

Marcus told me later that she had said this. "I never thought about it that way," he admitted.

From that point on, Lily had my gratitude. It was a tremendous relief to finally be acknowledged, even if it wasn't by an actual family member. Her generosity didn't stop there. Even though she had moved in with Marcus just that summer, and had only just met my father, she agreed to take over his full-time care. I showed them how to load the tanks into the oxygen machine. I showed them how to turn the machine on to refill the tanks, and how to attach the hoses. Lily was an astute learner. She had spent significant time in the medical community. She had been married to a doctor, and her brother was also a doctor. So as not to slam this outsider with what I knew to be an overwhelming task, I volunteered to come and stay at Marcus's for the duration of Dad's treatment. "We have plenty of room for everyone," Lily said.

I could feel a burgeoning pressure that could only be described as a sigh of relief. It was building, just not ready to escape yet. It seemed too good to be true that I would finally be getting some help and support with this enormous responsibility, and by someone who appeared to be sane, no less, and even kind.

Not everyone was so happy with the arrangement. R3, of course, was in rare form. She referred to Lily as, "Marcus's whore." When she found out Dad was slated for care at Spectrum, she wrote R2 a scathing email, "You picked a whore over me!"

R2 promptly shared the email, in which R3 also asserted that I was, "Freaking out because the gravy train is about to end."

I laughed, "That's right! I just want to live in Dad's castle with all its amenities, where my every need is provided for, and I'm lining my nest egg, too!"

I was determined that they weren't going to get a rise out of me. I thought it was like swimming upstream. "Keep kicking," I told myself. "You're not here for anyone's approval. Praise and acknowledgment are not the goal. Stay focused on the goal. Breathe. Keep kicking."

The three of us, Dad, Amanda and I, moved in with Marcus. I immediately resumed my dog show schedule. I kept what I considered my more needy dogs with me: Til, Ms. Rip and Este. Friends were keeping little Jack Johnson for me. Jennifer still had the brindle border collie puppy, whom I had named Havoc.

Marcus was a gracious host, cooking meals for all of us. Amanda and I had bedrooms upstairs, but Dad slept downstairs on a trundle bed, so he wouldn't have to lug his oxygen tank up to the second floor. One night he asked, "What is that blue light over there?"

It was the power light on a stereo. I unplugged it and later explained to Marcus that it had been keeping him awake. Dad was accustomed to total darkness and quiet at night. But Amanda could sleep anywhere. I could hear her snoring every night in the next room. She was content to socialize daily with her brother, and now that we had come downstate, she wanted to see other family members.

"I'm going to Rowena's for Thanksgiving," she said.

"I'm sorry," I quipped.

"Oh, very funny!"

"When you get there, be sure to tell them that 'Black Friday' is now, 'Celebrate President Obama Day,' and that you want a T-shirt."

"Okay, I will," she said.

I wondered if she really would. She was savvy enough to understand how well that would go over in a house full of religious Republicans.

Our Thanksgiving consisted of Marcus and Dad and me. That was fine with me. Dad sat watching football all afternoon, and feeding Este the majority of his pork sandwich. He and the little Chihuahua were good buddies again, I realized, now that R1 was out of the picture. He never yelled at her anymore. She would sit at his feet and look up at him, wagging her curly tail hopefully while he snacked on mixed nuts or dried fruit. When he watched TV, she would curl up beside him into a tiny ball and sleep with her forehead pressing into his leg. She was solid and radiated heat, and she grunted in her sleep like an infant. I hoped she brought some small comfort to him.

177

For Thanksgiving dinner, Marcus served a delectable meal for the three of us: Fresh squash, green bean casserole, and stuffing with generous helpings of venison heart. As I munched on the venison heart, I remembered the old Native American tradition of taking a bite of the heart of an animal to inherit some of its admirable qualities. I started having romantic notions that maybe the deer was a powerful buck, swift and smart, courageously testing the air before being struck down by my brother's crossbow. I could use some of those traits: Courage. Smarts. Strength. Beauty.

"What deer was this?" I asked.

"It's a road kill."

I laughed, but when he asked why, I just shook my head.

Lily came home later that night, from spending the holiday with relatives. She had noticed a brown spot, smaller than a dime, on the white carpet by the sliding glass door. "Marcus, what is that?"

Marcus wiped it with a piece of tissue and sniffed. "It's dried dog poop."

Lily said nothing. I didn't either. It could have come in on anyone's shoe.

But the next morning, the hammer came down.

"Nancy, those dogs are not going to be allowed inside this house anymore!" Marcus's tone was belligerent. He strode into the room and sat down opposite Dad at the breakfast table. Lily was sitting quietly on the end. I stood by the counter drinking a glass of juice.

"Marcus, it's November in Northern Michigan. It's freezing. I have two pencil-necked sheep herders and a Chihuahua."

"Well, that's just too bad," Marcus said. "I have to get this house set up to sell."

"Well, then what are you doing with a bunch of hillbilly Yooper house guests?" I said jokingly.

` "I'm not kidding here! You're going to have to do something with those dogs. I don't want them in here."

I looked at Dad. He was sitting there with his cereal bowl, watching me.

"Okay," I set the glass down. "I'll pack up and head out."

"Lily and I have a party to attend tonight. We need someone to stay with Dad."

"Fine. I will stay tonight and leave in the morning, then."

It was clear that the partnership wasn't going to work the same way as when Mom was sick. Marcus had a full-time, live-in woman now and didn't need me, I thought, as I pulled out of his driveway the next morning. It was only three hours back to DeTour, and I was actually looking forward to a break and some solitude.

It was a strange feeling leaving Dad in someone else's care. I didn't really like the idea, but I wasn't going to just sit by and allow my brother to verbally abuse me. I'd had enough. I didn't mind working around the dogs. After all, a lifestyle with animals wasn't everyone's choice. I remembered the winter prior, when Ms. Rip had sneaked behind the Christmas tree and deposited a smelly pile of dung. Dogs were like my sisters, I decided. It took a certain tolerance level to put up with their crap. Only the dogs were not as bitchy.

I could have found them temporary lodging elsewhere, but the real problem was Marcus's tone. It smacked of disrespect and was belligerent and obnoxious. There were kinder ways to approach a problem, unless you wanted to get rid of the person.

As I drove up the tree-lined road, my cell phone rang. It was Lily. I answered, "Hi."

"Hey," she said. "Listen, you don't really have to go. I don't mind the dogs – they will just have to stay in the basement, that's all."

It gave me a little jolt that she said, "I" as if the house was hers.

"Oh, it's okay," I said. "I just don't want to be underfoot. I'm sure you guys can handle things. He'll just need delivery to chemo and radiation, and he'll probably sleep most of the time. And Amanda's easy. She'll just sit and watch T.V. all day if you let her."

"Yeah, well, I told Marcus he could have handled things a little more nicely. He was pretty rude to you."

"Ya think?"

We both laughed a strained sort of laugh.

"Hey," I said. "I really appreciate you reaching out to me. That was nice. Thank you. Call me if you need anything."

"Okay," she said. "Take care."

I went back home across the Mackinac Bridge to the north country, breathing a sort of relief in the cold air, glad to be back, and so glad that there was finally an answer for Dad's pain. The day Dad began treatment to shrink the tumor, my cough, which had plagued me for months, disappeared overnight. My foot was healing, although it had never resumed its former lift and power. I wasn't sure if it ever would. There was a big scar and the heel wasn't pretty and it bulged out now, where it was supposed to curve in. The nurse had told me it would always look like that. I hadn't given it a lot of thought. It was just one more thing to worry about later. I had given up wearing earrings and dress shoes. I couldn't even remember the last time I had gone out for drinks with friends, or ridden my horse, or hiked in the woods. Dating was out of the question. I thought I couldn't possibly handle one more person needing my attention. My life was spent on futons and couches and motel beds, holding my pillow and grasping desperately for every bit of sleep. And there was the driving. Constant driving.

I didn't know how long Dad would be getting treatment. I was sure though, that he would need rest and would probably have to stay at Marcus's until spring. Amanda would have a bit of adjusting to do, I thought, since I was getting text messages from Marcus, "Amanda did eight sit-ups today!"

I laughed and shook my head at the thought of Marcus or Lily trying to Mandate an exercise program. It took a special technique to motivate Amanda. I wondered how long their efforts would last. "My money's on Amanda," I murmured, with a chuckle.

More texts came in, "Why didn't you tell me Amanda requested therapy?"

"Not my news to tell," I said.

"Well what was it about?"

"Not my place to say," I replied. "Why don't you ask Amanda?"

"How do you think I found out about it?"

At that point, I knew Amanda had probably said all that she wanted to say about it. I received more messages later, about how Amanda wasn't "cooperating" very well, but I thought there wasn't much I could do about that. In spite of Marcus's complaints, I thought it was good that Dad and Amanda were at his house. Cadillac seemed so far from everything, and the R's didn't like Marcus and didn't want to know Lily, and maybe they would just leave Dad alone for awhile.

Meanwhile, I was enjoying some respite. Life in DeTour was very lonely, but that was okay for now, I thought. I spent time on the beach with the dogs every day, and visited a little tavern called the Mainsail. It was an inviting saloon with a sprawling, shady deck as long as the building, where in warmer weather, one could sit and look across the street to the harbor. The inside was decorated with a nautical theme, with knotty pine walls and soft lights strung across the beams overhead. I wasn't much of a drinker, and with my introverted nature, not much for socializing in a barroom environment. But it was the only local business with free wi-fi. This offered plenty of fodder for Facebook humor. I would post, "Here I am, back at the bar again. It's only noon in the UP but it's five o'clock somewhere."

The Mainsail's proprietor, Desi Latocha, was an angelic-looking woman with a blonde braid that hung down past her waist. On occasion, Dad had stopped in to have a beer and to flirt with her, and now she asked me daily about his progress. "How's your Dad, Nancy? He's such a sweetie."

I would give her updates, which I knew would pass around the community. Desi was an efficient news source, one primary hub in the town's activities, and best of all, a friendly one.

One day I overheard her saying, "I want to hire someone to come in here and watch the bar next summer, so I can escape once in awhile."

I immediately looked up from my laptop. "Desi, you need some help? I'll come and help. I will need a job here next summer when Dad gets home."

She smiled, "Yeah, Nancy, you can come and work here."

It was such a relief. This, I thought, would solve a multitude of problems. I knew it wouldn't pay much, but it would save me from so much time on the road. I wasn't surprised that she had immediately and graciously given me the offer. Everyone in town knew Dad, and they all knew he was ill.

I was in the gas station looking at movie rentals and noticed a middle aged, roughened- looking man in a plaid coat staring at me.

"Hello," I said politely.

"Are you wunna Blaine's?" He spoke in heavy Yooper.

"Yes."

He grinned. "I could tell. How izzy?"

I smiled. "He's hanging in there. Thank you."

He turned to go, then looked back and added, "You look like yer brudder Jon, eh?"

I rolled my eyes. "Gee, thanks."

He laughed. "Aw, dat's nodda bad ting!"

Dad had asked me to pay some bills for him, so I went to the bank and the teller said, "How's your Dad doing? He's such a sweetie!"

It was the same thing at the credit union and the town hall. I later joked to Dad that I was going to get a T-shirt that read, "The Sweetie is fine."

Even from his station three hours away, Dad was able to stay focused on the tasks at home. He asked me to call Frank to see if he could fix the furnace. It had a habit of shutting off on its own. It would start again if you hit the reset button, but that was an unnerving glitch during a Northern Michigan winter. It sat in the kitchen by the bedroom hallway. On occasion it would make an unnerving bang, like a small explosion, and then it would just keep on chugging. It was just another idiosyncrasy in the ramshackle house that we had learned to live with, but probably shouldn't have.

But Frank was reliable as ever. "I've got a gadget attached to the answering machine that tells me when the furnace is off," he said.

"If the answering machine picks up, I know everything's okay. But if the phone rings and rings, I know I have to come over and reset the furnace. Are you going down below for the holidays? Give me a call when you head back home, so I know when to stop calling the house every day, eh?"

People in the Upper Peninsula call everything south of the Bridge, "Down Below," as though it is Hell.

My next trip Down Below was for Dad's birthday, near the end of November. I took him an ice cream cake and some gifts, some warm pajamas and socks. I arrived at Marcus's to find Amanda not there. They had sent her up to R1's.

"I just think Amanda should be getting used to life without your Dad, you know what I mean?" Lily said.

I shook my head. I thought it was a lame rationalization for a terrible idea. Lily only knew Dad as a sick, cranky old man. She had never known the real character who loved books and coffee and the smell of the woods, who flirted with waitresses and teased incessantly, who wasn't afraid to look the fool in order to get a big laugh. There would be no way to ever get used to life without Dad. One would go on, I thought, like a three-legged dog.

During my brief visits with Dad over the next few weeks, my other dogs stayed at home, but I always traveled with Til. Like most border collies, he was loaded with excessive energy that would lead to destructive habits if he became bored. In the car, he was content, happy to wait for hours in the back seat, probably secure in the knowledge that pretty soon we would be going somewhere. He was a nice traveling companion for me, too, because he was quiet and always cheerful. During my visits to Marcus's that winter, I was very conscious of Til waiting for me in the car. Periodically I would walk outside through the dusting of snow to start the engine and warm him up. He would greet me with a happily thumping tail, carefully accepting whatever treat I offered, and willing to snuggle down with his blanket again, or go out for a quick run among the trees.

Dad's mode was less cheerful. He was miserable being there. Marcus's house was generally cold, and his furniture was leather so that was cold, too. Dad sat on the big leather couch wrapped in blankets, watching TV all day. He kept the volume up to a deafening roar.

"I can't hear myself think," Lily murmured to me one day.

I nodded, remembering all those days of coming back from the beach to blaring episodes of, "Judge Judy."

"I feel your pain," I said.

"He's so crabby!" she whispered.

"Yeah, I know," I said. "I'm sorry about that. It's not normal for him. It's just that he hurts all the time. He doesn't like sitting still. And he doesn't like being away from the Island."

"I understand," she said.

"I can't wait for his radiation to start so he can finally have some relief," I said.

"Yeah, hopefully that will help."

I touched her arm. "I just want to say thank you for all you are doing for my Dad."

I was grateful to her. She was virtually a stranger to all of us, in a new relationship, trying to make it work. It took a special person, I thought, to be thrown into this mix and handle it graciously.

In December I moved Clifford and Trudy to my friend Kathleen's farm in Sault Ste. Marie. Kathleen had two young Morgans and a pony. "Clifford and Trudy can come and stay here," she said. "But my colts aren't gelded so they will have to be separated. We don't want any accidental babies! I have an extra pasture but the fence needs fixing."

After spending a long weekend mending horse fence in the cold, I packed up the dogs and headed south. I got to sit down with Dad for a visit. He has been at Marcus's for several weeks by that time, immersed in medical tests and preparing for his radiation therapy. The oncologist and radiologist blithely order more tests, without realizing the barrage of medical procedures Dad has already gone through.

Perhaps it was partly for this reason that Dad's face was wrenched and his disposition unhappy when I showed up. Probably it was more due to the ever-persistent stabbing pains he had been enduring since February, now dulled with constant medication. Maybe, and more likely, it was due to his forced immobility, his dependency on the oxygen hose and on the care of others, and his longing to get back to the woods. I thought he must be missing Amanda. Still, he looked up and gave me the same cheerful, "Hi!"

"Well, Clifford's in his new digs," I launched into the story of how some friends including cousin John Lowe had come out to help us get the fence up. John, I reported, had shown up with his new baby boy. "Did you know, when I found out they were having a baby I tried to get them to name him Clifford. I think Esther was seriously considering it! Well, they ended up calling him William. When I found out, I yelled at them. 'Why in the heck didn't you name that kid Clifford? Now his name is Will. Will Lowe. Willow!'"

It was great to see Dad start to brighten during the tales of how Clifford happily loaded, crammed into the little trailer next to his fat sister. He laughed when I talked about how they had never understood Clifford at the old place in Pickford anyway, due to his habit of going around with ears pinned, in his grumpy facade.

"Don't they know he's KIDDING?" I roared. "He's always just kidding! He's always joking around!"

Then he laughed some more when I told him how Clifford demonstrated his vicious teeth-baring face on cue, for his appreciative audience.

It only took a few new Clifford stories to cheer Dad visibly, and I marveled again at the healing power of beloved animals, even when they were not present. I wondered if it was my deep affection for Clifford that always sparked the happy reaction in Dad, and which caused this wonderful exchange between us, an ever-reliable triangle of humor and love. That may have been part of it. But after all my days with Clifford, and watching him interact with children, old people and people with disabilities, and his tremendous gentle insight and ever-present humor, I had to acknowledge that so much of it is due to the innate character of the horse, himself.

Clifford was magical, I thought. I left that night with a deep feeling of gratitude for years spent with such an unusual horse, and a Dad who could appreciate him.

I spent the holidays with Claire and Jay, who welcomed Til and Ms. Rip and Este and me. My other dogs stayed with their usual caretakers. Claire had mastered the technique of making me feel welcome with three dogs. She sent text messages. "When are you coming back? The boys miss Este! We love you!"

On occasions when I showed up with one less dog, she would pretend annoyance. "Where is Ms. Rip? She's my baby."

I knew I was very blessed to have such a friend. She cooked eggs for me in the morning and Jay would run out to the store looking for my favorite treat, coffee ice cream. I thought they were more like a family to me than my own was. But I always felt a self-imposed pressure of not belonging, of being temporary and yearning for my own space to call home. I missed my farm, dearly, and had disturbing dreams about strangers moving into my garage. Some mornings, I would wake up still thinking I was there. I missed my horses, now settled in at Kathleen's near Sault Ste. Marie. I missed Dad and Amanda. I missed that old feeling of unity that I thought only family could provide.

In January I learned that Theil and R2 were both flying in for a visit: Theil from Phoenix and R2 from Colorado. Dad's two brief rounds of chemo had gone very well and his prognosis was good. I debated going to visit while Theil was at Marcus's, but I decided Dad didn't need more confusion in the mix. I knew that radiation would have drained him and he really needed rest. I thought it was a terrible time for guests, and I wished Marcus had discouraged Theil and R2 from coming. There was a bit of niggling concern tugging at my brain, which became worse when I learned that while enroute to Michigan, Theil and R2 both had become sick with a virus. Now they were planning on taking Dad on a trip up to Drummond to visit relatives. I had mental imagery of them coughing and sneezing all over him, and dragging him the three hours North. I knew Dad had to be terribly homesick, but I thought socializing at this point was a bad idea.

Then I got a call from Lily. "Hey, Nancy, I'm in DeTour. You're not planning on heading home anytime soon are you?"

"At some point I will, yes," I said.

"Well, don't come up here. The pipes froze. Everything is frozen."

"What?"

"Yeah, it's bad. There's no water."

"Oh no! What happened to Frank's gadget?"

"I don't know," she said.

I immediately called Frank. "Did you know the pipes froze at the house?"

"Yes," he said.

"What happened to your gadget?"

"I guess it didn't work."

I was grateful that Lily had called to let me know about the condition of the house. None of my siblings bothered to. There was nothing to be done about the pipes until spring. There was no way to even know how bad the damage was until thaw. I knew that I had to be available for Dad again when he was ready to come home. Meanwhile, I would stay Down Below. The good thing was that there would be fewer miles to drive in order to meet Bud to go to the east coast for shows. But there still wouldn't be enough money to rent my own place. I sighed when I realized that I was going to have to spend the next three months sleeping in motel beds, or on Claire's futon. Luckily for me, my friends Steve and Myrri in Ann Arbor, seeing my dilemma, stepped forward.

"We cleaned out the spare room for you," Myrri said. "Come here. Make this your home base."

It was a relief. Steve and Myrri were both artists and had six dogs of their own, so I settled in there for the winter. They were glad to have the pet and house sitter, and I was glad to not have to worry about dogs. Steve, who was an animator, gave me a job helping him restore old films. It wasn't exactly life on the farm, and it was so far away from my horses, but I was grateful to have a place to stay and work to do.

About that time I got an email from R2, warning me that R1 was positioning herself to become Amanda's guardian. R2 said that R1,

"Has a history of doing this sort of thing with her own kids and with her granddaughter."

She said in light of this history, and "the way she shuts out other people of interest, I think it is imperative for you to mend fences with Marcus so you and he can show a united front when the time comes."

She added that my visitations would be limited to Raven's convenience and that it would never be convenient for her.

She said that while I was not in a position to take the guardianship myself, Marcus was, but he would need some emotional and actual hands on support. Theil, she added, would take the guardianship as Dad wishes, but since he is out of state, he will not have any legal standing in the state of Michigan.

She said that R1 stated that she doesn't think that Amanda should take extended visits out of state, so Theil would not have any standing should a judge hear the case.

"I am alerting you to this so you can organize yourself before this becomes a critical issue," she added. "At this point, we sibs have some leverage with Amanda, but that is sure to end once Dad has passed. Please find a way to make peace with Marcus before Amanda ends up in Raven's complete custody."

I replied, "I am not impressed that Marcus felt inconvenienced and almost immediately
shipped Amanda off to someone whom he knows abuses her.

"In fact, I am quite pissed about it.

"Amanda is the one most affected by Dad's illness (and loss) and she is the one who most needs emotional, physical and economic support. Obviously, she is not going to get this in any healthy way from Raven.

"Marcus's protests about Dad needing to be away from Amanda are unfounded since Amanda is a constant in Dad's life. Since Dad is ill and living under Marcus's roof, he will be passive about the way Marcus wants to do things.

"If Marcus wants to mend fences, he knows that the first step is to do the right thing and get Amanda back. He can start to deal with the pain in the ass issues that go along with Amanda, as we all do. Right now he is the only one who can do that.

"It's obvious I am the one most capable to care for Amanda on an emotional level. However, right now I can't fill her other needs. It is very unfortunate that I am not in a position to do more about her current situation, but as it stands, I am not.

"However, it is nice to see someone have a real perspective on the matter. Thank you!"

She wrote back. "Frankly, in watching the interaction and the effect that Amanda has on Dad, I concur with Marcus on the issue of needing to separate them on a daily basis until Dad is a little stronger. I noticed immediately that Dad is hyper-vigilant when he is around Amanda. It is stressful for him and the condition he is in warrants

193

limiting stress. I was very impressed with the genuine care Marcus demonstrated for Dad and his ongoing efforts to make the best decisions. His decision to send Amanda to Raven was difficult for him and he is constantly questioning if it is the right thing. In light of the options he had, it was the only thing he could do at that time. Dad was critical and his stress levels had to be brought under control. He barely survived what he was going through. While Amanda has needs, she was not on the verge of dying and her presence was a negative. I know it hasn't been easy for Marcus or for you and I know that my stepping in at this point is a little late in the game. However, I do still live in Colorado and that has made it a little difficult to be more involved. And by stepping in when I did, I saw the picture with a different perspective. Perhaps not a better perspective, but certainly unbiased."

She added, "I'm glad to see that you are at least admitting that Amanda is a pain in the ass to deal with. She is, quite simply, spoiled and expects to be catered to. Raven has a good handle on training her, but it may be too late to make much of a difference in that regard. I was not pleased with the environment that Amanda is now in, but at the same time, I realize that the options are pretty limited. My primary concern is that there is no means for any of us to check on Amanda or communicate with her. I am considering filing with the Board of Human Services. However, once that has happened, Raven is going to become very aggressive in asserting her status.

"So looking at options; I would take Amanda for a short time. Theil would take her for a while. Jon would take her for a while and Marcus is willing to take her as long as he isn't having to cope with Dad's medical care at the same time. Other than that, Raven offers a place to stay, though not the best environment. I don't think DeTour is going to be an option even this summer, as I don't think Dad should be living on his own anymore and obviously, Amanda can't be his primary caretaker.

"I think you have done your duty concerning Dad and Amanda. You don't have to change your life, just your communication and receptiveness with Marcus. Otherwise, you are playing right into Raven's hand.

"I can't dictate to anyone what to do or how to manage their lives. But I can alert you to the situation from my point of view and let you know that if you do not put aside your differences and put Amanda's future as a priority, you are sealing her fate with Raven. I am striving to keep all avenues of communication open so we can build an alliance which is what will be necessary to keep Raven from doing exactly what she did in the past. I hope you can find a way to align yourself with Marcus and help us manage that."

I was wishing she would have shown this much interest about two years prior. But I was glad at least finally someone was willing to discuss these issues. I wrote, "It is never too late for Amanda to change her bad habits. She changed them every time she came to stay with me for extended periods. She became helpful, clean, active and yes, lost weight. Then she would go back home and fall right back into her old habits. She needs to be stimulated, to be useful, and to be treated fairly. In the right environment, she can shine."

R2 wrote, "What I noticed while she was here, the few times she came to visit, she played Mom and Dad against each other, and against anyone who proposed to have her do anything she didn't want to do. When she was here with Dad, she did the same thing. She is passive aggressive with him and it was impossible for me to get any positive engagement with her. For example, she sulked if asked to set the table. Then Dad would hop up and do it for her. This is what she has experienced for 40 years.

"Living with Raven, she has cleaned up her act, to a degree. Whatever means Raven has used, is whatever she has at her disposal. (She isn't an animal trainer and doesn't change her ways very readily.) Keep in mind that her tactics are the same ones that Mom used with us when we were little, which was a different approach than Mom used with you. I am not judging Raven as being "good", just that she has affected a noticeable change in Amanda's behavior. I also realize that Amanda doesn't especially like being around Raven, but Amanda isn't going to like being expected to change her habits regardless of where that expectation is coming from.

"Her weight is a huge concern. I think she is heading for diabetes. I think that the diet and exercise Raven offers is lacking if not absolutely counter to what Amanda needs. This is another reason I think that Raven is not offering the best environment for her. Hell, it isn't the best environment for Raven."

Then she reverted the subject back to Marcus. "His report to me was that you haven't been talking to him since he banned your dogs from his house. I was surprised that you two are at odds as you were always so close. I always anticipated that you guys would show a united front when the chips were down."

I decided to avoid commenting on my relationship with Marcus. I thought it was none of her business. Besides, I thought anything I said would be sent to him immediately. So I replied, "Yes,

Amanda will avoid movement if possible, and Dad has enabled her lifestyle. Mom did too. And Raven does, too. Raven didn't think she should be walking with me outside, and always complained that I asked too much of Amanda physically.

"When Amanda came to stay with me I experienced a lot of resistance from her the first week. It got so that I could predict it. She would get downright bitchy. It hurts to move when you aren't used to it. After the first week, she would start feeling better, and getting happier, and having more energy. She thrives with rules and routines. It isn't that difficult when she is away from people who undermine the effort. (Like Dad.) Bullying her, however, will have the opposite effect and cause her to shut down, and rightly so. Unless you have the brains to develop a technique that is respectful to her, you will get nowhere. She is very stubborn. She also is very canny and knows when she is being played and patronized.

"But Amanda isn't evil. She has a good heart and really wants to get along with everyone. If shown the proper amount of respect, and given the right amount of space to make her own choices, she usually will do the right thing."

Then I added, "I really don't care what Raven's history is, what her degree is, what her job is or what kind of parent she is. She is abusive to Amanda and there is no excuse for it. Amanda should not be under her supervision."

"So what can you do about that?" she asked. "It's all good to make that assessment.
I'm not disagreeing with you, just asking if you have ideas that could be

implemented at this time and pointing out that Raven has worked the system and knows exactly how to implement her wishes into the custody of any person she decides she should be in charge of. Try to convince

any court that she isn't fit. Not gonna happen."

I wasn't sure what I could do about it, if anything. It was a good question, and certainly worth consideration. Hopefully, Dad would be around long enough to render the issue moot. In two years, Theil would be retired and spending summers on Drummond. That, I thought, would simplify Amanda's situation. It would be difficult, but depending on Dad's needs, I could hang in there until then. I hoped Dad could. I thought now he could use support and encouragement, which I could at least offer through the phone.

Then, one day when I called Marcus's house to speak to him, Lily said, "Your dad's not here."

"Where is he?"

"He went to spend the weekend with Raven and she never brought him back. Marcus is very pissed at her for doing this. We don't know where he is. We think at her place."

"What? Why?"

"I don't know. She said it was his choice."

I knew why. It was because he was worried about Amanda. As soon as his radiation treatments ended, he went to stay with her because he didn't want her to have to be alone. She was sitting by herself all day long in R1's modular house in the woods, while R1 worked long hours. I thought Dad staying there wouldn't be such a bad thing, except R1's schedule prohibited much freedom to get him to appointments. He was going to need after care.

There was nothing I could do about it but wait for the weather to break. Then the damage at the house could be assessed, so that I could help them come home. If the plumbing turned into a major job, we still had the Lodge on the Island. I had a job lined up this year, at least. I knew I could work with Desi and she would give me the freedom to do whatever I needed to do for Dad. I could quit the dog show and stop putting up with Bud's idiocy.

I received an elated voicemail from Amanda one day, "Nancy, your father is doing great. The tumor is shrinking. He is feeling strong like a Hartson. He is off the oxygen!"

"Strong like a Hartson," meant that Dad was taking after his mother's German side. Amanda had always described the German bloodline as the powerful one.

It was all going to be okay, I thought.

Chapter Nine

About the R's - Amanda

Raven and Rose had matching bride dolls. The hair on the dolls was too curly and stiff. They freaked me out. They had eyes that would close and open, and the dolls looked like they might come to life. Rowena chased me around the house with them. Rowena was jealous of me, because I caught everybody's eye. But Nancy taught me not to be afraid of the dolls. She grabbed my hand and made me feel their hair. It was kind of smooth and not so scary anymore.

About the R's - Nancy

In March, after the long road back from Long Island, I was exhausted. I was overwhelmed with crowds and running dogs and Bud's narcissistic yammering and drunkenness.   While on the road, I had a call from R1 where she blandly informed me that Dad had been admitted to the Soo hospital. Dr. Aiken had diagnosed him with pneumonia around mid-February, shortly after R1 had taken him home with her. When I learned that he had pneumonia, I immediately began bombarding R1 with emails. She worked long hours and there was no other way to reach her during the day. "How is he? What did the doctor say? Please, take him to Petoskey so he can see Dr. Underwood. He might need to be admitted."

Rather than answering me directly, Raven replied to Rose.

From: Raven
Sent: Tuesday, February 12, 2013 12:05 PM
 Subject: Dad

"Hi Rose,
"Please forward, if you will. Please do not have family inundate this email address with replies.
"Dad was seen by Dr. Aiken yesterday and, if he doesn't have pneumonia, is on the verge of it, along with some congestive heart problems that come with the heart attempting to push through fluid from the lungs. His feet are swollen with edema. He is on antibiotics and water pills along with his usual regiment. He is coughing a lot. Sputum is heavy and green. He slept the first night well but has been up a lot since. Dr. came close to sending him to ER but felt that

he needed to be treated with antibiotics whether it was pneumonia or drainage from sinuses that would settle and cause pneumonia."

I was frantic with worry. I couldn't call her at work. When I called her house, I would talk to Dad and he was tell me that he wasn't feeling well. Raven insisted that he was improving. At a loss for what else to do, I emailed Raven back.

From: Nancy Bailey
Sent: Wednesday, February 20, 2013 9:02 PM
Subject: Re: FW: Dad

"It is difficult to tell if his improvement is Raven's opinion or Dr. Aiken's. Has he seen Dr. Aiken again today? After reassessing this I am going to urge you Raven to take him to ER.

"Get him to Petoskey tomorrow. This is nothing to play around with. Dr. Underwood can check his pacemaker there. Dr. Aiken is very cautious in his recommendations and Dad will absolutely not want to go. You need to override him and insist before this goes any farther. He needs to see a specialist and possibly a different course of antibiotic since he is now on "second round" and still coughing up stuff.

"DO NOT mess with pneumonia or anything that looks like it!
"Please."

On 2/21/13, Raven wrote
"Again.....

"This email account is owned by the state of MI. It is not intended for my personal business. You have the house number. Please use it if you can afford the calls and minimize the use of this email account. I do have other accounts but cannot and will not at this time afford computer access at either of my homes.

"Thanks for your concerns. Things are progressing nicely. While it might seem necessary in the heat of receiving news to attempt to threaten, cajole, chastise, rebuke, or otherwise intrude into Dad's care, which is rarely done well or with Dad's consent. I am happy to entertain, and do entertain suggestions and will, at times, offer to delegate or defer to someone else's availability to chase something down. I will announce when I need some support. Thanks. Raven "

I was starting to get angry.

From: Nancy Bailey
Date: Thu, Feb 21, 2013 at 10:08 AM
Subject: Re: FW: Dad

"Apparently his primary care physician already did indicate it was necessary, and you have overruled him, and that is why I am alarmed.

"I have had experience with the Soo and although it may be a more convenient location for you, there are at least two misdiagnoses on Dad's condition last year (1 being a broken rib, 2 being CHF). I have every reason to believe and insist that he needs to be in Petoskey.

"I am emailing because I want other family members to be witness to your resistance in these matters. If you want to take care of Dad then you need to be available to us all and if this is not an acceptable email to use then you need to get one that is. There are free email accounts available via Yahoo and Gmail.

"Please get Dad the type of care he needs."

Again, Raven sent her response to Rose.

> From: Raven
> Sent: 2/28/2013 1:07:11 P.M. Mountain Standard Tome
> Subj: Dad
>
> Hi Rose,
>
> "Please forward, if you would. I have been monitoring Dad's recovery from his pneumonia and after his 2nd round noticed that he was still coughing up mucus…thinner and lighter green but too much to say he'd recovered. His ankles had resumed swelling as well. Dr. Aiken's office offered me to take him to an after hours clinic in Kinross rather than interfere with my work hours. I took him last night as the soonest I was available."

I noted that, in Raven's email of February 28th, she stated that *she* was monitoring Dad's "recovery". His condition was not being monitored by doctors. It was being monitored by Raven. Also, she made it clear that even though Dad had been symptomatic for over two weeks, she was still prioritizing her work hours over his health care. It was 17 days after Dr. Aiken first diagnosed him with pneumonia.

> From: Nancy Bailey
> Date: Thu, Feb 28, 2013 at 10:40 PM
> Subject: Re: Dad
> "Thanks. Be apprised (because Dr. Aiken has already forgotten at least once) that Dad's potassium levels are high and so he should not be placed on medications to heighten them to compensate for effects of lasix.
> "Please be aware that WMH has already misdiagnosed Dad

with CHF when instead he had lung cancer.

"A clinic is not the place for an 87 year old man with a heart condition who has pneumonia. He needs to be admitted in Petoskey where he can be properly treated while monitored by his cardiologist.

"Let me reiterate, I am very concerned about the quality of care Dad is receiving with his current condition."

Finally after two weeks of forwarding emails from Raven, Rose agreed with me.

From: Rose
Date: Fri, Mar 1, 2013 at 2:57 PM
Subject: Re: Dad

"I concur. Raven, please arrange for Dad to go to Petoskey. I'm sure Marcus will be willing to meet you at the bridge. Thanks for your efforts."

R1 argued that she was perfectly capable of handling the situation. She forbade me to email her anymore, since her account was owned by the state of Michigan and not available for private use. She was usually out of cell phone range. I just kept emailing. I sent copies to all the siblings so they could see what was happening. The weeks trickled by, and Dad did not improve. All the siblings were silent and there was no response to my pleadings. Even when R2 agreed with me and asked Raven to take Dad to Petoskey, she would not. Unbelievably, Raven allowed Dad's pneumonia to progress for nearly six weeks without having him admitted. When he started coughing up blood, she finally decided to take him to the ER.

By then, it was too late.

I had mixed emotions when seeing the "Welcome to Michigan" sign at the state line. Instead of heading back to Steve and Myrri's, I stopped in Ann Arbor at a motel. I did not want to see anyone or talk to anyone. I just wanted my dogs around me, and that was all.

After getting settled in my room, I did open my laptop and saw I had an email from R2. "I think it wouldn't make much difference where he went. Death only stays at bay for so long and when the time has come nobody can change the outcome."

I replied, "Agreed about the outcome, way too late to treat pneumonia now. We are all gonna die, but that doesn't mean we need to hasten the process thru negligence."

I had an email from Steve. "Where are you?"

"I'm at a motel."

"Are you okay?"

"I don't think so," I looked around me. Til was at my feet with a tennis ball, impatiently dropping it, over and over again, hoping I would notice. Ms. Rip was staring at me sadly from her spot by the door. The two Chihuahuas wrestled wildly on the bed. Havoc sprawled on the other bed, thumping his tail and grinning at me. "I think I have been accumulating these dysfunctional dogs because I can't fix my dysfunctional family. As the human family disintegrates, I add more animals. As I was heading over here this afternoon with the back seat crammed with dogs, I realized how strange my behavior is and started self-analyzing."

My dogs were so much easier than humans. They never placed blame. They were always loving. They were honest and simple with no hidden agendas.

I did not want to go north. I did not want to watch Dad die. I did not want to face a nasty pack of self-righteous siblings.

And yet, I knew his death would be my fault. I knew that R1 couldn't be trusted. I knew how irresponsible she was. I had railed at her to get him the right kind of care, when I should have just made the trip north and taken him to Petoskey. I had let economics get in the way of what really mattered. I had failed Dad, miserably, by failing myself. I knew I would kick myself for the rest of my life for this failure. If only I had kept my head above water. If only I still had my farm. If only…

But my self-pity was short-lived. The phone rang and I saw that it was Marcus's girlfriend, Lily. I answered, but then heard an unexpected voice, wavering, "Nancy?"

It was Amanda. "Well, hello Blood Sister!" I said.

She was weeping. It was heartbreaking to hear her cry. "Nancy… Can you come?"

"Yes! Yes, of course. I can come. I will be there."

She sniffled. "When can you get here?"

"Hmmm…" I looked at the clock. It was already late afternoon. I wouldn't be there until after 10 pm and I still had to make arrangements for a motel room. Better to leave in the morning. "Well, would tomorrow be too late?"

Immediately, her weeping stopped. "No," she said. "That's not too late."

"Okay then. I will see you then. Probably evening."

After we hung up, I became more and more restless. I packed up my things, loaded all the dogs and took off. While enroute I got a text from Marcus's son Justin, "Hi Aunt Nancy, I heard you were on the way up and we just wondered if you wanted to join us for dinner."

"I'll be too late," I replied. "But thanks for thinking of me! Love you guys."

His reply shot back. "Love you too."

When I arrived, he and his Taylor Swift doppelganger were sitting alone in Dad's room. This was a best case scenario for me. Two gentle, kind people, and one a cancer nurse, to boot. I wouldn't have to deal with any hostility tonight. I wonder if my relief showed. "Hey guys!"

"Hey!" They both rose up to hug me. I glanced over at Dad and saw him lying still with his eyes closed.

Their whispers told me to lower my voice, but I knew if Dad was asleep he wouldn't hear me.

"Katrina, how's he doing?" I said.

"He's doing okay. He's been very alert. You can talk to him if you want to."

I looked over at him. His eyes were closed and he was lying as peacefully as I had seen him all year. "I don't want to disturb him. I'll let him rest."

I bid them goodnight and went to find the motel.

When I arrived at the hospital the next day, Amanda met me in the doorway of Dad's room. She grabbed me around the neck, yanking me down to hug me tightly. She gasped and wept into my hair. R1 shushed us, ushering us out of the room.

"It's okay, Manda," I said. "We will figure everything out. Come on out here and let's talk a little bit, okay?"

I led her out into the hallway. We walked down into the lounge and I said, "Oh check this out! They have a pop machine. How lucky is this?"

I reached into my coat pocket for loose change and found some. "I hope this thing works." I dropped the quarters in, punched the button and heard the satisfying rattly "thunk" as the bottle dropped into the slot. I pulled it out and handed it to her. "One for you."

Several more quarters in, then another "thunk" for me.

"Let's have a seat," I said, motioning to the big leather couch by the window. We sat down, opening our colas. Amanda looked worn out, I thought, but okay. "So you want to tell me what's happening?"

"Dad's been coughing. Coughing and coughing. He had a bad night, that last night at Raven's. He came and woke me up. He sat down on the edge of my bed and said, 'I've got four more years.'"

I took a swig. "He did? You mean he thought he had four more years to live?"

"Yes. Then he said Raven was taking him to ER. He let me stay home."

"You went back to sleep?"

"Yes, I stayed in bed."

"That is just as well," I said. "ER is a lot of waiting around anyway."

"I know. But he was getting weak. He tripped over that fireplace. I watched him every day getting sicker and sicker. And she wouldn't take him to the doctor!"

Her eyes were welling up. I reached out and rubbed her arm. "Yes I know. That was frustrating me, too."

"It was?"

"Oh yes."

I grappled briefly with how to bring her some comfort. I remembered a similar dilemma with her, about Mom, and how I had handled it. Again I decided the best way was to assure her that she wasn't alone. I started bringing others into the conversation; others who cared about Dad. "Have you heard from Franklin?"

"Yes, he came and saw him yesterday."

"Oh, that's good. I think the only thing we can do right now is just be here for Padre. Help him through it. Just show him we love him and that we care."

"I agree."

"Theil is flying in tonight."

"He is?"

"Yes. With Katherine. And Jon and Judy are driving across the country. They should be here today."

"Oh, good!"

We lingered for a while, drinking our colas and chit-chatting in our own particular abbreviated sort of language. We drew great comfort from each other. I knew, for the rest of the day, she was not going to let me out of her sight, and that was fine with me. After awhile, I told her I would like to go and see Dad, and talk to him a little. "You can come with me," I said.

"Okay," she said.

I stood by the foot of his bed and he looked at me. "Hello Padre," I still remembered to smile. His eyes immediately filled and his face twisted. I walked in and put my arm around him, encircling his head carefully as not to bump his breathing tubes. R1 and R3 were sitting across from me at his bedside, looking at me. I ignored them and kept talking to Dad. "I'm here! I drove up last night but you were sleeping when I got here. I didn't want to wake you. Justin and Katrina were here when I arrived and they gave me the run-down on how you were doing."

R3 stood up. "We're going to get going, Dad. We'll be back a little bit later."

Dad reached out and took her hand in his left hand. He held mine in his right and he pushed our hands together. His eyes closed, pinching as the tears ran down his face. Unbelievably, R3 pulled her hand away from mine. I kept smiling. I patted him. "It's okay, Dad. We're still a family. We're a family."

R3 scowled and kept attempting to jerk her hand away. But Dad held on to her. "He wants us to hold hands," I said, not unkindly. I took her hand in mine and held it firmly. "It's okay Dad. See? Everything will be all right."

R3 yanked her hand from mine and left the room, leaving Dad openly weeping through his breathing tube. I was livid, but determined not to show it.

"Don't worry Dad," I said. "She has to make a scene. You know how she is. But everything will be okay. Anyway, Amanda's right here and she can hang out with me as long as she wants to."

He visibly relaxed. "Marcus's here too, and Jon's on his way," I continued. "He's driving here with Judy. And Theil and Katherine are flying in from Arizona today."

I just kept on talking for a little while, giving him updates on how I was doing and how Clifford was. He would nod and acknowledge me and squeeze my hand. His eyes were bright and alert. I could see him in there, feel his presence even through his wasted body. He was still the same force I had always known; the foundation of so much of who I was. He still emanated love.

"Are you okay here? I'm going to head downtown for a bit. I have to go to the courthouse."

I was sure he knew that I meant to go and pay property taxes. But I also wanted to give Amanda a break from the R's and the hospital environment. Dad nodded. I looked up. "Amanda do you want to come with me?"

She got up immediately and followed me out of the room. As we approached the elevator, R1 came hustling up, breathing in little huffs.

"If you're going to the courthouse to file for guardianship," she said in a stage whisper. "Don't worry about it. I've already taken care of it."

"What?"

"I filed a petition for guardianship for Amanda," she said.

I was becoming agitated, hoping I wasn't hearing her right. "I don't know what you are talking about."

"There wasn't anyone on file," she said.

"So? We all know who it is. It's Theil."

"Not necessarily." Her tone was high pitched, a little wrong-sounding, like a schoolgirl caught leaving the store with three packs of

Juicy Fruit in her pocket, when she had paid for only one. "Oh," the schoolgirl would say. "These other two are for charity. I didn't think you'd mind. Sure, I took them, but it was for the common good."

"Ding," said the elevator, and the doors opened. Amanda and I stepped inside. I hit the button as R1 turned away. As the elevator trundled us down a floor, I wondered what R1 was trying to do. Why would she file for guardianship when she wasn't the chosen guardian, and with Amanda's current guardian still alive? R2 had been correct in her prediction. I thought probably R1 had confided her intent to R2. There was a closeness between them. They were only a year apart in age and had often been mistaken for twins. It wouldn't surprise me if after learning this, R2 had turned right around and reported it to me.

I thought maybe I should go back and tell Dad what R1 had said. But it was probably best to not upset him. I decided to just wait until Theil arrived that night.

When Amanda and I returned to Dad's room that night, our cousin Polly was sitting in the chair by the doorway. She stood up to hug us. We saw that Dad had fallen into a fitful sleep. "I just didn't want him to be alone," Polly whispered.

A nurse came in and looked at his monitor.

"Mr. Bailey, do you want another blanket?" the nurse's voice resounded loudly through the room. Dad's eyes opened and he nodded yes. I was a little surprised, as one of the hospital's heated blankets was usually more than sufficient. But Dad was shifting, moving his legs and turning his body in different angles. I imagined that it was uncomfortable lying there among the tubes, on the sterile sheets between the cold metal bars. The whole room was white and grey, with sharp edges and corners. The feel of it was temporary, and even the pale light from the fluorescent tube above the cupboard was cold. The stack of machines next to the bed blipped with graphs and tiny red and green lights. Dad lay breathing deeply, looking miserable. At least, at his request, they had removed the breathing tube. His speech had become so garbled that it was nearly impossible to understand him. He had given up trying to talk, and now just lay there conserving his energy. I looked at his hands, thick and gnarled with age. They still looked the same. They might be holding a cup of coffee, tapping it on the table to tease a young waitress into filling it. Dad was wasted and pale, but his steely eyes were bright and knowing. He watched everything. The life force in him was still so powerful. It was hard to believe that he couldn't just get up out of the bed, rip the tubes out and throw them down and say, "The hell with this! Come on, girls, let's go get a sandreech."

Amanda and Polly and I would go after him, and he would pause in the hallway, lean over the countertop where the nurse was sitting, and pull a sucker out of his coat pocket. "Here's a present for you."

The nurse brought in another blanket and covered him, feet first, then carefully unfolding it and laying it over him. He nodded to her.

Polly visited with Amanda and me. Dad watched while Polly talked about her kids, and her numerous grandchildren. It must have been comforting to Dad, I thought, to hear stories of family and the next generations; babies coming and people starting new careers, new marriages, new families.

While Polly talked, Amanda hung on every word. If she paused, Amanda would prompt her. "How's Brittany doing? How are Traci and Fritz?"

Amanda, I thought, loved the name, "Fritz." She always said it in a sort of emphatic, happy way. I realized Mom had always said it that way.

After a little time had passed Dad gestured to me and I got up and went over to him. "Hot," he said.

I touched his forehead. "Good grief, you're sweating like crazy! Let's get rid of this second blanket."

I took it off him and tossed it into a chair. He was pushing the second cover down, weakly. I went out to the nurse's station and asked for a washcloth. "He's burning up in there."

She gave me a cool cloth, and I went in and began wiping Dad's head and around his eyes with it. He lay there, looking relieved. I patted his shoulder. I didn't say anything, just spent a long time wiping his face and head, hoping the touch would sooth him in some way.

He opened his mouth and pointed into it. "Thirsty?" I said. "I'll try to get you a drink."

I went back out to the nurse's station. "He is asking for water."

"He can't swallow," the nurse said.

"Well – then maybe some ice chips? Is there something we can do for him?"

"I'll come in with a swab," the nurse said.

She came in and swabbed all around Dad's lips and inside his mouth. When she was finished, he said to her, "Thank you." I was surprised, because his speech had become so slurred, but when he said this, his voice was perfectly clear and still had its old timber.

The hospital had grown quiet and it was getting later. Polly stood up and put her coat on. She went over to Dad and patted his arm. "I'll see you later."

She walked toward the door and in the doorway, she stopped and looked back. Dad raised his right hand in a wave, a salute to her.

"I'll be back tomorrow," she said.

She walked out.

I sat down by Amanda and we talked a little bit, softly. I was waiting for Dad to fall asleep. Dad turned his head, first one way and then the other. His legs thrashed in discomfort. I stood up. "Dad, Amanda and I are going to the bathroom," I said. "We'll be right back."

He nodded to me. Amanda got up and followed me out to the nurse's station. I leaned over to the nurse. "Can he have something to help him rest? Maybe some morphine? He's just terribly uncomfortable," I said softly.

"Yes," she said kindly. "I will see that he gets some, right now."

"Another thing, can you turn that light off that's above his head? I know it's keeping him up."

"Sure," she said.

Amanda and I went down the hall to the waiting room. We loitered there, and I put more change into the pop machine.

"I'm just giving him a little time," I explained to Amanda. "I think he might actually go to sleep if there is no one in the room with him, especially if she turns that light off."

"I agree," Amanda said.

We waited about ten minutes and then went back. I looked into the room and saw the light was out. Dad was lying at an angle in the dark, with his head on one side, and was fast asleep.

I breathed a sigh of relief. "Thank you," I told the nurse.

At around 8:30 the next morning, I had just let the dogs back into the motel room when a text message chimed in from Marcus. "Breathing getting shallow, Raven says get to hospital."

Amanda was still sleeping.

"Amanda," I said.

She stirred, but her deep breathing continued. My eyes flicked around the room, taking in her suitcase, her pile of clothes on the chair, assessing what she would need and the fastest way to get her ready. I wanted to wake her gently, without adding any elements of panic. The day was going to be hard enough. Just then, my cell phone buzzed and I saw Marcus's name.

"Shit," I said.

I picked it up and pushed the button.

"Hi," I said.

His voice was tight and he choked out the words. "I am just calling to tell you that Dad passed away."

"I know," I said. "I knew it when I saw you were calling me. What happened? Did he say anything?"

"No. Raven said he never woke up."

"Okay," I felt perfectly calm. "Thanks for letting me know. I'll tell Amanda."

"Is she doing okay?"

"Yes. She's still asleep. Are you okay?"

"I'll be okay."

"All right. We will get there as soon as we can. Thanks for calling me. I love you."

"I love you too."

We hung up. I turned and pulled the curtain away from the window, looking out at the smooth grey sky. I turned back and looked at Amanda's quiet, blanket-covered form. She hadn't moved. The dogs were all watching me and their expressions seemed sad and knowing. I began pacing around the room, trying to think of a way to wake this girl up and tell her that her dad was dead. I suddenly understood why people become smokers. I couldn't think of what to do with my hands. As I paced, I was shaking them as if they were wet rags. It would have been more productive to pick up a cellophane-wrapped packet and smack, smack it against my palm, as I had seen people do. I could slide out a cigarette, and then snap open the lighter. I could hold the cigarette between two fingers while I sucked the hot toxins into my lungs. Plus I could flick the ashes, and wave the little white stick around so it drew blue smoke circles in the air. There was safety in preoccupying oneself with small, self-important gestures.

Amanda still lay on her bed with her head covered. From beneath the cheap bedspread came a gentle snore.

I grabbed my cell phone and stepped outside.

When Mom had died, it hadn't even occurred to me to reach out to my cousin, Polly. But the fact that Dad had so loved her, and since we had shared his last evening with her, it seemed like the natural thing to do.

Her voice answered, and I realized I was standing outside in my bare feet and pajamas. The pavement was cold. I was looking across the parking lot at a crusty pile of blackened snow that towered higher than the motel roof. It had been pushed there by the plows and now remained, a sort of obscene reminder that it was the end of March and there was no hint of any change in the weather.

"Polly? It's Nancy." I spoke softly, because I didn't want to walk away from the door, but I didn't want Amanda to hear me either.

"Oh, uh huh?" Her voice, though soft, had a little edge to it, an uneasy anticipation.

"Dad passed away this morning. I just wanted you to know."

She drew a sharp breath. "Oh, I was afraid you were going to say that. I just had a bad feeling when I left there last night."

I remembered Dad's salute to her, how he had raised his right hand as she paused to look back and smile from the doorway. "I'll be back tomorrow," she had told him.

"You and Amanda and I were the last ones to talk to him," I said.

"How is Amanda doing? Is she handling it all right?"

"She's still asleep. I haven't told her yet."

She sighed. "Oh, dear."

"Yes. I am not looking forward to it."

"Amanda has been through so much already. And she is so much better since you came back. I am so glad you are here for her. And that your dad had that time with you last night."

"Yes, me too."

"Did Theil get here okay?"

"Theil and Katherine drove all the way up from Detroit last night. They were so tired after the flight and all. They checked in to their hotel room and they were going to see Dad this morning. They didn't get to see him."

"Oh dear," she said again.

"I know."

She kept asking me questions, effortless and soothing, as empathic people do when someone needs to talk. I told her that I thought Marcus was at the hospital, and R1 and R3 had been with Dad when he took his last breath. But he had never awakened after I had asked the nurse to give him the additional morphine the night before.

"That's a blessing, in a way," she said.

"Yes, it really is." I sighed. I suddenly felt exhausted. "Well, I guess I had better go try to talk to Amanda."

"Well, thank you for calling me. Will you call me when you know what the plans are?"

"Yes, I for sure will."

I stepped back into the room and Amanda was peeking out, just one eye showing from under the blanket. The eye quickly shut again.

"Hi," I said.

She didn't answer. I wandered over to the bathroom, picked up the dog bowl and filled it with water.

I was thinking about how Dad had waited for us to leave the room before he started his departure. He had been a true gentleman, always. I was thinking he was making it easy on me. There was no way I could have done for him what I had done for Mom. I had held her hand on her deathbed, telling her that it was okay for her to go; setting her free. She had died minutes later. I knew that Dad was suffering, but I wasn't sure that I would ever be able to say those words to him. I remembered him talking of his mother's death. Grandma had died at home, in her bed. Dad sat by her side, and she kept hugging him, telling him, "I will be leaving you now."

He had said, "Mom, now don't you talk like that."

He told me he had left the room for a minute, and when he came back, she was gone. She had turned over on her side, he said, and she was lying there peacefully, looking as if she had just drifted into a deep sleep.

"I can't remember why I left the room," he had said to me.

"Maybe you left because she needed your permission to go," I said.

He had paused, thoughtfully, and said, "You might be right."

It was occurring to me now that we had relived this intimate history. Dad had gone softly and politely, just like his mother.

The dogs lapped at their water. Amanda finally rose, letting the cover fall, heaving herself forward with a grunt. She sat upright, staring sleepily straight ahead.

"Are you awake?" I said.

"No." Her expression was peaceful.

"I just talked with Marcus on the phone," I said.

"You did? What did he have to say?"

"He told me Dad passed away."

I sat down on the bed next to her. She didn't move. Her expression didn't change. She was staring at the blank TV screen. Finally, she yawned and said, "Well, I guess I better get some coffee."

Curse the poor hearing. I had to tell her again. "Amanda. Did you hear what I said?"

"No. What."

"I said our father passed away."

Her reaction was instant. She flopped backwards onto the bed and pulled the covers up over her head. She was still for a long moment. Finally, she began to cry. She lay there on her back, bleating in heartbroken staccato squeaks, as one would imagine a dolphin might cry. Her whole body shook.

"Four more years! Four more years," she sobbed. And then, in a tiny, plaintive whimper, she said, "Dad."

That was too much for me. I lay down next to her and put my arm over her wide, trembling girth, and I began to sob. Our voices united in misery. Finally, she paused, holding her breath, listening from beneath the rumpled bedspread while I wept.

"It's okay to say, 'Dad'," she said.

I hesitated. "It is?"

"Yeah."

She was helping me, supporting me, understanding that I needed to grieve, giving me permission to realize my own loss. At that moment, I lost whatever control I was trying to maintain for her sake. I let the pain hammer into me, a punch crashing deep into my chest. "Daaaaa-ad!" I wailed. "My Padre!"

Amanda began to weep again. We howled. We mourned. The great man was gone. The fight to keep him safe was over, and I had lost. Our trio was splintered, shattered beyond repair. Grief spilled out of us like a spring, gurgling up from the deep, deep earth, washing over the surface, seemingly with no end. We cried and cried, holding each other, sharing the terrible knowledge that the most important person in our lives was, with each moment, slipping farther into our past.

Finally, she took a deep breath and lay still. I lay next to her and we were quiet for a moment. Then she said, "What do you want to do?"

"I don't know," I said. "What do you think we should do?"

"I think we should go see Polly."

"You do?"

"Well… She makes really good coffee."

She had not asked to go to the hospital. She knew Dad was gone. Her acceptance was immediate and complete. Now she was guiding me, showing me the way, and like me, she was reaching for the person who had shared his last conscious moments with us.

"Okay," I said. "I'll call her right now."

We didn't tell anyone where we were going. We sat in Polly's house and had coffee, and talked about the usual things. "Talk about nothing," Polly had called it. Amanda was calm and seemed peaceful. We were there for about an hour and my phone began to buzz. It was Marcus.

"We have to go meet the sibs," I sighed.

The Reamer Funeral Home was the same one that had handled Mom's service and cremation. It was situated in a little farm town called Pickford, between Cedarville and the Soo.   R2 was making plans to fly in from Colorado. The remaining seven of us crammed into a tiny office with the funeral director and his wife. We agreed to have Dad's viewing at that location, but to move him to the Drummond Town Hall for the funeral. The R's dominated the meeting. I sat silently in the corner, except for when the question of flowers came up.

"Tulips," I said. "They're his favorite."

I was mildly surprised when no one argued over it. Afterward, we all left and walked in a sort of stunned silence out of the building. Amanda and I got in the car.

"Nancy," R1 was approaching. Amanda immediately reached over and locked her door.

I opened the car door and stood up, leaning over it. R1 continued. "Amanda needs to come home now."

"Amanda has asked to stay with me. So, we are heading back to the motel room."

"She needs to come with me."

"Why?"

She appeared irritated that I would even ask. "Because she has been running around here long enough. She has her own bed and her own things and she needs to pick out some clothes for the funeral."

"She has clothes. I bought her an outfit and some new underwear. She wants to hang out with me. It's no problem."

"It's time for her to come home."

"That's not her home."

Theil and Katherine pulled up next to me in their rental car. They had the window down and were listening in silence. I stood defiantly, keeping the open car door between R1 and myself. Out of the corner of my eye, I watched as if in slow motion, Marcus was getting out of his car and approaching us. I felt a wave of relief.

Marcus said, "What's the problem with Amanda hanging out with Nancy? That's where she wants to be right now."

"She needs to get her things organized."

"Well, if there are things at your house, maybe Nancy could come by and pick them up."

"Yes, of course," I said. "I'm happy to run over there and get whatever she needs. Not a problem."

Amanda remained seated, unmoving, in the car. Theil and Katherine watched in silence.

"Well, we have a rhythm to our days here. Amanda needs to come home now."

"That's not her home," I said again. "Amanda has made her choice. She wants to stay with me."

"I know what's best for her, and she needs to be home getting organized right now. We have a lot to do."

"Look," I said. "Amanda has been through a lot. We all have. But she especially has. She is going to need some time. I think it is important to respect her wishes and give her the chance to grieve in the way that she chooses. She is, after all, an adult."

"She's a disabled adult."

"So?" The fact that R1 made this distinction infuriated me. Did Amanda's disability make her less of an adult? Was she incapable of feeling her loss or of needing to mourn? Could she not express herself or make her own choices? All my senses were heightened. My face was growing hot. I imagined the hair on the back of my neck standing erect, my cheeks puffing out. I was rising up on my toes, holding onto the car door for balance, like a mother bear instinctively making herself appear larger.

"I am her primary caretaker," R1 said.

I shook my head. "That's not the case."

"Yes, I am," R1 looked through the windshield at Amanda. "Come on, Amanda."

Amanda didn't move. I was livid. Dad would have never permitted this. At that point, he had been gone about six hours. I turned to Marcus. "Is Dad even cold yet?"

"That's not appropriate," Marcus said.

"Sorry," I said.

But my question had the desired effect. R1 spun around and walked away. I went over to where Theil and Katherine sat in their rental vehicle. "Can we have a meeting? We need to get this guardianship thing straightened out, pronto."

"Yes. We will organize that."

"Thank you! Let me know if you need any help."

I got back in the car with Amanda. Her eyes were wide. She said, "Did you notice I locked the door?"

"Yes. I noticed. Why did you do that?"

"I was afraid she was going to open the door and drag me out of the car."

I sighed. I started the car.

"Why does she call that place my home?" Amanda said. "I don't have a home. I'm homeless."

I looked at her in astonishment. "Oh my gosh. I hope you don't really believe that."

"Yes I do." She was sitting with her arms folded. A scowl darkened her face while she stared out the window at the road.

"Well, I can understand why you feel that way. And sometimes I feel that way too."

"I know you do!" she said immediately. I understood then that she was joining me voluntarily. Her stance wasn't merely because she needed me, but from her perception of how isolated I was. I needed her. If I was displaced, she was too. If I was unwelcome, she was too. If I was an orphan, so was she. 'I am Spartacus.' I could feel the tears welling up. How was it that this tremendous insight and compassion was most evident in one family member – the "disabled" one?

I swallowed. "Well, I will tell you something. There are lots of people who won't let you be homeless. There are people who care about you. I mean, even besides brothers and sisters. You have Frank and Polly and Aunt Sue. You have lots of relatives who love you."

"Like Jack," she said.

"Yes, there's Jack too. It's just like me. I have friends who would never permit me to be out in the street. I have Claire. I have Steve and Myrri. I have Cindy. You have people, too. We don't have our mother and father any more. But as long as there are people who love us, we will always have a home. And you know, wherever I am, you will always be welcome."

We spent that evening and part of the next day trying to adjust to the idea of Dad's absence. It was a strange time, with an ache akin to hunger in my middle. Amanda was quiet but she didn't ask to go to Raven's, or even to go home to DeTour. She seemed content to hang out with me in, "our apartment," as she liked to call the motel room. She would sit on her bed and hold and scratch Este, and throw the ball for Til. We went to the movies and visited with Polly, and we had dinner with Theil and Katherine. His hotel had a pool, but despite our cajoling, we could not get Amanda to swim. "I don't feel like it," she said.

She stayed in "our apartment" with the dogs when the meeting time arrived. Marcus had rented a conference room in a hotel down by the Soo Locks.

When I walked into the meeting the siblings had already assembled, with my brothers spaced evenly along the window near the back wall. R1 and R3 perched tightly together, off at their own side table. I smiled at everyone. I wasn't optimistic about the results, but I was grateful that we all were at least making the effort. I was carrying my laptop case and it bumped against the wall as I edged through the narrow space to sit close to Marcus. Jon sat on the end, directly across from me. Theil was presiding, in the center of the long end table. He had a notebook and pen. He said, "I guess we can start now. I want to thank everyone for coming. Since I called the meeting I want to start off with a couple of ground rules."

Ground rules. An excellent plan for a volatile group.

"Rule number one," he said. "Show respect. Rule number two is to stick to the topic. We have a couple of topics that I want to cover.

One is Dad's trust, and the other is Amanda's guardianship. Since Marcus has had power of attorney and served as Dad's financial advisor, I will let him address the matter of the trust."

"That's simple," Marcus said. "The trust is empty. There's nothing in it."

"Empty," R3 said.

"That's right," Marcus said. "He created a trust, but he was terrible at managing his money. The trust was there, but there was nothing in it."

This didn't surprise me and I was sure Marcus spoke the truth.

"I will want some documentation of that," R3 said.

"No problem," Marcus replied.

"What about the properties? What about the Drummond lot with the trailer?"

I looked at Marcus. We hadn't discussed it, so I was interested in what the response would be, and if he planned to tell them that Dad had left it to me, and what their reaction would be to that news.

"The Drummond property is deeded to me," Marcus said.

What! My horse corral, my sanctuary? But what about Dad's little diagram with my name on it? I felt like someone had just punched me in the gut. I worked very hard not to show any reaction or surprise. I just sat there, but my head was spinning. What had Dad done? How had this happened?

"It's deeded to you. So you now own all the Drummond property. The entire thirteen acres," R3 said.

"Yes," Marcus said.

"Well, that's just great!" R3 snapped her laptop shut. "Praise Jesus! Thank you God! Thanks a lot Marcus. You just made my job a whole lot easier."

She turned her face away from us and muttered, "Shyster!"

To me the whole situation was beginning to look ridiculous. I had been sitting in my seat for five minutes, had already lost Clifford and Trudy's summer home, and in fact had lost my only remaining home. I made a mental note to talk to Marcus about this. It was not a good sign that he had kept this very important fact a secret, even from me. Hopefully he was just keeping it safe for me. In years past, I would not have even questioned him. But the family had shattered and relationships were not what they had been. The first two rules of the meeting were already broken. These people! What was the point of even having rules? We were the Baileys, now split into two factions. We had degraded from the Waltons to an up-north version of the Hatfields and McCoys. Goodnight, John-Boy. I stifled a chuckle by biting my lip. My retainer had a sharp edge on it and I busied myself with popping it on my teeth. If I sucked it hard enough on one side, I could force it down from my molars and give it a pretty substantial snap. I knew this was very bad for it, as it had already developed a huge crack and probably wouldn't stay in place much longer. But it still offered me a bit of stress relief.

"Good. Maybe Marcus can get a copy of the trust to everyone," Theil said. "Our next order of business is about Amanda's guardianship."

Marcus said, "Raven, Theil's here now and he can file for guardianship. But he can't file unless you withdraw your petition. We need you to withdraw your petition."

"I can't do that," R1 said.

"Why?"

"Because Amanda won't have any coverage if she leaves Michigan. Her benefits don't translate to other states. I just filed for guardianship to make sure she was covered. If no one had stepped up, she would have ended up as a ward of the state. You have to be Johnny-on-the-Spot on this stuff."

I knew this wasn't true. Amanda was covered by Medicaid and Medicare. They were nationwide programs. But R1 was a social worker now employed by the state, so no one was going to argue with her. Her misinformation would be easy enough to prove, so I said nothing. Instead, I sat and popped my retainer.

"Okay," Theil said. "I will do some research on it. But when I retire, my health insurance will apply to her."

Marcus turned to R1 again. "If Theil were the only one in the family, Amanda would be traveling back to Arizona with him. Please withdraw your petition."

"I can't do that."

R1 and R3 sat united in their determination to have their way. It was obvious at that point that we were doomed to further legal action. There would be no cooperation, no discussion of how Amanda felt or what would be best to usher her through her grief. No one had asked me how she was doing. I realized then that to them, this was about something other than Amanda. Was it about money? Was R1 so needy, with her two homes and drama with her adult children, that she was desperate for Amanda's SSI? Was all this really worth $700 per month?

When I looked up at the R's, both were glaring at me. I turned my gaze away so not to be rude, but every time I looked back, they were staring at me, each with a pudgy grimace. I didn't understand why their focus was on me. I had been silent the whole time. Their expressions reminded me of the Hecklers on the Muppet Show. The Hecklers were two old men, each with a perpetual glare, who sat side by side in the balcony and criticized all the puppets in the cast. I was fighting off the urge to laugh. Years prior, Marcus and I had been prone to giggling fits in church, and it felt exactly the same as this. Laughter was utterly forbidden, and so wrong, and therefore there was no way to stop it. I looked away and said nothing.

"If Amanda lives in my home, she is my dependent," R1 said.

Finally I piped up. "Actually," I said politely. "Amanda's permanent address is the same as mine. It's in DeTour. If it works as you say, I guess that makes her my dependent."

"Oh, give us a break, Nancy!" R3 screamed. "You don't even have a home!"

"Uhm, yes I do. I've been living there for two years. It's just that right now it isn't livable."

"It isn't livable because you froze the pipes!"

I rolled my eyes. Theil sat looking down at his notes. Marcus sighed. "Well, it seems a shame that we can't all come to some kind of agreement on this."

"That's not going to happen in a group this large," R1 said.

I felt a word of encouragement might help. "Certainly it can happen. The size of the group has nothing to do with it. If Dad's wishes are honored, in a group of people who are sane enough to –"

"Sane enough?" R1 got up and left the room.

R3 leaped to her feet. "In a 'sane' group, Nancy? Are you saying we're insane?"

I just shook my head, speechless, struggling to maintain my composure in a meeting that had seemed like a good idea, but was fast becoming merely theatrical. With R3's yelling and gesticulating, she was only solidifying her Heckler persona. Any thought of the Muppets immediately hurled my mind back to a summer day, some fifteen years prior, when I had taken Amanda to a carnival. She hadn't gone completely bald yet, and there was just a single large tuft of hair growing out of the top of her head, like a friar's. She knew I wouldn't go on any roller coasters, but she loved them, so she would ride by herself. She decided to try one that traveled in undulating circles, through a tunnel and back out again. She sat down in one of the cars next to a little kid, and pulled the bar down in front of them. When the machine began to move, it was playing head-booming rock and roll music. Amanda was loving it, holding her arms above her head and singing. Every time they came out of the tunnel, the coaster was going faster. Amanda was still singing with her arms up, but the little kid next to her was gripping the bar so tightly his arm muscles stuck out in little cords. Finally, they came out at top speed and Amanda at last had resorted to holding the bar. Her eyes were bulging and her mouth was a big half-moon hole, and that hair was standing straight up on top of her head.

There were parents, the faint of heart like me, standing around me, watching as my sister whizzed by with her popping eyes and gaping mouth.

"She looks like Beaker on the Muppets!" I yelled, to nobody in particular. I was laughing so hard I could barely see. Amanda was leaning over to one side and the little kid was squashing beneath her, but with the inertia there was nothing they could do about it. They did a few rounds like that and I realized everyone around me was laughing because I was yelling, "It's the Muppet Show! It's the Muppet Show!"

I tried to stop because I didn't want people to see me making fun of my disabled sister, but I was beyond help at that point. Finally the thing slowed down and Amanda could see I was in tears. She got off the ride and came strutting past me and said, "Laugh it up, there, Fozzie!"

The group around us screamed with delight and began to applaud her. Even years later, I still can't relive that day without laughing.

"Wipe that smirk off your face!" R3 shrieked. As she yelled, her jaw yammered up and down between the folds of her cheeks, exactly as the Heckler's did. I thought our meeting was fast becoming, "The Muppets" meet "Jerry Springer." I had to look away.

She turned to Marcus. "Way to go, Puppet Master!"

That did it. I was ruined. My head fell into my folded arms, and I dissolved into helpless gales of smothered hilarity. R3 was still the little kid running upstairs with a butcher knife and a red sock. My reaction was enough to send her over the edge. She stood in the middle of the room, screeching at me. "Now you're laughing at us? You think this is funny? What is wrong with you? Shame on you, you… You sociopath!"

Unfortunately her yelling only escalated my reaction. I was wiping tears away by the time she went crashing out of the room. I could hear her out in the hallway, still yelling. She stormed out of the building, and we could see her through the window as she got into her car and roared off.

With both R's gone, the room was suddenly quiet. Jon was still sitting at the end of the table. His face was clouded into a deep scowl. He turned to Theil, "Back when I did air traffic control, I used to sit in military briefings between pilots that were similar. Very little got accomplished."

Just then, R3 stormed back in. She must have circled the building and come flying back into the hotel, but no one had noticed. "To hell with you, Marcus! This is my family and I am going to be here!"

"Okay," Marcus said.

"Dad's been gone 24 hours and we're already in a legal dispute?" she said as she sat down.

"Thank you," I said. "That was exactly my point!"

"Shut up, Nancy!"

Theil cleared his throat. "So the hearing is set to determine who will be Amanda's guardian."

"What is the date again, for the hearing?" Marcus said.

"It's April 11th," Theil said.

I looked up. "It's the eleventh? I thought it was the tenth."

"It's the eleventh," Marcus said.

I shrugged, joking, "I dunno. I'm probably told the wrong date so I don't show up."

R3 screeched at me from her seat. "Everyone's put on notice, Nancy, don't be so stupid!"

I ignored her and looked at Theil. "Can you be here?"

"I can't."

"I wonder if there's some kind of absentee thing you can do."

"I'm sure there is."

"Cuz it looks like the train's leaving the station," I said.

"Yep."

Theil got up and walked out, and I could hear him asking R1 to come back in. She followed him into the room and sat down. The R's were reunited then, side by side, a virtual wall of self-righteous hostility. I carefully kept my eyes averted from them. It was better not to look.

Theil said, "We have to remember that this is a hard time for all of us. We all have defense mechanisms that we use to handle stress. Some of us yell. Others handle it in other ways. I know that my defense mechanism is in making jokes that are considered inappropriate. I know some others use that, too."

He looked over at me, but his expression was not unkind. I smiled, still wiping my eyes.

After the meeting, the R's roared off together. Jon said that he was going to catch the boat and rejoin Judy on Drummond. I went back to the hotel room to pick up Amanda, and the remaining group of us went to Applebee's for lunch. After we had ordered, Marcus stood up and said, "Nancy, come with me, I want to talk to you about something." He held out his hand and I hopped up and took his hand and followed him to the front of the building.

Near the door, by the hostess's station, he turned. His smile had vanished. "I want to talk to you about what you said in front of the funeral home. That thing you said about Dad being cold. Ya know, if you had been a man, and said that, I would have knocked your block off!"

"Way to control yourself," I snapped. "Lucky for me I have a vagina!"

He turned to walk toward the door. He gave my hand a yank, pulling me up in front of him. As he pushed me roughly toward the entrance, my shoulder slammed into a woman who was entering the restaurant.

"Marcus, stop it!" I jerked my hand away from him and strode into the other side of the building, the large dining room. I was practically running, looking around for a ladies' room to escape into.

"Come here and sit down and talk to me!" he said.

"I am not talking to you. You are too scary right now."

Just then the restaurant manager approached. "You two need to take this outside."

"We're okay. I'm good." Marcus waved him off. I was a little surprised when the manager just nodded and walked away. I thought he might be more forceful. In fact, I would have welcomed the interruption. This was off to a bad start.

Marcus motioned to a bench. "Just sit down here, will you?"

I sat down, thinking, "Sit here, like a good little girl. Be the big ol' figurative toilet we all know you are."

I looked at him.

He said, "You know, in the meeting at the funeral home, Raven was trying to ask you something and you walked right away from her. She was calling your name and you went out of the room. I know you heard her. I saw you do it."

"So?"

"What is wrong with you?"

I stared at him. "Oh, I don't know. Let's see. Uhm, my dad is dead?"

I stopped myself from saying the last part, the part I was thinking. "And she killed him."

His expression softened. "I know. I miss him too. But you know, we've all lost him. We all miss him. How could you be so disrespectful toward Raven? How could you say that horrible thing to her? Asking if Dad is even cold yet! How could you say that?"

"It got rid of her, didn't it?"

"That's beside the point. She's our sister."

"I don't give a shit."

It was true. I had checked out. I had truly taken Jennifer's advice to, "get a cold heart." Dad was gone. The only person that mattered now was Amanda. Nobody else mattered. My days of trying to keep everyone happy were over. I was not the person Marcus remembered, and he could see it. He shifted in frustration. "You must."

I shook my head. "Not anymore. Not with what she is putting Amanda and all of us through."

"She's doing what she thinks is best."

"You're starting to sound like Rose. Whose side are you on? We have a dead father and now this crazy bitch is dragging us all into her drama."

"You see, that language isn't necessary."

I shrugged.

He could see he wasn't reaching me. "Well, that's just great."

"Well, what exactly do you want from me, Marcus?"

He said nothing. He stood up and walked outside into the cold. Vastly relieved, I immediately went back to the table. Theil was in rare form; making Amanda laugh, maybe trying too hard. But I smiled. It was a strange contrast to be in such gentle company, after the weird and semi-violent encounter in the restaurant entrance. A few minutes later, Marcus came back in. He leaned over and whispered in my ear, "I hope you and I understand each other."

I patted his cheek, but said nothing. It was clear that, for the first time in our lives, we no longer did.

After the strange Applebee episode, Amanda and I went back to Theil's hotel room. R2 was due to arrive from Colorado at any time. I stopped first at our "apartment" to let my dogs out, and then grabbed Este and put her in the car. When we arrived in Theil's room, I pulled Este out from under my coat and tossed her on the bed. Theil and Katherine loved dogs, including small ones. They had owned poodles for years. "Oh look!" Katherine said.

"That's Este," Amanda said. "Our Cheeeee-wowa!"

We laughed. Este bounced back and forth on the bed, her curly tail wagging, ears flattened, doing her Chihuahua happy dance. "Hey," Theil said. "She's cute!"

He got down on his knees and patted the bed, imitating a doggy play bow. Elated, Este spun in circles and did a mad dash off the bed, around the room and then jumped back up on the bed again.

"She does tricks," I said. "Dad loved her. He was always laughing at her."

Just then came a knock at the door. Este exploded into barks. I called her over and picked her up to quiet her. "That's Rose," Theil said.

He opened the door and there stood R2, clad in a coat and tight jeans and thick hiking boots. She greeted him with a big hug. She entered the room and gave hugs all around. I could see her eyes flicking from face to face, assessing the level of sadness. When she noted that we all seemed cheerful, she smiled.

"Hi!" she said. "How is everyone? Gosh it's so good to be off that plane, ugh."

She flopped down on a chair and looked at me. "That's a cute little dog. I have a Chihuahua too. Mine is longhaired."

"L.D., for 'Little Dog', yes, I know. I've seen his pictures. He's very cute," I said.

"What is her name?" R2 said.

"Her name is Este," Amanda said.

R2 patted her leg. "Come here Este!"

I put Este on the floor. To my surprise, her hair rose up along her spine in a spiked mohawk. She lowered her head and growled.

"Oh, she's one of THOSE Chihuahuas," R2 laughed.

"Actually no, she isn't. I've never seen her like this," I said.

Este's tail uncurled and clung close to her body. She slinked in a wide arc around R2's feet and then she barked once. Then, she decided to keep barking and she ran back and forth, pointing at R2 with her nose, yapping and growling.

I was mortified. I felt like a parent whose four-year-old blurts out the complete truth about how her mother feels. "My mom doesn't like you!" Este barked. "She thinks you are two-faced! Two-faced! Two-faced! Two two two! Face face face!"

I could feel the back of my neck getting hot. I leaned down and scooped Este up, but she just kept growling and snarling at R2. My only hope was that no one else in the room had the intuition to see what was really happening, and would just write it off as behavior typical of a yappy breed.

"Darn Chihuahuas," I grinned.

We spent the evening making plans on how best to use the next few days. Theil and R2 wanted to go visit the DeTour house. I had no desire to go there. Amanda didn't either, so the next day, we stayed in the Soo at our "apartment." But it wasn't long before I got a call from R2.

"You need to come down here."

I loaded Amanda into the car and we took the drive. It was evening when we arrived. "Wait out here," I said.

I walked into the house and stopped in disbelief. R2 was in tears. The walls were nearly bare. The furniture had been moved, with Dad's chair sitting askew in the middle of the room. The floor was covered with books and papers and old photos.

I suddenly understood why Mom had been so insistent on having her jewelry on hand when she was admitted to the Manor. Her worst fears were now realized.

"I need you to look around in here and tell me everything that's missing," R2 said.

"Oh my God," I said. "Where do I start?"

I heard the front door slam and Amanda's limping, heavy step coming through the hallway. R2 jumped up. "No! No! Get out!"

She met her in the doorway and blocked her path. "Okay, okay, jeesh," Amanda said.

She turned and went back outside.

"It's okay, Rose," I said. "She can handle this. It will upset her at first, but she will actually be better at the inventory. She's got a better memory than I have."

R2 shook her head. "She doesn't need this."

I looked around. The place was in a shambles. It reminded me of the time a black bear had broken into Dad's camper, and torn the door off the refrigerator. The floor was completely covered with paper and trash. That was how the house looked now. The things that meant the most to me were the first to come to mind. The book I had given Dad about Lewis and Clark. Mom's watercolors that she had done during the phase we were both painting birds. The framed photo of Dad and his father that I had given him one Father's Day. The framed photo of Amanda that I had taken when she was about twelve years old. All were gone.

"I don't know where to start," I said.

Theil came in through the front door. "Amanda just fell down on the ice."

"Is she okay?"

"I think so. She's sitting in the car."

I went outside and got in the car with her and turned on the engine.

"Why did Rose kick me out of my own house?" she said.

"She's trying to protect you. I think she thinks you can't handle it. The house has been ransacked. It looks like a tornado hit. There is a lot of stuff missing."

"Who did that? Raven and Rowena!" She immediately answered her own question.

I shook my head. "Don't worry, we'll get it all straightened out."

"I hope they didn't touch my stuff," she said.

"Me too!" I said. "Theil said you fell. Are you okay?"

"I'm fine."

"We are all heading over to Drummond now to meet Jon and Judy for dinner."

"Oh, good," she said.

But when we arrived at the Island, Amanda couldn't even get out of the car. Her knee had swelled up and she was in so much pain she couldn't move.

"Get her to the hospital," Jon said. "This isn't worth it."

I was frankly disappointed to miss out on the socializing. I wanted to have dinner and visit with Judy. The duty to take Amanda just naturally fell to me. I thought, why hadn't anyone else offered to go, or at least ride along and keep us company? I resented the fact that they all were going to socialize and eat good food, and I once again was stuck in the role as caretaker. As much as I loved Amanda, it seemed terribly unfair. In all the years spent watching over Amanda, it was the first time I could ever remember feeling this way.

Then, when I was preparing to back out of the snowy parking lot and head the ten miles back to the ferry, R2 came out to the car. "Hey, Marcus has passed the role as executor over to me. Just thought you should know. I'll need your signature."

I wasn't happy with this news. I didn't trust R2. My face must have given me away, because she said, "I hope you'll go along with it. Everyone else is."

She pulled out her wallet and handed me $50.00. "Here, this is to help you with gas."

"Hey, thanks!" I was pleasantly surprised. Finally, someone was chipping in. Finally someone was noticing my efforts. It cheered me immeasurably. Maybe there was some hope for this family. Maybe, just maybe some of them were beginning to see what was really important.

As we drove to the Soo that night, I said, "Hey. I had an idea."

Amanda said, "Oh, what was it?"

"Well, you know how I wanted to write that screenplay about you and me being bank robbers, and you didn't like the idea?"

"Yes."

"My friend Kelly said that only vampire movies work right now anyway. She thinks we should be vampires."

"Hey, that's more like it!"

"I'm tellin ya!" I said. "Is that inspired, or what? A whole group of people with Down's Syndrome, as vampires!"

"I told you we were blood sisters!" she said.

"Gives new meaning to the phrase!"

"That's right!" she agreed.

"We'll have to name one of the cast members, 'Special Edward'."

I pulled the car up to the Emergency Room door.

"Haha! Very funny!" Amanda said.

"Well, here we are, back at the hospital, again! Oh joy, eh?" I opened the door and got out. "You wait here. You need a wheelchair."

She had bruised the knee badly. The knee was subluxated, but we already knew that. It had given her problems since the time she had learned to walk.

"Amanda," I said. "Where is your knee brace?"

"It's at home."

"Are you sure? Or did you take it to Raven's?"

"No, it's at home."

"Do you know where?"

"I'd have to look for it."

I knew she couldn't look for it, because she'd never get up the rickety stairs. Plus, with the mess that house was in, who knew where it was now. "We should just order you a new one."

I called R2 to give her the update on Amanda's condition. "She's okay. She's on crutches though. It's just a new development to an old problem."

R2's gift of gas money had encouraged me. I thought maybe part of the family's problem was they just didn't have a real perception of what was happening. I decided it was time to start speaking out, and stop assuming people knew enough to do the right thing.

I was pining for the island. I had told Marcus, years prior, that once Dad was gone, I might never want to go back. But now the opposite was happening. I thought being there was the only way to feel closer to Dad, to make some sense of the loss, and to truly say goodbye. There was sure to be great comfort in the rocks and trees that he had loved. They held steadfast, the landscape remaining the same when nothing else did.

That night, when Amanda and I returned to our "apartment", I wrote an email to Jon, Theil, R2 and Marcus.

"Dear Sibs,

"It pains me a little that I should even have to point this out, but the camp should be plowed and opened up for Amanda and me to stay there. I understand all the legal reasons for shutting everyone out, especially considering the pillaging that's happened in DeTour, but these are rather extenuating circumstances.

"I have spent $55 per night for a room since getting up here, which is now extending due to the guardianship issue, so that I can be present for court and provide Amanda a safe haven.

"Obviously this is very expensive, especially for me.

"Further, Dad and I had a conversation in fall of 2011 wherein he offered to leave me the Drummond property including trailer, gazebo and corral area. He also mentioned the tractor (advising me I'd have to have the tire fixed) and his shotgun because, "You will need to protect yourself." (He didn't specify from whom.) Dad remained steadfast about these issues all through last year.

"Drummond has been summer home to the horses and me since 1989. I have a lot invested in the property, even beyond the shingles on the shelter and gazebo, many other things which I paid for and both buildings I helped construct.

"Were the situation reversed, I would never allow any sibling of mine to live the way I have been doing these past months. Now that Dad's care is no longer an issue, I will be able to concentrate on my own life and proceed with some ventures I am planning. In the meantime I will need to have a home base. I think I have well earned my place in the Drummond property and no sane person would begrudge me that.

"Thanks,
"Nancy"

Not a single person replied to the email.

The next day, Amanda and I went shopping for clothes. Theil and Katherine went with us and they picked out a black blouse for her to wear to the funeral. Nobody mentioned the email I had sent, and I didn't bring it up either. I realized that it wasn't Theil's decision if I could stay at the Lodge. It was now up to Marcus. And Marcus had said nothing. I did wish that, just out of decency, other siblings would advocate the right course of action at times like this. They never spoke up. It frustrated me.

We drove to Pickford for the viewing that afternoon, and as soon as Amanda and I were inside the funeral home, Lily pulled me aside. "We have to file those objections today," she whispered. "I'll take Marcus's and you can ride with me."

I had my letter, a short paragraph, written already. "Amanda, do you want to go?"

"Yes," Amanda was sitting on a couch in the lobby and she reached for her crutches.

"Well, then we won't get to talk," Lily said softly.

"Oh," I said. "Okay. Amanda, how about you stay here and greet relatives? Lily and I will be back shortly."

A look of urgency crossed Amanda's face. "I think I better stay with you."

R2 intervened then. "Amanda, if you stay here, you can hang out with me."

"Okay," Amanda seemed fine with that. I was just as happy to not have to deal with the other two R's.

"Thanks, Rose," I said. As Lily and I left the funeral home, I said, "What did you want to talk about?"

"Oh, nothing specific. I just want to be able to talk freely," Lily said.

"Oh, I see."

We gossiped about various family members until we arrived at the courthouse. We walked in and presented our respective letters of protest to the court clerk. "We can't file these," she said. "There is a fee, and a form you have to fill out."

"How much is it?" Lily said.

We looked at each other. Neither of us had enough cash.

"Theil has filed his, anyway," I said. "That's the important thing. We may be out of time after today."

"Are you in a big hurry to get back? I'd like to go have a drink," Lily said.

I sighed. "God, I would love nothing better."

We went to a bar down by the Locks. I didn't blame Lily for not wanting to go right back. The R's had been horrible to her. "Is it true that Rowena screamed at you when you went to the house?"

"Yes," Lily said. "I had just come in the door and she started yelling, 'Get out of my parents' house!'"

"Wow." I took a sip of my rum and cola. "What did you say?"

"I told her, 'Rowena, I don't want anything, I'm just here to help.'"

"Marcus must have been livid."

"He was. I just told him, 'Marcus, I don't care. Let's just go.'"

I shook my head. It was terrible. I thought it gave no credit to the grief Lily may have been feeling. After all, she had lived with Dad, too. "There's really no excuse," I said. "I would apologize for them, but I gave up on that a few years ago."

She shrugged. "I don't care."

I swirled my glass, clinking the ice cubes. "I guess it's weird for me to be sitting here during my Dad's viewing."

"So?" she smiled.

She was so charming, I thought. So nice. I hoped Marcus didn't screw it up. I could use a sister like her. I needed a sister like her. I took a sip. "You're right. Grief is weird. Nothing is normal right now."

We had two drinks and then drove back to the viewing. I was relieved in thinking there were only a couple of hours left to go. I was determined that no one was going to see me cry today. In a way, I thought, it was like being on stage. I had the costume, with the skirt and boots and scarf. Amanda was the leading lady and I was the

255

supporting actress. It didn't matter what the audience reaction was. My job was to stay in character. This was like an improv theatre where I had to make up my lines as I went along, and my role was a woman with a cold heart.

I didn't go into the room with the casket and flowers. I went straight downstairs to the basement. Amanda was sitting in the room where all the food was, snacking on donuts and talking to Frank.

When I walked in, Frank immediately turned to me. "Nancy, I know you are blaming your sister for this happening. And I know you wish your dad was still here. Well, I wish that too. But don't you be holding this against anyone. That's just how life is."

I nodded my head and said nothing. The alcohol had relaxed me. I sat down and smiled at Amanda. "Who did you see today?"

She gave me an enthused list of friends and neighbors that had stopped in to pay their respects. Amanda seemed fine, I thought. It was a social hour and she was in all her glory. Besides, there was all this food: Ham and cheese, crackers and donuts.

"Well girls, I'm gonna go find Sue," Frank said. "I'll talk to ya later."

He trudged out the door, passing my friend Claire who was on her way in with her two little boys, Beck and Cameron. She looked disheveled and tired. I jumped up to fling my arms around her. "Oh my God!" I said. "Did you drive up today?"

"Yes!" she groaned. "Five hours with two kids in the car, ugh! Jay couldn't watch them. He's too bogged down with work. Are you okay? Do you want to come over to my room for drinks later?"

"I would love to, but I don't know what's happening." I struggled for a way to phrase it so that Amanda wouldn't feel badly. "I know that's what we did when you came up for Mom's funeral. But this time I am not thus unencumbered."

Her eyes never left my face, but she nodded, comprehending my dilemma. "Amanda is welcome too."

Amanda looked up from the sandwich she was making. "Oh, thank you! Would you guys like a sandwich? "

"Thanks Amanda, I can't. I promised them pizza. And we are gonna go because they want to swim in the pool." She squeezed my arm, "Call me if you need anything."

The hour crawled by. I just kept hiding in the basement. I did not want to go upstairs and deal with the R's. I stayed in the room with Amanda and the food and greeted whatever stragglers came in.

Finally, when I thought it could no longer be avoided, I crept upstairs and peered into the large, softly lit parlor. The open casket was on the other side of the room and at first, I carefully avoided looking at it. There was an easel near the doorway, holding a board covered with photos. I recognized the one I had taken of Dad and Grandpa, years ago, and some others that I had taken and given to Amanda. Apparently the R's had gone through her things and helped themselves. I noticed there was not one photo of Clifford, who had been a significant part of Dad's life and summers on Drummond, for nearly 20 years. Nor were there any of Dad's beloved Newfoundland, Lewis, nor any of our pets, for that matter. It was all about children, grandchildren, and great-grandchildren, and mostly those descending from the R's. There were very few pictures of Jon's kids, or Theil's, or Marcus's. It was definitely the R's show, I thought.

The Drug Baby came blasting up to me, banging against my knees. "Hi! Hi! Hi!" she screeched.

"Well, hello," I said. She was immediately called away. The R's, and whatever descendants of R's were present, were just blank shapes that I barely noticed. I saw Marcus and Lily standing by the wall, talking with Lily's brother.

I took a deep breath and walked over to the casket. It was covered in a mass of white tulips. Dad lay like a waxen figure, his once powerful hands now crossed in repose, his wire-rimmed glasses perched upon his powdered face. I looked at his crooked mouth, the scar where he had been burned as a child. It was Dad, but it was not. He was not there. I stood stiffly, gazing at the shell of him, wondering what life was going to be like from now on. I wondered if anyone would stop and listen when I spoke.

I felt a hand on my shoulder, and knew it was Marcus. His arms went around me, and he was hugging me. "Thanks," I said.

I looked up at him, "How you doing?"

"Hanging in there," he said.

I appreciated his attempt to give me comfort. But I did not cry, even for him. I smiled up at him and said, "You look good."

I walked away. There was another day of this to prepare for, a funeral to attend on Drummond Island. And after that, thanks to R1, we would still have no relief. We had to go to court.

That night, Amanda said, "I have to ask you something. I would like to write something for the funeral."

"Oh, what a great idea!" I said. "What do you want to say?"

"I want to talk about what happens when we die."

"Okay."

"I want you to read it for me. Will you?"

"You know I will. But it would probably mean more coming from you."

She shook her head. "I can't do it. I would be too nervous."

"You mean to tell me you can go on a microphone and sing 'God Bless America' to the whole world, but you can't read a simple statement?"

She laughed. "I just want you to do it, okay? It's hard for me to explain."

"Okay. I will do it."

She labored over it that night. I helped her with spelling, but the rest was her own creation.

When it was finished, I read it and said, "This is tremendous."

"It is?"

259

"Oh yeah. You are going to have people bawling their eyes out."

She smiled.

"This part is my favorite," I said. "About the dead – they are not just souls, they are heart and soul. I love that."

"Yes, that's right." She nodded wisely. "They are heart and soul. When you get to the end, be sure to say, 'God bless you all, and thank you for coming.'"

"God bless you all, and thank you for coming," I recited obediently.

She seemed comforted by this, I thought.

The Drummond Town Hall had a scooter that enabled Amanda to leave her crutches in the car. It even had a little basket on the front of it, for our purses. She parked it on the end of the front row next to my chair. She was wearing the new black blouse from Theil and Katherine. She sat calmly looking around and greeting whomever came to speak to her. She was the picture of composure.

Dad's casket stood draped in the American flag, near the podium on one end of the room. There was a crowd of about thirty people. I had expected more, but I realized that many had traveled south for winter, and others among Dad's peers had passed on. Jon had offered to give the eulogy, but it was very hard for him. My heart went out to him as he struggled through it haltingly.

When he finished, the minister returned and asked if anyone else wanted to say a few words. No one moved. I stood up and walked to the front. I put on my reading glasses and unfolded Amanda's little slip of paper.

"After Life, by Amanda Bailey," I read. "It is so amazing to believe in God and Heaven, angels and ghosts. It's okay to think about the dead, every night and every day, too. One way to be happy is to have family. Family can be anyone. Good friends are your family. Animals can be family. Anyone you love can be your family and you decide this, the same way you decide to be happy. The most important thing about the dead is that they are peaceful."

At that point, I looked straight at the three R's, who all sat together, glaring at me. "Not mad about anything, not trying to cope."

They just continued glaring, so I broke off and kept reading. "I'm trying to cope. But the dead aren't. They love being up there. I think they are trying to be like angels to us. They look after us. When they look around, they see other people. Dead people. They are not just souls. They are heart and soul."

I looked over at Amanda and she nodded to me reassuringly.

"They can see us in our dreams, they talk to us then. They have fun. They eat, they drink, they dance. They like music. And they love us for who we are."

I looked up and folded the paper, and said, "God bless you all. Thank you for coming."

I walked back to sit down next to Amanda and she gave me the "thumbs up" sign.

At that point, a small group of soldiers outside fired off a twenty-one gun salute. The mournful trumpet sound of "Taps" echoed throughout the hall. Two soldiers in dress uniform, both in their forties and I imagined seasoned veterans, took the flag off Dad's casket and folded it into a neat triangle. One of them marched over to Amanda and stood before her. He held it out and she took it from him carefully. He stood up straight and then saluted her. She immediately snapped back a perfect salute.

I knew instantly that this would remain one of the most poignant moments in my life. I swallowed it, hard, and turned to Marcus who was sitting beside me, and gave him a smile.

Amanda kept the flag in her little basket, and she remained composed and elegant for the rest of that afternoon. I maintained my resolve to show no emotion, even when R1 marched over and took a little green plant out of Lily's hands, saying, "My co-workers sent that."

"Oh," Lily said. "Marcus told me I could have it."

"It's mine," she snapped, and carried it away.

We stood there in silence for a moment, and then burst out laughing when Polly backed out the door concealing a single tulip under her coat.

The next morning, R2 called. "Marcus said that Brandon wants to have a meeting with us today. He wants to meet with Amanda and talk to all of us about who we think her guardian should be."

"Where is the meeting?" I said.

"I suggested Antlers."

Antlers was an ancient restaurant near the top of the Saint Lily's River, just east of the Soo Locks. The ambiance of Antlers was legendary. Its walls and ceiling beams were covered with animal pelts and the stuffed remains of all varieties of wildlife. It had been a popular hang-out in my college days, then having notoriety for offering, "The World's Largest Hamburger."

Or maybe it was the largest hamburger in the state of Michigan. I couldn't remember. Anyway, the hamburgers were delicious.

Getting Amanda in and out of the car was less cumbersome than it had been with Dad and his oxygen tank, or Mom when her legs started to fail. She was adept with her crutches, at least, and more than happy to go into a restaurant. The floor in Antlers was a little uneven, but she managed it well. I pulled out a chair for her and leaned her crutches against the wall. "Here ya go," I said. "You just sit right here and I am sure Brandon will be here any minute to talk to you."

I sat down beside her and R2 pulled up a chair next to me. She opened a folder with paperwork. "I just need your signature."

Encouraged by her generosity of the night prior, I signed the form agreeing to name her executor, hoping I wouldn't regret it later.

Even though Marcus hadn't seemed himself lately, I would have much preferred he remain in the role.

"Good," she said. "Our first order of business is to give you $300. This is to help you with Amanda's expenses."

I thought I was dreaming. I wanted to pinch myself. "Wow, thank you!"

I was touched. Maybe this was a real family, after all.

Brandon came in then, dressed in "Lawyer," not his usual backwoods flannel that I was so accustomed to. He sat down across from us. "Hi Amanda! How are you, Nancy?"

"I'm good, Brandon. How are you?"

I felt that for some reason, Brandon hated me. I didn't know why, other than the R's had buddied up to his mother, Sue, and there was plenty of what I called, "bad press" about me among them. Brandon was always civil, but when he greeted me it was with an aloof, "Hello, Nancy," that called to mind Jerry Seinfeld's famous, contemptuous, "Hello, Newman." But today, I noticed he had dropped his normal Seinfeld-esque salutation. He seemed friendlier.

"I'm good," he said. "I just need to speak to Amanda privately. I've already talked with Marcus and Rose."

"Of course," I got up and R2 followed. We walked through the door, where Marcus and Lily were sitting at a table, waiting by the entrance to the building. As we approached, Lily smiled at us and got up to leave, I assumed for the restroom.

Marcus gestured to an empty seat. "Sit down."

I sat down. "Brandon didn't talk to me about Amanda."

"That's because he already knows how you feel."

I digested this, willing to concede to it. Marcus didn't mention the email I had sent, so I said, "I want to stay in the camper, so that I can be available for Amanda. This motel is costing me an arm and a leg."

"Well, I'm not sure anyone should be staying over there," Marcus said.

I looked at him. "What?"

"I don't think anyone should be staying there."

"Why not? I am happy to pay the electric, if that's what you're worried about."

He shook his head. "I'm going to give it a year before I decide what to do. I want to see how everyone behaves in that year."

"Just a minute. Why does it matter how anyone 'behaves'? Dad had drawn out a map of that thirteen acres and he put my name on the campsite. He showed it to me last fall. Dad intended that camp for Amanda and me. That's why he left me the tractor, and shotgun, just as he said he would."

R2 was silent, staring at me.

"He also left a mortgage," Marcus said. "And he signed the deed over to me."

"I am sure that there was some arrangement. But I am just as sure he would not want me kept away from there."

"Nobody is staying there. I just want to do what's fair to our siblings."

"Seriously? Our siblings all have a home to go to. Mine is gone. Theil is leaving before the court date and he can't take Amanda with him. Do you know how much a month in a motel up here is going to cost me?"

"I'm just trying to be fair," he said.

"You all have a place to go home to! I don't! How is that fair? How is that fair, Marcus?"

He just shook his head.

I was livid. I got up and crossed the room and sat down at a table by myself. Brandon walked by, looked straight at me, and then exited the building. He hadn't taken time to talk to me. No big surprise there. Then Lily appeared. Noticing I was upset, she sat down with me. "You okay?"

"I just want to go home," I said.

"You mean the Drummond camp?"

"Yes. Camp. Camp is my home."

"Marcus has plans for the camp," she said.

"Oh yeah?"

"Yeah. I'm not going to tell you what they are. But you're not going to like it."

I sighed. "Lily, Dad designated that camp for Amanda and me. I've been bringing my horses there for 20 years."

She shook her head. "You're not going to be bringing them anymore."

I looked at her. This, I thought, was really weird. Lily had been living with Marcus for all of eight months. Even after being married for eleven years, I would have never presumed to talk to my husband's siblings this way.

I said, "Well, maybe Marcus will sell it to me."

She shrugged. "Sure, if you've got the money to buy it. You know, when my family sold property, we just sold it and moved on. We didn't hang on to it."

"That property has been in my family for four generations," I said.

She sat looking straight at me, with her mouth in a tight, determined line. At that moment I decided Marcus had been right, after all. She didn't look anything like me.

I got up and left the building. I couldn't believe what was happening. I knew things hadn't been the same between Marcus and me over the past year, but I never thought he would betray me. There was a bizarre element to the day, like walking on the beach when the wind-whipped sand kept sifting beneath my feet, so that every step was moving me sideways.

I sat in the car, waiting for Amanda to crutch out. Finally she hobbled out with R2, who opened the car door.

"Here ya go," R2 said cheerfully. She placed Amanda's crutches in the back seat. She shut the door and waved. I waved back, dismissively.

I started the car. "Let's go see a movie. I can suddenly afford it."

"Sweet!" Amanda said.

That evening I typed out another email.

"Hi All,

"Amanda is EXTREMELY depressed. I am letting her make her own choices every day, but she has been clinging to me like velcro. I think it is important for her right now to feel that she has at least some control over her situation. I finally got her to stay in the hotel room by herself for a half hour when I went to Wal-mart last night. Her grief is just heart wrenching and she has been very upset about the fighting among siblings. She keeps apologizing to me about it.

"I am livid about the fact that she is being dragged through volatile legal proceedings at a time like this, but I am going to try to keep things quiet for her over the next few days.

"Jon called me today and asked me if I was getting her to bathe, saying he knows how hard it is to motivate her. I know where that came from, and it is an insult. I have been Amanda's caretaker just about every summer for periods since 1989. I know how to motivate Amanda, probably better than anybody else does. Yes, she is bathing and wearing clean clothes. It would have been nice if Raven had delivered a few of her things to the house when she showed up there, or to the wake, or to the funeral, but we are making due.

"After our meeting with Brandon I am still very concerned about how court is going to go. I talked to Marcus and Lily both a little bit about bringing the horses back to Drummond while the property is in a sort of limbo state this year -- and I think we need to be able to tell the judge that Amanda will have a home with me again on the Island this spring/summer/fall. She is welcome to stay with me as much and as long as I can physically keep her. I have already invited her on the Clifford tour and still working on that.

"I understand that Marcus and Lily are willing and available to have her in Cadillac.

"Since I will be present in court, I think it is very important that I be able to say I too can accommodate her if asked.

"Thanks."

R2 replied that it was unfortunate that a judge had to decide Amanda's fate, but that was unavoidable. It was a requirement.

She said she was confident R1 would provide appropriate care for Amanda.

She said that she was leaving for Colorado next day, and disappointed that she didn't get to spend more time with Amanda.

I was starting to feel like the only rational kid in, "Lord of the Flies." I replied, "Let me make this absolutely clear. Raven does not provide 'appropriate care' to Amanda. I am not sure why you even say that. Raven abuses Amanda. This is why I am adamant that she not be assigned legal guardianship. I agree that Amanda needed to be taken out of the mix of arguments and volatile behavior among siblings. In the interest of civility, I personally am not ready to have any kind of interaction with Raven, therefore I have not requested anything. But as I said, we are making do."

"And another thing," I added. "Let's stay honest, please! Securing Amanda's guardianship may be 'necessary and unavoidable.' But this court dispute is not 'necessary', nor is it 'unavoidable'. It should have been handled per Dad's wishes, quietly with a signature. She did not need to drag Amanda and the rest of us through this crap and all the extra expense. I know for me personally, Raven's fiasco is costing hundreds of dollars. It is causing a lot of additional anxiety and grief for me, not to mention Amanda. What she is doing is wrong and Dad never would have tolerated this. And I agree that it's too bad you and Jon didn't get to see more of her. I am sure she would have enjoyed that. It's too bad she smacked her knee and had to go to ER. In fact I was thinking it would be nice if I didn't have to be the only one to run her up here. If a few other family members could have come along and made a night of it. Unfortunately there is only so much money and time to spread around. Oh well. Hopefully there will be better times ahead. Wishing safe travels to ya'all. And, thanks for the reply!"

R2 said, "Dad did not document his wishes and told different people different things." She admitted that he had left a list, designating me to receive the tractor and shotgun.

She promised to seek a solution that considers all concerned parties with Amanda's interests in the forefront. Then she added, "Please send any ideas to me and be patient so I can process equally."

I wrote back, "I am aware of the list. I am also aware that Dad drew a diagram of the 13 acres in which he left the trailer, corral and gazebo to me. He did show me this diagram and informed me that he gave it to Brandon. I am trying to be patient but I do not like playing games and would prefer everyone to be as honest and up front as I am being. Dad intended the trailer for me and Amanda to use, and we will need to use it, ASAP."

She said the diagram predated the deed. Therefore, there was no obligation to let me use the property. She said it wasn't the estate's job to provide me with a domicile.

I wrote, "So.... Going against the patriarch's wishes, this family would put his caretaker of two years, now rendered homeless by his death, out in the street when there is a disabled sister who needs care, and a habitable property sitting there empty, that Dad directed Brandon to leave to me? I really don't believe that. I will trust it all works out and that Dad's wishes will be honored."

The $300 was the last bit of help I got from R2. As tax time rolled around, I asked her, "Who has keys to the house? I need to get in there. I would suggest the key be placed in a hidden location at the house so that Michigan residents can have access to items for Amanda as well as our own possessions."

"Raven has the only one but was supposed to make a copy to leave with Brandon."

"Why in the world would you leave Raven the only key when you intentionally changed locks to keep her out? You're fired!" I was only half joking.

"That is not the reason I installed the locks. I did it for the shock effect and to get everyone's attention. "

"Let a fox in a hen house, and ask him to count the chickens?" Then I admitted, "It's probably moot, as they cleaned out anything of value on the first day (if not prior) anyway. The hens are all the gnarly ones by now. So, who cares, right. My concern right now is to get what I need while there is still time to do taxes."

"Please arrange to remove all of your belongings so they aren't confused in the inventory. Or worse, added to the pile of good will donations."

I shook my head. Well, I thought, there's a chicken and egg problem. Speaking of chickens. If they lock me out of my own house, how am I supposed to remove anything?

"I need to go stay at camp until Theil comes back, at least," I said.

"What do you do for a living?" she asked.

What the heck was this about? She knew exactly what I did for a living. She knew I was a struggling artist and animal trainer who barely made ends meet. "I'm an independent contractor," I said. "Don't worry, I am fully capable of paying the electric bill, and happy to do it."

Apparently the answer was not satisfactory enough. There was no more discussion about camp, from anyone.

April 11th dawned with a tension snapping through the grey sky. Amanda crutched in and I led her to a seat near the back of the room on a bench with Marcus. I was relieved when Tom West walked in. He had told me he didn't know the judge, Betty Temple, so his appearance wouldn't have any political impact. But he would be there for moral support.

Judge Temple marched in, a diminutive woman with a mop of brown curls that bounced when she walked. Her stride was forceful, perhaps orchestrated so to override her childlike appearance. She reminded me so much of one of my old college roommates, who had been a dear friend, that I took an immediate liking to her. She walked up on the bench and said, "Is this the Bailey family? Amanda Bailey?"

"Yes," Marcus replied. He moved up to the front table and Amanda accompanied him, leaving Tom and me sitting on the bench seat.

R1 had not appeared. A text message chimed in from Katherine, in Arizona, "Nancy, thanks so much for all your care for Amanda during this time. What are you all doing in court now? Love, Katherine."

She always signed her texts.

"Waiting. R1 is late," I texted back.

"Please, God," I thought. "Let her have a flat tire. Let her run out of gas. Let her be hit by a bus. Anything."

But just then, she walked in, accompanied by our cousin, attorney Brandon Farley, and they were laughing together. "How convenient," I thought.

Worse, then Brandon took a seat next to her at defendant's table.

"Brandon, these are your relatives, right?" Judge Temple said.

"Yes, that's right."

"First of all, let me say I am very sorry to hear about the death of your father," the judge said. "I think I may have met him once. By all accounts, he was a good man."

"Thank you," Amanda said.

The judge riffled through some papers on her desk. "Let's see. There is a petition for guardianship by Raven, and an objection to the petition by Theil. Is Theil here?"

"He's in Arizona," Amanda piped up.

"Well, Amanda, you certainly have a lot of people who care about you."

"Yes, I do," Amanda said.

The judge turned to Brandon. "Who are you representing, here? Raven, or Amanda?"

"Oh, I'm representing Amanda," Brandon said. "However guardianship is a little out of my scope of experience and I suggest we assign a guardian ad litem."

"A guardian ad litem, yes, that's a good idea," the judge said.

"Meanwhile I recommend that Amanda be placed under Raven's supervision for the 30 days until the hearing," Brandon said.

I couldn't believe it. Thirty days with R1? Brandon was throwing Amanda under a bus! My hand shot up in the air. "Can I object to that?"

"Sure you can," the judge said. "But it won't make any difference. Amanda can go stay with Raven until the hearing which is scheduled for May 21. Meanwhile, Amanda, I want you to think about where you want to live."

Amanda started to speak, but the judge interrupted. "Don't tell me! You have a month to think it over. I will see you on May 21."

That was longer than a month, I thought bitterly. There would be no mixup on the date this time. May 21 would be Marcus's 50th birthday. We all got up and filed out of the courtroom. Marcus motioned us into a small meeting room down the hall. R1 entered the room and sat down at the table by the wall. Marcus sat next to her. Amanda took the remaining seat at the table. I stood on the end, bouncing on the balls of my feet, feeling the Achilles tendon stretch. Tom sat a little apart from us. Brandon walked in.

I immediately whirled on him, "Brandon, why didn't you ask Amanda where she would like to spend the thirty days?"

He snapped back. "Oh come on, do you think it's going to do Amanda any harm to stay with Raven for thirty days?"

"Yes," I said.

I thought it was the attorney's tactic to always be sure of the answer before you ask a question. If that was the case, he had misjudged me. His expression registered surprise, but he said, "Oh, bullshit! Raven is perfectly capable of caring for Amanda."

Brandon was about the same age as Amanda. Dad loved to tell the story about how once when they were little he had been bullying Amanda, and pushed her down, and Grandpa Bailey, with one swipe of his long arm, had sent Brandon flying. I had laughingly brought it up once to Brandon, years before. He laughed too. "Everyone says I was a bratty kid," he had admitted.

"Nancy, do you want to sit here?" Marcus asked. He was perched right next to R1, rocking back on his chair legs.

"No, thanks." I wanted to remain standing, and besides, I thought, I might be tempted to strangle her if I had to sit that close.

"What do you have to say, Amanda?" R1's tone was self-satisfactory, edging on smug.

"I just want Theil to be my guardian," Amanda said in a tiny voice. Her lower lip was shaking, and she put her face into her hands and began to cry.

Since I have been homeless, and therefore classified among the ranks of society's misfits, I understand now what it is like to be universally underestimated. It is to have people talk down to you, to overlook you, to rebuke you and yes, make fun of you. When you are anywhere outside of what is considered the norm, even if the circumstances are beyond your control, it does not bode well for your confidence. It is to know intimately the feeling of utter frustration, of horrific anger, of terrible discouragement. It is demeaning. It is an insult to you, and those around you. It can sometimes be worse when confronted by those who mean well. You become a charity. You are catered to and treated as though you were incapable of any more. Unless you experience this sort of helpless degradation firsthand, even the sincerest form of empathy will never present it to you in any genuine way.

Even so, I had the enviable ability to communicate. I couldn't imagine what it was like for those who could not easily express themselves. I remembered Amanda's catch phrase, "I will let Nancy explain it."

And Dad, in the hospital bed, pointing to his mouth.

So Amanda sat there weeping, and I felt a hot flood of rage, boiling up through my neck and slamming inside my head. I couldn't remember ever being so angry. I grabbed Amanda and hugged her. I thought how I had permitted R1 to destroy what had remained of Dad's life. I was not about to let her do the same to Amanda. I made a silent vow, standing with my arms around my weeping little sister, that I would never allow such a thing again.

"Well, this was necessary," R1 said in her nasally snip.

"That's crap!" I squeezed Amanda and whispered to her, "Be brave, okay? Be brave in the attempt."

She inhaled sharply, and then immediately stopped crying. I stood up and faced R1. She recoiled a little when our eyes met. I can only imagine the look on my face. I wanted to fly across the room and kick off her head.

"I hope you're happy, you heartless scumbag," I said.

"Whoa!" Marcus said.

I turned and walked out of the room. Marcus followed me. He immediately began a lecture. "You have got to calm down in there."

His lips were moving, but all I could really hear was, "You're a fucking retard." I had a fleeting thought about his tantrum in the Applebee's, but decided now was not the time to discuss hypocrisy. I looked over at Brandon, who had followed us out and was now sitting on a chair in the hallway, smirking at me. I turned to Marcus. "Can we do this somewhere else?"

We walked down to the end of the hallway and through the door into the stairwell. He turned. "Your attitude is getting us nowhere. You are smarter than any of these people. You have to play the game."

I nodded. I knew he was patronizing me, but he was right. This was all a big game, and there was no place for brutal honesty in this negotiation. It was ducking and jabbing. It was a match. We were maneuvering and posturing for possession of Amanda's soul. He was telling me to, "Get a cold heart."

So, I forced myself to calm down and listen to his advice on how to handle R1. Rule number one was to stay calm at all costs. Appearances were going to be important. If I cared too much, if I let my emotions get the best of me, she would come out looking like the sane one.

I realized then that I was going to have to do the very thing that I had always scorned, and that was to be artificial in the face of despicable people. But if I treated it like a stage, much as I had at Dad's funeral, maybe it would work. I thought, "Okay. It begins now."

We walked back down the hall and into the room where R1 still sat across from a miserable-looking Amanda.

"Now Amanda, what do you want to do today?" R1 said.

"Well," Amanda said. She kept her eyes down, and then very humbly said, "I would just like to spend more time with Nancy."

R1 nodded like a benevolent queen. "You may do that. I'll pick you up on Friday."

That gave us two more nights together. I was a bit surprised that R1 had conceded that, but she did have to work those days.

When we left the courthouse, Amanda's expression was pure, heartbreaking dejection. "Look," I told her. "I'm not going anywhere.

I am staying right here. We will still have our Girl's Day Out. You're not in this alone."

"I know," she said. "I just wish I could stay with you."

"We can still hang out here. Raven can pick you up after work."

When we got back to the room, I ripped a sheet of paper out of one of her tablets. "Here is what I want."

I wrote on the paper, in big letters, while practically shouting the words. "Dear Brandon, You are fired. Love, Amanda."

I thrust it at her. "Sign it!"

She took the sheet and read it. She laid it down gently on the bed. "I'll talk to him."

"Talk to him?" I screeched. "You would do better with a court appointed lawyer! He's totally on Raven's side!"

"Well, he is my cousin, you know."

"That's my point! It's completely inappropriate for him to represent you! It's a total conflict of interest!"

She shook her head. "I'm not signing that. I don't want to fire Brandon."

I sat down and sighed. "I don't understand this faith in Brandon. Dad was the same way. He trusted him with your guardianship information, and with the Drummond property, and look what happened."

She patted my arm. "You gotta love him for who he is. He's family."

"That's not a compliment," I said.

Chapter 10

About Life with Down's Syndrome – Amanda

How I could put this? People with Down's are lucky because they are not alone. There are lots of others with Down's and lots of families and groups who love them, and the spirits love them too. They are special. They are honest. They don't lie. They can have lots of fun in their lifetime. I like to be who I am. I love people. I know how to read and write. I know how to use the remote. I know how to dial the phone. I know how to use the microwave. Some things I wish were different. I wish I could drive a car. I used to wish I could get married, but now I don't want to. I don't want to live alone though. I like having family around me. I'm just the baby of the family. Forever and always.

About Life - Nancy

I was beginning to understand how hard it was for people who divorce and are forced to share custody of their children. I met R1 to deliver Amanda that Friday, and from that point on, I was all smiles every time I came in contact with her. I just kept that damn smile painted on my face. Everything she said was greeted with a chirpy, "Uh huh!"

It was my normal mode to be cheerful, so she didn't even seem suspicious. But inside I was clenching my teeth. In fact, it felt as if everything inside me was clenched.

After relinquishing Amanda that first weekend, I got in the car and called Bud. "Listen, you are going to have to come up with some of that back pay on those shows we did last summer. The sibs are being as kind and helpful as usual. Amanda and I won't be able to stay at home on Drummond. I need money for a motel."

He was uncharacteristically sympathetic. "Well, I have a date retainer coming from the east coast tour. I will call it in to the motel."

I drove back to the motel and checked us in for the coming week. I was going to be available to Amanda, every day until her court date, no matter what. I knew it was probably going to be a battle with Bud to get the rest of the money he owed me, but I would do whatever it took. I couldn't allow Amanda to languish out there in the woods, alone, in the same house where she had watched Dad get sicker and sicker. She would have appreciated going to stay at the camp with me on Drummond until Theil was able to come and get her. It would have brought Amanda tremendous comfort and it would have saved me so much money. But, I thought bitterly, now everything was an asset. Apparently Amanda was, too.

I met R1 one evening at the McDonald's and she said, "I will have to meet you here tomorrow at 4. Amanda has an appointment."

"Oh, is she going to see the doctor about her knee?"

She shifted uncomfortably. "No, the meeting is about a legal matter."

"You mean about court?"

"Yes, the meeting is with court people."

Why was I having to drag this out of her? I was becoming annoyed. But I kept my tone patient and civil. "What court people?"

"It's about her guardianship."

"You are meeting with the Guardian Ad Litem tomorrow? Great, I would like to be there. What time?"

She just shook her head. "Come on, Amanda."

She ushered Amanda into her car and took off.

I had gotten the Guardian Ad Litem's name and phone number from Theil. I called her that night and left her a message. She called me back the next morning around nine. "Sure," she said. "You can come in. There won't be a lot of time, as I have to leave by five, but you are welcome to come."

I drove out to Raven's that morning and had a talk with Amanda. "Listen. The meeting with this Guardian Ad Litem is today. She might be able to help you. You are gonna have to get serious."

"Well, I might just have to crack her up," she said.

I said, "Look, this is important. It's not a game. It's your life. You have to tell this lady what you really want. And you know how you always go, 'I'll let Nancy explain it to you.' Well, I won't be there to explain it!"

R2 had sent me an email asking what time the meeting was, and to have R1 call her if I saw her. I wrote back, "Meeting at 4:20. And I will see Raven since I have to deliver Amanda at 4, because God forbid I should be seen taking her to the meeting."

Since I thought R1 knew where the office was, I decided to just follow her. She pulled up in a parking lot across the street from the building. I pulled in next to her to answer a text message from R2, asking me to have R1 call her. I looked through the window at Amanda, sitting in the passenger seat. She was making motions of slitting her own throat and putting a gun in her mouth.

"So much for my lecture about how this is serious business," I sighed.

A moment later my phone rang. R1 was calling me. "Do you know where this office is?" she asked.

"Follow me," I said.

I pulled up to it and R1 pulled in beside me. Like most of the buildings in Sault Ste Marie, it was old, but reminiscent of the Frank

Lloyd Wright design, being long and flat. I was carrying a manila envelope that contained a seven-page letter I had written the night before. We walked down the narrow, creaky hallway and took a seat at a table in the lobby. The sun angled through a glass door nearby. It was nearing the end of the business day and I was remembering that Valerie said she wouldn't have much time. A smiling woman in a grey suit appeared around the corner. "Hi! I'm Valerie Swift. Are you the Baileys?"

She held out her hand and we all shook it. "Amanda, why don't you come with me?"

"Oh, sure," Amanda said, standing up and taking her crutches. "I get to be first!"

She followed Valerie slowly down the hall. That left me sitting with R1 at the table. I knew R1 was accustomed to these legal meetings with estranged extended family members. I was not. I would rather be just about anywhere else.

"Have you spoken with Rose? She wants you to call her," I said.

"I haven't." R1 dialed her cell.

I noticed a bathroom near the corner and stood up. I had placed my envelope on the table, but now I took it with me. I didn't want to chance it disappearing. I loitered in the tiny restroom, checking my hair, looking at my teeth. I took my retainer out and rinsed it. I came out, but R1 still sat there alone. I sat down again at the table opposite her. I had nothing to say.

Finally, Valerie reappeared, alone, with a big grin. "Your sister is delightful!"

"Great," I thought.

R1 stood up. "Thanks for meeting with me, Valerie."

"Oh, I am going to speak to Nancy first, since I talked to you at length on the phone. If you would, just wait right here and make yourself comfortable." She motioned me to follow her.

"Two points for Valerie," I thought, as I walked back down the hallway. Amanda was sitting in a chair by Valerie's door. We went into her cramped little office and I sat down, and she sat down across from me.

"I brought you a letter," I held it out to her. "It's kind of long. You don't have to read it right now. But you will read it, won't you?"

"Yes," she said.

I decided to get right to the point. "Do you know Judge Temple?"

"No," she said.

I could not suppress a disappointed sigh. "I am just a little concerned because my cousin, who is an attorney representing Amanda, claims to be friends with her. And he seems to have a very strong bias toward Raven."

She said, "Maybe so, but I was hired for a reason. Amanda has talked about Arizona and that's where she wants to be. Usually, if the person with the disability is able to express what they want, the court will go along with it. As long as Theil's not some kind of evil person, I see no reason why Amanda wouldn't be given what she asks for."

My relief must have been obvious. She said, "Amanda talks about you a lot."

I nodded. "I know."

I didn't want to take up any more of her time. I thanked her and stepped out of the office, where Amanda was seated on a chair in the lobby. "I will see you tomorrow, Amanda," I said.

"Why don't you sit here and keep me company?" Amanda said.

Valerie paused by her door. "Here, let me get you another chair."

She dragged a chair out for me and I plopped down next to Amanda. Valerie walked off down the hall to get Raven. Amanda leaned toward me conspiratorially. "How did I do?"

I gave her a thumbs-up. "You did great."

She beamed. "Well, I did crack her up, anyway."

That night, I thought about the letter I had written, and hoped it would make a difference.

Valerie J. Swift

Michigan Probate Court

April 18, 2013

On behalf of Amanda Bailey

Dear Ms. Swift,

First , I want to explain to you why five out of seven of Amanda's siblings object to Raven as her guardian, yet no one managed to file a formal objection to the court.

Raven kind of swooped in while Dad was on his deathbed, and was first to file the motion for guardianship. Of course none of us were home to get the written notice, so by the time we found out, we were in the throes of grief and funeral arrangements. Theil did attempt to file guardianship upon his arrival in Michigan but Raven had already filed. I took three letters to the court from sibs to try to file an objection but found out that there was a format to follow. By then it was too late and our 5 day window closed.

I am Amanda's "blood sister", arguably her favorite sibling, and I was arguably Dad's favorite also. This has led to a lot of expressed jealousy and even hostility from my other sisters over the years. There is an almost unbelievable amount of dysfunction in this family.

Of all her siblings, I have spent the most time with Amanda. I myself would gladly make a bid for Amanda's guardianship, were Theil not available. My financial status is not stable right now. I am recovering from a publishing deal gone awry, which cost me my life savings and foreclosed my home.

I am 9 years older than Amanda and I basically raised her, since my mother was too depressed to do much after she was born. She was a humongous accident. She came along after Mom had surgery for sterilization, which the surgeon botched. Later, of course, we were glad that this happened because we could not imagine life without Amanda!

Raven left for college when Amanda was just turning 2 years old. Rose left two years later, but she did not take much active interest in Amanda. I changed Amanda's diapers and later walked her to school every morning. I came home to play with her after school. I spent hours teaching her to pronounce words and other small functions like tying her shoes.

Like the others, I eventually moved away to attend college. When I moved back to Michigan in 1989, we were still just as close. Amanda came to my home and spent time with me nearly every summer, sometimes for as long as six weeks. During this time I initiated an exercise program which employed behavior modification through positive reinforcement techniques. She lost weight and felt great. I took walks with her and encouraged her. It was not always easy, but we made it fun for each other. We would go to movies and out to eat.

I took care of her health issues. I took her to the podiatrist and the orthopedic doctor and the dentist's office and had her teeth cleaned. As is the wont of many people with Down's, she has a plethora of physical problems.

While at my house, she was responsible for daily chores, referring to a list that I had posted on my refrigerator. She had a personal hygiene regimen that was posted there also. She did well with this visual guideline. I would outfit her in a new wardrobe every fall. She is still wearing a lot of the clothes I gave her. I taught her to read, both by working with her and by acquiring a "Hooked on Phonics" program which I donated to her school.

I also spent a lot of time with her in her own home with Mom and Dad, as I would bring my horses up to Drummond Island every summer. I took her swimming, one of her favorite pastimes and the things she is best at. Amanda and I have a weekly, "Girl's Day Out" with trips to the Soo for movies and pizza. I initiated her current job at Goodwill through a meeting with Tom West at Hiawatha Community Health.

When my mom got sick during fall of 2010, I moved in with Dad and Amanda on a permanent basis. I lived with them (minus their winter trip to Washington for several months in 2011) until Dad started his radiation treatment in November 2012. In summer 2012 Raven took the prison job in the Soo and left her former position in Gladstone and moved in with us. Raven was working full time with an hour commute each way, and I was still Dad and Amanda's primary caretaker.

If you talk to Amanda, it won't take long for you to find out how close we are.

I have never asked for any monetary compensation for any time spent with Amanda, and until this past week (when I was given $300 from her SSI by the family's executor because I kept her in the motel with me for two weeks), I have never been compensated for any of it.

I have the unique perspective of having lived with both parties who are contending for guardianship. I lived with my brother Theil and his wife Katherine in Arizona years ago, and last summer I lived with Raven after she moved in with Dad and Amanda and me.

Here are the reasons why Theil is the best candidate for Amanda's guardianship.

- *He is smart, kind and fair to everyone.*

- *He is loaded with empathy.*

- *He is patient and doesn't lose his temper.*

- *He has a great sense of humor.*

- *He is financially stable.*

- *He will retire in a year's time and for now, Katherine his wife is home all day so Amanda would not have to be alone.*

- *Amanda gets along great with Katherine.*

- *After retirement, Theil will have a summer home on Drummond Island where Amanda can be back home and available to see relatives.*

- *In the winter, he will be in Mesa where Amanda can enjoy opportunities not available to her here, like participating in Special Olympics, as well as visit with relatives out West that she rarely gets to see.*

- *He will be generous with Amanda's time and allow her to visit siblings.*

- *He will respect Amanda's wishes and treat her like an adult.*

- *He will be conscientious with her health care and she will be covered by his insurance.*

- *He is interested in her emotional health, having already mentioned grief counseling to me.*

- *Theil was my Dad's choice to be Amanda's guardian.*

- *Theil is Amanda's choice to be Amanda's guardian.*

Here are the reasons why Raven is not a good candidate for Amanda's guardianship.

- *She abuses Amanda verbally and emotionally. (Using punishment and threats.)*

- *According to Amanda, she abuses her physically. (Snatching things out of her hands, stomping up to her aggressively.)*

- *There may be other safety issues with regard to Amanda's health, such as timely and appropriate medical care. Raven allowed my Dad's pneumonia to progress without adequate treatment. (See emails below.)*

- *Raven lives an hour from the hospital.*

- *Raven lives in an area (Raber) with no 911 service.*

- *Raven lives in an area where there are few resources for specialists (such as podiatrists) for Amanda's physical problems.*

- *Raven is very disrespectful to Amanda. She "talks down" to Amanda and treats her like a child. Often, if you ask Amanda a question, Raven will interrupt with the answer.*

- *She underestimates Amanda's ability to think for herself.*

- *She has no respect for Amanda's dignity or privacy, ie, asking in a room with mixed company, in a loud voice, "Amanda, did you get your period?"*

- *She will force Amanda to stay alone all day while she is at work.*

- *Communication is a major problem for Raven as she cannot be reached by phone during the day and she does not accept email at work.*

- *She will ration Amanda's time with siblings, if we get to see her at all.*

- *She is not as financially viable.*

- *When in her care, Amanda becomes depressed.*

- *Amanda requested counseling to help deal with her issues with Raven.*

- *Amanda emphatically does not want to live with her, even to the point of tears.*

- *It is not what Dad wanted.*

- *It is not what Amanda wants.*

Raven is very good at selling herself as a professional with her MSW. She will avoid questions and important issues with a lot of verbiage. But she is dragging Amanda through these painful legal proceedings, immediately following the death of her father. This is something that could have been handled with a signature. It shows no consideration for Amanda's wishes or respect for her period of intense grief. This tells me that Raven has a skewed vision of what is best for Amanda.

Raven took Dad home with her after his radiation, during what was supposed to be a weekend visit. She ended up just keeping him. His radiation had gone well and the oncologist had given him a two-year or longer prognosis. He had a strong will and desire to live. While at Raven's he developed pneumonia. As I was Dad's primary caretaker for the better part of two years, I was familiar with his medical history. I was not in a position to house Dad myself, or I would have. Despite my pleading, (I'm including some emails pertaining to this) Raven refused to take him to Petoskey (where his specialists were) and have him checked or admitted. Raven indicated that he was getting better, perhaps to get me off her back. But the pneumonia was allowed to progress while Dad and Amanda sat alone in that trailer all day. Within weeks, he was gone.

Please see emails. (You will probably notice the tone of my apprehension and frustration coming through):

Here, I injected the a batch of emails from February 13 through the beginning of March, wherein I begged Raven to get Dad some medical care for his illness. Then I added:

There are more emails. Despite our pleading, Raven waited three more weeks before taking Dad to the hospital. (At WMH in the Soo.) He died several days later, on March 30.

At this point, I hope you can see how alarming it is for me, to think of Raven becoming Amanda's guardian. On top of Raven's household's isolation and her communication issues, her very high opinion of her own abilities and education causes her to make poor decisions.

Amanda is not a child. She is very adept intellectually and socially. Here are a few examples of recent conversations I have had with her, so you have an idea of how she interacts. (And to lighten the subject!):

Me: Amanda, your eye is red. Does it hurt?

Amanda: No.

Me: Look that way. Look this way. Look up.

Amanda: It's okay.

Me: How many fingers am I holding up?

Amanda: Two. (Making the shape of an L on her forehead) How many fingers am *I* holding up?

And:

Amanda and I are driving. My dog, Til scoots up from the back seat, putting his head on her shoulder. She scratches him.

Amanda: Hi Til. You take after your mother.

Me: HEY!

Amanda: Well, would it be better if I said, "You got your mother's good looks"?

During the time of Dad's death I spent two weeks in a hotel and let Amanda stay with me, by her choice. I maintained the room until the court date because Amanda kept asking to stay with me. Now that Raven has been appointed temporary guardian, I have maintained the room so I can go to her house and pick up Amanda every day while Raven is at work. Amanda has never lived alone and I don't want her to have to be alone during this period of grief.

Amanda was nervous about today's meeting and asked me to be present. I could not get the meeting location and time from Raven, which is why I called you.

Amanda has a mind of her own and she knows exactly what is going on.

Thank you for helping our family during this painful phase. I hope the judge will make the obvious right decision and choose Theil. Amanda deserves to have a happy, safe, productive life and to preserve her magnificent spirit.

Respectfully,

Nancy J. Bailey

The next day I had an email from R2 asking how the meeting with the Guardian Ad Litem went.

"It went well. I had been concerned that the Guardian Ad Litem might be some kind of power-heady redneck Yooper (with, as Marcus put it, "a bunch of alphabet soup behind her name") but she seems pretty sane. So far so good."

Then I sent another note, with a copy to Marcus.

"Hello --

"I am checking out tomorrow since Amanda is going downstate to Rowena's. My total hotel bill is $1,030.40. This is their discounted weekly rate. Theil did pick up two nights of this, which left me at $940.80. Martyrdom isn't my thing, but the days are past where I sacrifice my ass for this family and say nothing. There may be some argument about whether this is a necessary expense, and considering Amanda's mental state (very depressed) plus the apparent lack of cheaper accommodations, it should be a given."

I still was livid about being kept out of the Lodge. Every time I paid my hotel bill, it felt like I was flushing money down the toilet.

R2 did answer this time, saying that was only half of her travel expenses, and that Theil was spending money too, and what did I want?

I wrote, "Actually all I want (besides to vent) is to fire up the trailer and go live there until Amanda is settled and I (hopefully) get my tour running. You guys all get to go home now. Amanda and I do not. We are both stuck in this wretched phase of grief and limbo. And I know Theil is going to be forced to spend a lot more before it's over. I am irreconcilably pissed at Raven, both for Dad's death and for this sequel she has now served up, and the drama she keeps dishing out every time I have to see her. I will never forgive her. There is a lot to vent about! Now I have a show in Virginia so at least I can get away from it... Sorta."

Bud and I were traveling the next day. Dad had been gone three weeks by that time. One evening that weekend, my cell phone lit up with the name, "Tina Bailey." I had talked to Tina only twice in the past ten years. She was my cousin Dave's wife, and they lived in Maine. Tina had missed Dad's funeral and I thought she must be calling to express condolences. I answered, "Hey, Tina! How are you? Nice to hear from you. It was good to see Dave at the funeral, but I missed you."

"Uh, well," she hesitated, seeming a little taken aback by my enthusiasm. I thought it must be because she wasn't expecting me to sound so happy. "My reasons for calling you are twofold."

"You don't need a reason!" I said. "Just call to say hi! Call anytime."

"Yeah, well, that's not surprising you would say that." Her tone was ugly. "Because you have a need to be needed, a need to use people, and a need to play your little games with people, but you don't fool me. If you're so stupid –"

"Whoa!" I said. "Just a minute! That's enough! Goodbye."

I hung up. With an introduction like that, I wasn't going to give her time to say more. I knew that she talked regularly with R3 and thought she was now acting as R3's microphone. People were different now that Dad was gone.

Tina called back immediately, but I didn't answer. She ranted into my voicemail, "Nancy, if you don't straighten this out, this is all gonna come down around you. There's a bunch of names for what Amanda has. But she is a child. And I'm hoping that if you keep pressing your sisters, and doing what you're doing with them, that they press charges against you."

"There's a bunch of names for what you are, too," I muttered. She never got specific about how I was "pressing" my sisters or what I was supposedly doing.

The voicemail went on. "Well, maybe we'll turn the internet around on you! And we'll put out there what you've done as far as being a sibling."

Sure enough, it wasn't long before I was alerted to the ways in which I was accused of "pressing" my sisters. A friend forwarded me a long email from R3. It said that I had racked up a huge hotel room bill, then "dashed out on it without paying it these past 3 weeks." R3 went on to accuse me of stealing money from Amanda's account, stealing Mom's oil paintings, jewelry box, and the flag that covered Dad's coffin. Then she said, "But by God, she makes sure she feeds her dogs!"

She added that I took Amanda out to, "ply her with liquor" and, despite Amanda's bad knees and other physical problems, I still "take chances with getting her drunk."

The letter was good for a laugh. I thought it was interesting that she was accusing me of stealing things from the house. But I was stumped as to why she would be spreading rumors that I hadn't paid my hotel bill. That made no sense, because I was still staying there. Furthermore, even if I ever had done such a thing, how would she know about it? It just seemed like an accusation made up by someone who couldn't come up with anything better.

It was no secret that I still had Dad's flag. Amanda had asked me to keep it safe for her, until her court date on May 21st. R1 had asked for it several times, but I had politely declined. The flag was so important to Amanda, and I was worried it would go the way of Mom's opal ring, her paintings and other treasured items.

After reading the email from R3, I sat in the hotel room thinking it over. When someone has to make up lies to further their weird agenda, doesn't that tell them that something is inherently wrong with the agenda?

I have never really understood liars.

Is the idea to lash out at someone, no matter what? And if there isn't any real ammunition, then you have to make it up?

And why so much hatred to begin with?

The most telling part of her email, I thought, was when she said, "Nancy has made it sound as though Amanda has capabilities that reach far beyond what they truly are."

All I really wanted was for Amanda to be allowed to speak for herself.

Bud overstepped his boundaries too, that weekend. He got drunk as usual, but then made the mistake of slurring, "You're a retard, just like your sister."

"Thank you," I said. "You just lost a trainer."

I was whacking people out of my life left and right, I thought wryly. I was becoming an expert at it. I thought of one of my favorite TV characters, Samantha Jones on "Sex and the City," who once said, "You can't swing a Fendi bag without knocking over five losers."

I was well rid of them, I knew. I really was getting a cold heart. I wondered though, when it all was over, how I was going to keep from being too angry and bitter. I decided I would worry about that later. I was focused on the business at hand, which was to do everything in my power to make sure Amanda was safe and happy. I learned that Theil's lawyer, Casey Fountain, had an office in Lansing and I decided to request a meeting with her while I was still downstate.

"I just think it would be good if she met one of us in person," I told Theil.

"Keep it brief," he said. "She's $150 an hour!"

When I walked into the little coffee shop, I noticed a beautiful dark haired woman sitting at a table by the window. She was wearing a dark blue business suit with a polka-dotted blouse. She looked up and said, "Are you Nancy? Hi!"

She shook my hand. I liked her immediately. She seemed warm and genuine. She sat down and opened up a folder with some paperwork. "I am so glad you called me because I have some questions."

She wanted a list of all family members, and the birth order, and where each stood in terms of Theil's guardianship. "Sorry about all the questions," she said.

"No, that's okay. I'm happy to help. It's just that Theil has asked me to keep it short. He has already spent so much money on all this, and now he has to get another plane ticket to fly back here again. It has been a very expensive endeavor for him."

"Oh I understand," she said. "I won't gouge him on this."

By the time we left the coffee shop, we were laughing and talking about families. She had been so artful about making me feel at ease. I thought Amanda would love her. I was able to travel back up North feeling good about our resources, through Valerie Swift, and now Casey.

Meanwhile, my position as co-signor on Dad's credit union account had ignited a whole new rumor that I was siphoning money from it, and that it was being drained automatically to pay bills and depriving the family of their inheritance. I found this amusing, because Dad was always so broke. But R2 was in an uproar over it. With my focus on Amanda, I hadn't worried about it.

As soon as I went back up north, I met R1 to pick Amanda up after an appointment. We met in the Wendy's parking lot and R1 got out of the car and stood in front of the passenger door as if to block Amanda from getting out. She handed me her cell phone. "Here. Rose wants to talk to you."

I took the phone. "Hi. What's up?"

"Can you please go to the credit union and talk to them about Dad's account?" she wailed. "They won't give me any information because your name is on it."

"It's gonna close," I said. "By the time I get there it will be after five."

"Not if you hurry."

I sighed and looked at the clock. "Okay, I guess we will do our matinee tomorrow."

I was looking right at R1 when I said it. She just stared at me.

We hung up and R1 finally permitted Amanda to get out of the car. "See you later," I said cheerfully.

Amanda and I took the hour's drive, listening to our music and laughing.

"I hate driving fast when I'm this tired," I said. "My judgment is like the weather: A little cloudy."

"It's not THAT bad."

"Aw, thanks Manda!"

"I meant the weather," she said.

"Ha, ha, ha. Very funny."

I turned the music up. "Sister Golden Hair" was playing on a CD my friend Steve had made for me. Amanda said, "Nancy do you get it? Will you meet me in the middle." She pointed at me.

"Will you meet me in the end," she pointed to herself.

We were indeed the middle child and the "end" child. I smiled. "Brilliant!"

We pulled in to the Credit Union lot that overlooked the ferry dock. "Wait here. We can go over to Desi's afterward," I said.

Dori in the credit union informed me that as estate executor, in order to get account information, all R2 needed to do was submit a copy of the death certificate. I smiled and thanked her, and asked her to print me a copy of the account's activity. It showed the account was empty, and had been for some time. I kept a copy in case I needed to face any more accusations.

I held the door to the Mainsail open as Amanda crutched up the ramp and inside. I left her near my usual table and went into the restroom. When I came out, Amanda had bellied up to the bar and was surrounded by a half dozen locals. They were all laughing boisterously. "My family is crazy!" Amanda was saying, then she spotted me coming around the corner. "Oops. I guess I better go sit down now."

There was more raucous laughter from the group. "Nice!" I said, and followed her to the table.

We only had a couple of hours to hang out until R1 was supposed to meet us. But she was running late. Meanwhile, I bought

Amanda a late lunch and while I sat there with my computer, Desi came over and said, "Amanda, do you want a magazine to look at?"

"Yes, please," Amanda said.

Desi gave her a gossip rag so Amanda had some celebrities to catch up on, while I skimmed Facebook. "You can keep that," Desi said.

"Hey thanks!" Amanda said. She stood up.

"Where are you going?" I said.

"I'm going to the bathroom. And I'm not speaking to my guardianship. I'm going whether anyone likes it or not!"

As the afternoon waned, we sat together and Amanda gave me updates on the celebrities featured in her magazine, and showed me pictures of various people, and who they were dating, and who looked best in the same dress.

Two hours later, R1 finally arrived. "Okay Amanda, let's go."

As I unplugged my computer and wrapped up the cord, I watched while Amanda stood up. Her crutches were leaning against the wall. She fumbled with her coat while R1 stood in front of her, making no move to help her. I put my computer in its bag and put my own coat on, meanwhile watching as Amanda struggled with her box of leftovers, her magazine, and her crutches. R1 simply stood there with her hands hanging by her sides, looking on. Who in their right mind would do that? I was starting to wonder if R1 was developing a brain tumor or some other physical ailment. A lot of her actions – or inactions – just didn't seem normal to me. I couldn't stand watching Amanda struggle anymore.

"Here," I said to Amanda. "Give me that."

I carried her magazine, her lunch box and my gear, and held the door for her while she crutched outside. I put her items and her crutches in the back seat and helped her into the car. "See ya tomorrow, Blood Sister," I said.

The next day I was greeted by a thousand white blobs of petals as the trillium bloomed all around R1's trailer in the woods. There was a small cluster of daffodils near her front step. The hardwoods were covered in a bright green mist. There was nothing so beautiful as spring in the UP, I thought. Amanda and I drove to the Soo listening to our music. This time it was Michael Jackson and Paul McCartney, "The Girl is Mine."

"She's mine, mine, mine. Hey! That sounds like you and Raven," Amanda said.

"That's not funny!" I snapped. She chortled with glee.

When we came out of the theatre, the sun blasted through the front entrance, revealing a sky so deep I felt we could dissolve into it. The birds regaled us, cheering en masse from their budding heights. Even though it was mid-May, the air was still and smelled like snow.

"Let's take a drive down by the Locks," Amanda said.

"Okay."

We drove down the hill, through the aged brick-and-mortar town, past the corner bars and the fudge shops, down by where the ships pulled carefully in to the massive stalls known as the Soo Locks. Tulips bloomed along the walkways, bright splashes of color against the cement.

"Let's take a little walk," Amanda suggested.

"Okay."

I glanced at my cell phone. It was a little after 3. If she was getting off work on time, R1 would arrive at her trailer ahead of us. But Amanda still would be back in plenty of time for dinner. I pulled over and parked, helping Amanda out with her crutches. "I just didn't want to go back yet," Amanda confessed.

"I understand. It is such a beautiful day for a walk. Hey, I've got an idea. Grab one of those little flags I got you, and I will take your picture by the tulips!"

The flags were in a small packet, tucked inside Amanda's purse. I had spotted them at Wal-Mart and instantly thought of her. Portable patriotism.

Amanda obligingly crutched over by the flower bed. I took the crutches and leaned them against the fence, and aimed the camera. She posed with her little flag, smiling against the backdrop of bright colors.

"Perfect!"

We walked through the iron gates, into the park by the Locks. "Hey! Let's pose by that big anchor!" I set the camera up on a trash can, hitting the timer button. I ran over to Amanda and we stood together, waving our flags. "Great shot," I said.

I looked up and down the river in both directions. "No freighters today! Dang it! Go figure."

She was quiet, not her usual buoyant self. She was heading for the stairs of the viewing platform. "They have a ramp," I said. "Do you want to go up there?"

"No," she said. "I'm just looking at what this says."

She had stopped and was facing a square of concrete, an engraved plaque on the wall below the viewing deck. I stepped over and began to read aloud.

When I finished, I said, "Isn't that nice? They give money to the families of lost sailors."

"That is great," she said. We turned and walked along the fence line by the water's edge.

I nodded toward a grassy area where picnic tables were scattered. "We were here about this time last year. Remember I set up the camera and took our picture? I think we were right over there."

"Yes I do remember that!" She crutched along in silence for a moment, holding tightly to her little American flag. The young leaves above us moved softly as the Lake Superior wind touched them. Suddenly, Amanda added, "We are gonna be okay, Nancy."

I looked at her. Her eyes were down, concentrating on her steps. "Yes," I said. "We are."

The walk angled sharply and took us back to the gate near where the truck was parked. We followed it reluctantly and climbed back in.

"I wish I could come to your dog class on Saturday," she said as I started the engine. I would be teaching an obedience workshop at JD Kennels, a new business that had opened up in Cedarville. I was quickly becoming fast friends with Jane Doty, the proprietor.

"I know you'd like to be there. You can ask Raven. I would come and pick you up. But I am sure she has plans for you Saturday."

She looked out the window. The corners of her mouth turned down a little. There were tiny lines on her forehead, long and fine as hairs. It was hard to see her looking so sad. I was developing a new appreciation for people forced to share custody of their children. I thought it ironic that, even though I wasn't a parent, I was enduring this kind of separation, possibly the same type of pain. The difference, of course, was that Amanda was an adult. The law had stripped her of her freedom to make choices; even choices as simple as where to spend her Saturday.

"I don't know how you do it," I said. "I don't know where you find this strength."

"I don't think I am strong."

"Well, you are. You are so composed. You are so calm."

"But on the inside, I am not."

I knew it wasn't the weekend that was bothering her. It was the whole business. It was the idea that a mere sister, who should have been her peer, had complete control over her every moment. It was degrading. It was depressing. She had to be wishing that Dad would come back and set everything right. There had to be some way to make these next few days easier for her. I searched for something that would help. Suddenly, I knew the thing.

"Do you remember what I said to you, at the meeting following the hearing? When you started to cry, and I was hugging you, and I whispered something in your ear?"

"No, I don't remember what it was."

"I said to be brave. And you stopped crying. Do you know why I said that?"

"No."

"Do you remember the Special Olympics creed?"

"Oh, yes. Uhm... Let's see. 'Let me win. If I cannot win, let me be brave in the attempt.'"

"Yes. Do you remember the time I was waterskiing? And I had lost a ski and I was getting scared, floundering around in the deep? And you and Marcus were in the boat?"

"Oh, yeah!" She was laughing now, amused at the memory, so confident in her own swimming abilities. "You are really scared of deep water."

"That's right. I was starting to panic. And you called out, 'Be brave, Nancy, be brave in the attempt!'"

"Oh yeah. That's right."

"It really helped me! So, that's what I was thinking about when I whispered in your ear that day."

"Okay. But Special Olympics isn't the same. That's not what they meant."

"That's true. But it still works. Because there are all kinds of bravery."

She was silent for a bit, pondering this. Finally, she said, "Okay, I know what you mean. But I still don't want to go back there."

"I know you don't. But just think. Tomorrow is Saturday. On Sunday, Theil is flying in from Arizona." I knew R1 would keep Amanda to herself all weekend. The dog class wasn't going to happen for her. She needed something to look forward to. So I added, "On Monday, Theil will be here in Michigan and on Tuesday is court. It's supposed to rain on Monday. That could be our next movie day! We could see the new Star Trek movie."

"That would be good!" She brightened visibly. "Thanks for taking me to the Locks. You sure made my Memorial Day."

Memorial Day was still a week away. "I did?"

"Yes. Giving me the flags, and then reading that sign down by the Locks, about the lost sailors."

"Oh, yeah. That was a good Memorial Day thing." I hadn't thought about it. She was right, though. If she went with Theil, they would be flying out the Sunday preceding Memorial Day and she wouldn't be able to visit Mom's grave, or see any parades, hang Dad's flag out, or enjoy any of her other rituals. A simple walk by the Locks for me had been something much more significant for her. She was seizing the moment. She had been thinking of our Dad, our fallen Merchant Marine, and carrying her little flag in his honor.

"I'm glad I could help," I said.

"You still have Dad's flag, right?"

"Yes. It is in a safe place. But you can have it back now if you want it."

"No. You keep it until May 21st."

"Okay."

"I was just checking up on it."

"I see."

We drove on, along the road lined with misty green trees, through the woods spattered with clouds of white trillium. We pulled up in R1's driveway. Her car was parked there, long and black, like something a dour reverend might be driving when he shows up to deliver the worst kind of news. We got out of the car and I helped Amanda hobble slowly up the steps. I ran back to the car and got her coat. As I trotted back with her coat, R1 flung the door open.

"Hi!" I said, handing her the coat.

R1's face rumpled into an ugly scowl. "Nancy, I am gonna be straight with you."

"No. Don't be straight." Whatever this was about, I wasn't going to allow it within Amanda's earshot, especially with her fragile state of mind. Amanda put her head down and crutched through the open door past R1. I turned around and walked back to the car.

"Come back here!" R1 yelled.

I waved. "Have a nice weekend."

Nearly an hour later, as I headed back into the tenuous cell phone range of the Cedarville community, my voice mail chimed in. It was R1. "If you don't call me back within five minutes and tell me where you are with Amanda, I'm calling the sheriff!"

I hung up. She should have known we were out of range. Cell phones were useless throughout most of the Eastern U.P. I forgot about her threat as I pulled in at Jane's and proceeded to walk around her kennel, discussing our plans for Saturday's class. Later that night, my phone rang.

"Uhm, is this Nancy Bailey?"

"Yes."

"This is officer West from the Chippewa County Sheriff's Department."

I stifled a laugh. She had actually done it.

"Hi," I said.

"Are you in Sault Ste Marie?"

"No, right now I am closer to Cedarville."

A half hour from him. He hesitated.

"Can you pick a time to meet me, or if it's okay, can you discuss something with me over the phone?"

"Sure, we can do it right now."

"We had a call from your sister, uhm – "

"Raven."

Better known as R1.

"Yes. Raven. She said that apparently you had taken your other sister to the movies?"

"Yes."

"She said that you did this without her consent, and she is the guardian."

Temporary – God willing, knock wood, cross your fingers – temporary guardian.

"Okay."

"Well, I just called to get your side of the story. I did talk to your other sister, Amanda, who said- "

"You talked to Amanda?"

Great. Just great. The poor girl had obviously not suffered enough. I immediately started thinking of ways to help her deal with this new punishment. I decided that slapstick would be our best defense. Blood sisters at the movies. A felony. No, a Miss - Demeanor. De more movies we miss, demeanor we get. We were going to have a field day with this one.

"Yes," he said. "I talked to her. She said she looked forward to Girl's Day Out. She said that you went to the movies and took a walk down by the Soo Locks."

Fun at the Soo Locks – sue me!

"Yes."

"Well, you do understand that you need Raven's consent to take Amanda. I don't know if you could get proof, or whatnot. But she has the paperwork and you could go to jail."

"Oh yes, I understand."

Girl's Day Out turns to Girl's Day In – in the slammer, that is.

"Do you have anything to say?"

I sighed. Why bother? Was the whole thing even deserving of a response? It was ludicrous, but, to at least one person, this appeared like a rational course of action. Maybe the best thing to do was clarify it, for the record. "Yes. First of all, I want to apologize for you having to spend time on this trivial issue. I know there are other things you could be doing. Raven is lying. She thrives on drama. She absolutely knew I was picking Amanda up. I told her yesterday that we would be seeing the earlier matinee, because we missed yesterday's movie. I did it out of consideration for her work schedule. We have a court date pending on the 21st and she is getting panicky. I think she is angry because I was an hour late taking Amanda back and then I wouldn't stand on her porch and listen to her squall about it. Now, it's her word against mine, so she's decided to do a little chest-thumping."

"Okay," his half-distracted voice told me he was writing. "So you say she's a drama queen?"

I laughed. "Yeah, put that."

"Well, you know it is your word against hers." He was polite, and sounded completely unbiased. I could tell he was young. I thought an older cop would have said something like, "Yeah, I agree it's crazy, but just cut me a break and play along."

"And Amanda has no say in the matter?" I asked.

"No, none whatsoever."

"Interesting."

"So unless you have some documentation, or whatnot, proving that you have Raven's consent to take Amanda, if it happens again, you could go to jail. Do you understand this?"

"Oh, yes, I understand very well."

Hit the Soo Locks, then throw away the key.

I thanked him and hung up. It immediately occurred to me that, in a normal community, this wouldn't help R1's case at all. She had been acting more and more irrationally, I thought. I remembered an email I had sent to Theil, complaining about her texting me during a movie with Amanda.

"I texted Raven and told her Amanda and I were running late and could not meet until after 6. Right at 6 (we were still in the movies) I started getting texts from her. She was done with her errands. She wanted her right now. I answered that the movie would end in about 15. She kept texting! She was hungry. She was still at Polly's and needed her right away. Etc. Anyway we watched the rest of the movie. Finally just as we were arriving at Polly's I got another text that she was coming to the cinema to get her. We drove in just as Raven was pulling out. She packed Amanda into that car and took off. She was in a huff!" Then I added, "Amanda is very depressed and just does not want to go back with Raven. I am stymied how to help her other than just keep getting her out of there as much as I can."

Theil replied, "You need to comply with Raven's directions. She is the temporary guardian. Be patient. There is a light at the end of the tunnel."

"Yes but it was 15 minutes before the end of the movie! Did she seriously expect us to walk out on it? That is crazy talk."

I was starting to think that maybe Raven needed to be on some kind of prescription medication. Poor Amanda! I knew that strange things could happen in a courtroom. I didn't have a lot of faith in this judge, based on what I had already seen. I could only hope that what was glaringly obvious to me – that being in this person's control was very unhealthy for Amanda – would be obvious to Judge Temple.

First thing Monday morning, the day she could talk freely, I had a voicemail from Amanda. "Hey Nancy what's up? I just wanna find out how you're doing this morning. I missed you the other day. You know why, the other day, because Raven's been calling the cops! And I was scared. And she approached them in the house. They asked me the questions. I wondered why they asked me the questions about you, Nancy. Ugh. I can't handle this. I was scared. So I hope you get my message. This is your baby sister. I hope you call back soon. Bye."

My reaction to this phone call was pure, unadulterated rage. I thought I could feel blood swelling up in my ears. It was as if R1 was now inventing ways to further traumatize Amanda. I realized her actions were due to her own agenda. But the fact that she had no inclination to put her weird impulses aside at a time like this, even for Amanda's sake, infuriated me. I had decided to treat the situation with humor, but Amanda didn't have a full understanding of why the police were involved. Apparently no one had bothered to explain it to her. And really, it defied reason. It was no wonder she was confused.

The first thing I did was forward her voicemail to Theil, thinking he may need it to help his case. Once I had calmed down enough to where I could make light of the situation, I called her back. "Hello? Amanda? It's me, your blood sister. I'm in the klink. They gave me one phone call. Can you come and bail me out?"

"Oh, very funny!" she said. But she was starting to laugh.

"Can you believe she called the cops because we went to the movies?"

"I can't believe it!"

"Was the cop at least a good looking guy?"

"Oh yes."

"Hot cops! Okay, that's good. Was he nice to you?"

"Yes. He was very nice. He said his wife has horses."

"Oh, you told him about Clifford?"

"Yes, I did. I told him my sister was an author, and artist, and trains animals, and does dog shows."

"Nice! Thank you!"

"You're welcome!"

"Well, you know why she called them, right? Did they explain it?"

"I think so. But I still don't get it."

"Actually it doesn't make much sense to me, either. But what happened was, Raven got mad for whatever reason. Who knows. Maybe because we stayed out too long. And then I didn't call her back, because we were out of signal range when she called."

"I see."

"So she called the cops and told them that I didn't have permission to take you to the movies. Because she has a court order stating that she is your guardian – "

"Temporary guardian," she corrected me.

"Yes. She showed them the court order saying she is your temporary guardian. So she has the legal right to keep you from going to the movies. If she claims she didn't give permission, the cops could take me to jail."

"They could?"

"Yes. It's not their fault. They are just doing their job. But they have to do what the court orders."

"I see."

"Yes. When I picked you up at Wendy's on Thursday, I told Raven we would see the earlier matinee on Friday. So she knew we were going to the movies."

"Yes, I remember that! Nancy. Do you know what she said to me? She said, 'I forbid you to go to the movies!'" Amanda's tone was angry. She was practically spitting the words.

"She did?"

"Yes! 'I forbid you!' she said! How can she forbid me, Nancy?"

"I do agree that is pretty extreme. It's a good thing we will be in court tomorrow. We need to get this straightened out."

"Yes we do!"

"Here's what I think you should do. When you get a chance to speak to the judge tomorrow, ask to talk to her in private."

"Ask to speak with Betty?"

"Yes. But you can't call her that. It's considered disrespectful. You have to call her, 'Judge' or 'Your Honor'."

"Oh, okay."

"And I think you should have a private meeting with her so you can speak your mind, just like you did with Valerie, remember?"

"Oh yeah."

"So, go in by yourself. No Theil, no Raven, no Brandon. No Nancy."

"No Casey?"

She had rattled off the name of Theil's lawyer even though they had never met. I wished I were as good with names. "Nope, no Casey, either. Just you and the judge. Then you will be less nervous, and you won't have to worry about hurting anyone's feelings, and you can speak your mind about what you want."

"That's good advice."

"Now I need to talk to you about today. "

"Okay."

"I know we said today was going to be Girl's Day Out. But I think we should wait."

"Oh." Her tone was disappointed. I hated to let her down. But I was thinking R1 would love nothing better than to put me in jail overnight, so that I couldn't attend tomorrow's hearing. I couldn't risk missing the hearing.

"Yep. I think today we will lay low, and celebrate with a movie after the hearing."

"Okay."

I thought she could use a little distraction to help her get through these last hours. Assigning her a task might help. "Today I want you to make some notes about what you think you should tell the judge. Try to get your thoughts organized so that you will be mentally prepared."

"Okay."

"Theil is in town now."

"He is?" Her tone brightened.

"Yes. I haven't seen him yet. But we will see him tomorrow. So get yourself ready and, as they say in the movies, I'll see you in court!"

That afternoon it stopped raining long enough for me to take the dogs to the beach. They ran madly along the water's edge, huffing with joy as the waves curled toward us. As I watched the sunlight flashing on the ragged grey surface of the great Lake Huron, I remembered Amanda's bald head popping up, and the splashing as she kicked. She had shouted to me from the sand bar, "It feels great!"

I thought how R1 had written of Amanda in her answer to Theil's objection. Her document, now filed with the court, described Amanda as, "a stubborn individual." It was peppered with assertions like, "She does not understand what is in her best interests due to limited cognitive function", and that she had a, "Poor scope of knowledge base or ability to perceive ulterior motivations in others," and, "Her cognitive function did not allow her to visualize living in Arizona."

Walking along the shore, watching the waves foam up toward me, I knew that if R1 were to become her permanent guardian, this type of limited thinking would prevent Amanda from ever fully achieving her potential. According to R1's document, my Dad had failed to provide Amanda with adequate health care, failed to supervise nutrition and hygiene, failed to provide a stable and safe environment for her, among other things. Even if the accusations were entirely true, which they weren't, Dad had given Amanda the best gift of all: The freedom to express herself, to sharpen her rapier wit, to visit with and relate to others and often go where she wished. He had listened when she spoke. He had allowed her to forge a true sense of self. The other things were just details.

"Well, done, Padre!" I called to the sky, thinking Amanda would approve of me speaking to him.

The dogs and I left our beach, and drove into DeTour to check my mailbox. I found a package from my friend Tori. I knew the package was a gift for Amanda, but Tori had addressed it to me to circumvent R1's interference. I opened it to find a book about Bon Jovi. Tori had been to a concert and knew that Amanda was a huge fan.

I decided I had better deliver it. There was still a good hour left before R1 came home. I stopped at the little town grocery, bought some Cola and chocolate, and took the twenty minute drive out to the woods. I walked up on the porch and knocked on the door, but heard nothing. I opened the door and yelled. "Amanda! Are you here?"

She answered me. "Yes!"

I walked in. She was nowhere in sight. "Well, what are you doing?"

"I just been napping."

She opened the bedroom door and moseyed out, smiling sleepily. She sat down and blinked at me. Sleep: Sanctuary for the depressed.

"I brought you something." I handed her the package. She opened it and pulled the book out, flipping it open and turning the pages.

"Oh my god! It's Bon Jovi!"

"Yes. It's from my friend Tori in Ohio. She went to a concert and she was thinking of you."

"Sweet! Thank you!"

"I also brought you this dark chocolate, to help calm your nerves. And I brought us a cola." I reached into the plastic grocery bag, pulling out a bottle of cola and handing it to her. She twisted off the top immediately and took a huge swig. Normally, unless it was Girl's Day Out, I didn't ply her with junk food. But I thought if anyone deserved the kind of comfort that only caffeine and sugar can offer, she did. She sat carefully holding her cola. There was some kind of orange stain all over her rumpled shirt front. Mustard? Her bald head was glowing in the soft light like a boiled egg, her crinkling eyes staring back at me. She smiled, and I realized that I was smiling. I cracked open my soda and held it up. "What do you want to toast to?"

"A new guardian."

"Hallelujah! I'll drink to that."

We clicked our bottles together and both took an enormous gulp.

Later that day I called Casey Fountain. I told her about the episode with the "Movie Police."

"Wow. Well, I'm glad you called because I wanted to ask if I can call you as a witness," she said.

"Absolutely."

"Our goal will be to make Theil look good. We don't necessarily want to make Raven look bad."

She sure doesn't need any help with that, I thought.

"I will have a few questions to ask you, and Brandon probably will too, and the judge may, and the most important thing is to keep your answers brief and succinct without getting too emotional."

"Okay. I can do that. Is the police report a factor in this? I mean, does that help us at all?"

"Oh, yes." She hesitated, stifling a chuckle. I could almost hear her shaking her head. "I hope it was a good movie."

I laughed. "Oh yes, it was the Great Gatsby. We both liked it. Leo DiCaprio... Amanda loves him."

"Ooh, I do too."

Our big day dawned. When I arrived at the courthouse, Marcus and Lily had just arrived and were heading up the sidewalk. When I caught up to them, they both greeted me with a smile and hug. What a relief. Life as it should be. As we approached the courthouse, we spotted R1 in her flat-footed gait, coming down the tree-lined walkway. She was wearing a big black jacket. With all she had put us through, and as despicable as I found her actions to be, I still felt nothing when I looked at her. No hatred. No revulsion. No love. My emotions were reserved for Amanda, toddling by her side, a vessel of goodwill, a capsule of hope. A curly brown wig perched crookedly on her head, spreading over her like a giant mushroom. She was looking at us and waving madly. She yelled, "Happy Birthday Marcus!"

"Thank you Amanda!" Marcus said. We all paused, smiling, waiting for them to catch up. Amanda and Marcus embraced enthusiastically. Our voices rose in happy greetings. For a moment, it felt like we were attending a family picnic. But then R1 stepped in front of Lily and me with her back to us. She was blocking us from Amanda, making herself into a big black wall. Lily simply circled around her and went to give Amanda a hug. I followed suit. As I was reaching for Amanda, R1 said, "Amanda come on. Amanda come on. We have to go. We're late. We have to get going. Amanda come on."

"All right!" Amanda hugged me and then started walking, and I fell in beside her.

"You know, I forgot all about this being Marc's birthday," I said. "I didn't even bring him a card! How embarrassing."

"Oh, that's all right," she said. "He-"

Just then, the black wall was planted straight in front of me, blocking my steps. R1 turned her head to address me over her shoulder. "Excuse me!" she snarled.

"Oh, sorry, was I actually talking to my sister? You'd better call the cops!" I patted Amanda on the back. "I'll see you inside."

I followed Marcus and Lily up the sprawling steps of the courthouse. Since Amanda had trouble with stairs, she and R1 proceeded around the corner to the ramp. Marcus turned to me. "I saw what just happened. And if they put me on the stand I am going to bring it up. That's ridiculous!"

I rolled my eyes. "Did you hear she called the police because we went to the movies? Gotta make use of those tax dollars."

The courtroom was ancient, with thick wooden doors and darkly polished window sills. Its floorboards cracked and squeaked, broadcasting every step. Despite the creaky high ceilings, it was large enough only for two rows of chairs where interested parties could see the proceedings. The chairs themselves were the folding office type, the kind known for becoming uncomfortable after sitting for short periods. It was a courtroom designed for the decisive action often required in the backwoods lifestyle. Drunk driving cases. Quickie divorces. Small claims.

Judge Temple strode in. Even though she was probably not much taller than Amanda, she exuded a take-charge air. Her footfalls stomped authoritatively across the groaning old courthouse boards. Her hair was a mass of dark curls. She looked like she could be at home in a pair of rubber wading boots, holding a dip net and scouting Albany Creek for smelt. Again it occurred to me that she seemed like someone who could be a friend to me. Not a tall, elegant shopping buddy like Casey. More like a hiking or drinking buddy.

"Is Brandon Farley here yet?" she asked.

"Not yet," her clerk replied.

She slammed back into her office. The minutes ticked by, torturously, while we waited in silence.

"Nancy, don't look so worried!" Theil whispered. He was leaning forward, looking across Casey at me. He smiled at me reassuringly. He was the picture of confidence. I wished I had his faith.

Amanda sat at the table next to R1, but she kept turning around to look back at the group of us. I knew that she had to be feeling anxious, but her expression was warm and affectionate. I imagined how we looked, her entourage of five, all lined up here to support her, hoping for the best.

The judge opened her office door again and looked at her clerk. "Mr. Farley here yet?"

The clerk shook her head.

"Okay, come on in here." The clerk jumped up and went into judge's office, carrying her clipboard. The judge looked at Amanda, her expression friendly. "I would like to talk to you for a minute."

"Okay," Amanda said pleasantly. She got up and wobbled into the office after the judge. The creaky wooden door slammed.

I drew a big sigh of relief. A private meeting, just as Amanda and I had talked about. No R1. No Brandon. Just Amanda, the judge, and the simple truth. Beautiful.

It wasn't long before gales of laughter erupted behind the door. I slapped my hand to my forehead. Dear God, not again. I hoped the judge was taking her seriously. Then, to make matters worse, Brandon Farley appeared, slightly rumpled-looking in his suit and tie. He tapped on the office door. It opened and he slipped inside. There was silence, then suddenly, more laughter boomed from behind the door. I perched on the edge of my seat, wringing my hands. Oh, Manda. We all love to laugh, but now, I feared, wasn't the time to be distracting the court with one-liners.

Suddenly the door flung open and Judge Temple strode out with a big grin. "Your sister is delightful," she said as she approached the bench.

I remembered Valerie, the Guardian Ad Litem, saying the same when she came out of her meeting with Amanda. It wasn't much of a comfort to at this point. Amanda hobbled out of the office behind her, followed by Brandon and the clerk. Amanda resumed her seat beside R1, but Brandon waved her over to a chair by the wall, next to where he was sitting. She got up and obliged him. When she was settled, the judge said, "This is to address the guardianship of Amanda Bailey, wherein there has been a petition filed to replace her original guardian, who was her father, Blaine Bailey. Raven had filed this petition, which now has an objection by Amanda's brother Theil. I see Amanda has a lot of family members here and I would like to know who's who. We'll start with you."

She pointed to me.

"I'm Amanda's sister, Nancy," I said.

The judge indicated Casey, who was sitting beside me. Casey spoke up. "I'm Theil's attorney, Casey Fountain."

"From Lansing, right?" Judge Temple said.

"Yes."

Next in line was Theil, then Marcus, then Lily. All alone in the row ahead of us was Amanda's Guardian Ad Litem, Valerie Swift.

"Okay, now that we know who's who, the first thing I want to address is foster care. Amanda, I don't want you to be concerned about this. Foster care is for people who don't have other alternatives. As you can see, there are lots of people here who care about you." She gestured to the lot of us against the back wall. I appreciated her attempt

331

to assuage Amanda's fears. But I knew, as Amanda did, that the fear of foster care wasn't the real problem. Marcus, Theil, Jon and I had already assured her that it would never happen. The issue was that someone had threatened her. No one seemed to understand that Amanda was offended more than frightened. She was aware that to threaten her in such a manner was abusive. The abuse, unfortunately, was now emblazoned in her personal history. The "foster home" threat would keep coming up forever. It was just like all those years ago when R3 had chased her with the bride dolls or called her, "fat ass". The deed was done, and Amanda would never forget it.

The judge went on, "I've read all the reports, including the reports from the Guardian Ad Litem. Amanda, I've been hearing about your wig collection. You probably have more wigs than Dolly Parton."

Amanda laughed. "Maybe!"

"With all due respect," R1 said. "All of her wigs, except for this one, are over fifteen years old."

"Well, your dad kept claiming wigs every year," the judge said, with a smile.

I smiled. Stick up for Padre. That's the way, Judge.

She added, "I have read your answer to the court, Raven, and I appreciate your position. But she's not a two year old."

At this point it was tough to resist doing a fist pump. Yes!

The judge continued. "I have reports from the other siblings and I had a nice letter from Rowena… Er… Rose? Who is in Colorado?

"Rose," R1 sniffed.

"Too many 'R's'," the judge laughed.

"You have no idea," I muttered under my breath.

"Rose gave a whole list of reasons why Theil or Raven would be a good choice as guardian, and why each would not be such a good choice."

"Why is this not a surprise?" my muttering voice said.

"Anyway, I am going to address the other siblings, the first being Nancy."

My muttering voice was startled into silence.

" You are not being considered for Amanda's guardianship. You are a wonderful sister to Amanda but your bookkeeping skills are inadequate. Fun is very important, but there are business matters to consider. Okay?"

I hadn't filed a petition to be Amanda's guardian. I said nothing. I just sat there looking at the judge. Bookkeeping was moot, since I had nothing to record; no savings to keep track of at this point. This day wasn't about me.

"You are a good friend to Amanda but you don't have the skills it takes to be a guardian. Okay?"

There was no way I was going to agree with this, so I said nothing. I had been a guardian to Amanda her entire life. This judge had never spent any time with us. What I was hearing was not the judge, but the voices of my siblings. With my current financial struggles, I had no expectations of being named her legal guardian. I was never in the running. But I was certain that the subject was coming up because Amanda had probably asked her to consider me as a backup. I understood why I was her choice. In the event of the demise of the primary guardian, an alternate guardian could immediately begin to make legal decisions on her behalf. This would have prevented a myriad of problems the first time around, and Amanda was trusting me to make those decisions. And now the judge was explaining to her why the answer was no. The explanation, however, seemed to be dragging on and on.

Even now she wasn't finished. "You're a free spirit!"

I think my shoulders sank a little.

"Stop looking so sad," she added. Despite my humiliation, I thought it was a good sign that she didn't want to hurt my feelings. Empathy was an essential quality, especially in a case like this. She said, "Amanda is very lucky to have a sister like you. Fun is very important. You have to be able to enjoy your life."

It wasn't Judge Temple's fault. She was going on information from siblings, and not one of them had endorsed me. Not one, except for Amanda. I glanced over at Amanda and she was smiling reassuringly at me, holding up her pinky finger and forefinger and thumb. "I love you," her hand said.

I immediately raised my hand to reciprocate, but I fumbled nervously and for a split second I accidentally flipped her off. Amanda apparently didn't see well enough to tell, because that for sure would have cracked her up. I looked up quickly, but the judge hadn't noticed either. That would have been contempt of court. Call the bailiff. I rearranged my fingers and got it right, and gave the, "I love you" sign back to Amanda. She grinned.

I thought these were the two issues Amanda must have raised in their meeting, because the judge then went on to say, "I have the reports here from Hiawatha Behavioral Health."

R1 piped up. "I took Amanda in for a meeting with them last week and here is the new report. Have you seen it yet?"

She handed it up to the judge.

"Thank you," Judge Temple took it.

"Those other reports are full of misinformation," R1 added.

I knew what the other reports were. They included the four visits Amanda and I had made to HBH the summer before, wherein Amanda was asking for help in coping with living with R1. Unfortunately for R1, she couldn't erase the past.

Judge Temple said, "I have made my decision based on information given me and I just want to tell Amanda that I understand you wanted to go to Arizona, right?"

335

My heart sank. I didn't like the use of the word, "wanted" in the past tense, but Amanda's response was calm and pleasant. "That's right."

"I am very sorry to tell you this, Raven, but my decision is to go with Theil as Amanda's guardian."

I could feel the air escaping me in a long hiss, like a popped tire. I hadn't realized I was holding my breath. All of us along the back wall visibly relaxed. R1 did not move. While the judge was speaking, Amanda's head flung back and her arms reached toward the ceiling in a gesture of pure elation. She mouthed the words, "Thank you! Thank you God!"

The judge continued, "This will be in place for one year, after which time it will be reassessed. The transfer will take place immediately. I am giving you the alternate guardianship, Raven."

At that moment, Marcus leaned forward in his seat and looked at me. Our eyes met in the same sentiment. Oh, God no.

Judge Temple continued, "Amanda, I know your life span may be shortened, and you want to travel. So have fun in Arizona! You should be able to enjoy your life. You should be happy. We never know how much time any of us have."

"Thank you!" Amanda said.

The judge stood up. "Theil and Raven, you two can meet in the office to discuss transferring Amanda's things. Good luck and safe travels, Amanda."

She marched out of the room.

Theil rose and followed the judge into the office. Casey immediately went after him. R1 hugged Amanda and said, "I have to go to work after this. I will see you later, okay?"

From her seat in front of me, Valerie Swift stood up, turning around to collect her coat and purse. She saw me watching and she winked.

"Valerie!" I whispered. "What does that mean? If Raven is the alternate guardian, does that give her any control over Amanda?"

"You can ask Theil's's lawyer," Valerie said. "But I don't think so. I think that is only if something happens to Theil."

"So if Theil gets hit by a bus, then what?"

"Well, then, someone would have to object and you get to do this all over again."

Oh, no. At least now we knew how to file the objection. I glanced up at R1. She walked out of the room into the office without looking at any of us. Amanda was glowing. She started toward us. "Happy Birthday Marcus!" she brayed. She grabbed Marcus and he scooped her up in a big hug. Lily was next.

Then, she saw me. She was crying now, elated tears puddling up in her eyes. The awful wig perched crookedly on her crown and I could see by the way the ringlets were bouncing that she was trembling. She yelled something, one syllable, unintelligible, as she approached me. She grabbed me around the neck, weeping, shuddering with joy, and said, "Now we can go to the movies!"

"Yes," I said, hugging her tightly. "Now we can go to the movies."

As Amanda and I left the courthouse and drove toward the cinema, I received a text message from Lily: "FYI the judge was rude and very insensitive toward you today. I found it very distasteful. Sorry you had to go through that. Celebrate with Amanda."

I was grateful for Lily's compassion. But I felt only gratitude toward the judge. She had handled the whole thing lightly, with humor, with no accusations, carefully skirting arguments and best of all, she had kept the session brief. She had addressed Amanda directly and with respect. She hadn't asked for any of us to take the stand or put Amanda through any added stress. I thought her performance that day had been exemplary.

We had a grand time that evening, with our movie and popcorn. Our relief was palpable. We were giddy.

After the movie, we took a last ride out to our bluff. "It's Marcus's birthday, and he's not here, but that's okay," I said. "And, we can celebrate your independence. That's another good reason for a bluff yell."

We got out of the car and I opened the trunk and pulled out Dad's flag, still folded in its immaculate triangle. I placed it carefully in Amanda's arms. We walked across the road to the edge of the hill and stood looking over the trees that were foggy with green buds, and the giant columns of steam rising over the Canadian Soo, and the evening sun dripping into the Great Lake, Superior.

Amanda held the flag up. "Hey Mom and Dad! I'm free!" she yelled. "I'm FREE!"

I looked on with a catch in my throat. "Thank you!" I whispered.

We drove back to our apartment and I found the box of Amanda's things that she had left in my care: Some of the clothes I had bought her, photos of us with Dad, and some extra tablets of writing paper. Later, Theil met us for the traditional pizza dinner.

"I have to go to Raven's tomorrow and get Amanda's things. Raven has specifically asked that you not come with us," he explained.

"No worries there!" I was sincerely hoping the court session would be one of the last times, if not the last, that I would ever have to see R1.

Thinking of her, I felt the old familiar tension mounting through the back of my neck. My anger had become a living thing, sprouting roots deep in my center and growing wildly, piercing my heart and lungs, branching into my veins and blooming through my hair and sending shoots through my fingertips. I could feel it coursing and pulsating, throbbing in my brain. It kept me awake at night and gobbled up my daily hours, ever insatiable, greedy and ruthless. I vaguely wondered if this was how R3 had felt her whole life. I didn't want to live like that. It was only through Jennifer's advice to, "get a cold heart," that I was able to tamp the rage down, smothering it, choking it out like a layer of smooth concrete that still developed

339

cracks and chinks and had to be constantly maintained. But I knew the root system was still there.

Amanda had never gotten a cold heart. She had remained eternally loving, almost divine in her gentleness.

"I just don't want to talk bad about her," she had said to me of R1, even in the midst of the personal disaster the woman was wreaking and all the pain she had caused. She loved R1 despite everything. She loved all her siblings, yet she was able to discern who was capable of truly loving her back. It was like that day in the woods when she had seen me hugging Trudy, and come outside to be closer to us. She had turned to Theil, not only because she felt it was her duty, but because she recognized him as the right choice. She had followed the love.

We spent that last night together in "our apartment." She sat on her bed throwing the ball for Til, bouncing it over and over off the wall. "Til is my part of my primary family," she said.

"Aw, that's sweet!" Then I hesitated. "Hey. Do you even know what 'primary' means?"

"No," she admitted. "It sounds good though."

"Well, what do you think it means?"

She thought for a moment. "Is it like, 'Rolling On the River'?"

I had to think about that one for a second. "Uhm, no. That would be 'Proud Mary'. Not 'Primary'."

"Oh."

"Primary is like your immediate family. Like your mother, father, sisters, brothers. But I think primary can also be someone who is very close to you. Primary can be Til or Este or Clifford, or Franklin or Polly. But Proud Mary is a boat."

Inevitably, we had to sing it while Amanda played her "air sax":

Big wheels keep on turnin'

Primary keep on burnin'

Rollin, rollin, rollin on the river!

We talked about Arizona, with its mountains and desert and cactus, and I said, "Hey, you know sometime we ought to go shout our ages off the Grand Canyon. Now that's a bluff!"

"Ooh, great idea!" she said.

She wanted to use Theil's hotel pool the next morning just before he checked out. I explained to the maid when we met her in the hall.

"We have a few minutes, but she really can use a swim," I said.

"Oh that's okay," she said. "I saw your husband was all dressed up yesterday in a suit and tie. He said it would impress his wife. That must be you!"

"No, that was my brother."

"Oh, sorry."

"It's okay," Amanda said, nodding toward me. "She could be my mother."

"Shut up!" I roared.

"YOU shut up!" Amanda said.

The maid laughed and walked away. We proceeded down the hallway toward the pool. As Amanda took her shoes off, I tossed three quarters into the water and watched them shimmy to the bottom. "How come you didn't come swimming the last time Theil was here?"

"Because I was too depressed."

I nodded. "I understand. It was very depressing. But now! Well actually, I'm jealous of you. Arizona! You're getting a whole new life! You're going to have a LIFE! How great is that? I wish I had a LIFE!"

Amanda smiled up at me. "You can share mine."

Later, when we were packing up to head for Drummond Island one last time, she seemed a little nonplussed. I asked her what was wrong, and she said, "How am I going to tell these people I am leaving? How am I going to say goodbye?"

I sighed. Here again, she was thinking of others. She had such an excellent perspective on how much she was loved.

"Well, let's see," I said. "You can tell them that it's not forever, and you'll be back. And that you will see them later."

As Theil and I took her to the home of each relative, I heard her follow my suggestions to the letter. She hugged Franklin tightly, saying, "It's not forever, Franklin. I will be back soon."

She did the same thing with Aunt Sue, and Brandon Farley. "Thank you for everything, Brandon. I will see you soon. I'm leaving now, but it's not forever."

As she repeated the phrase, I realized that it was becoming her mantra.

I followed Theil's car to the parking lot of DeTour's little grocery store, where we were finally parting ways. I was going back to Dad's house to finish packing out whatever remnants of my possessions I could still find there. Theil was heading downstate to Marcus's, and then the airport next day.

I pulled into the parking lot at Sune's market and climbed out of the car. Amanda got out of Theil's rental car and toddled over to me. She was smiling bravely. I hoped my own smile was disguising the terrible wrenching twist in the middle of my chest. We stood face to face for a moment. She reached up, standing on her toes, and pressed her nose against mine. She wrapped her arms around my neck, and I heard her say the words. "It's not forever, Nancy. It's not forever."

She got into the car and I watched as they pulled away. She kept her face turned toward me, her countenance beaming, her pudgy hand raised in a salute, acknowledging her new adventure. I held my hand up, pointing my forefinger and pinky at the sky. "I love you," the gesture said. As I watched them drive off, her fingers were pressed firmly against the glass.

343

She was gone. Gone with her, this time, was the customary worry that I felt when she was away from me. Now there was only an aching emptiness.

I drove back to Dad's house, walked past the realtor's sign near the front door, and confronted the mess. There was no sign of anyone. The walls were stripped bare, the rooms laid waste with only magazines and a few cardboard boxes left.

Normally, I thought, I would have been invited along to Marcus's. But there was bad blood between us now. Marcus admitted that he had convinced Dad to sign the deed to the Drummond lot over by claiming he may need to liquidate it to pay for Dad's health care, or Amanda's.

"Why would he need to sell it for that?" I screeched. "He's been all over the boards with health care for two years and his insurance covers everything!"

"I am going to haul the trailer off the land and build a cabin," Marcus said.

"How convenient!" I snapped. "Do you know what this looks like? It looks like you grifted a sick old man into turning over property he intended for two daughters: One disabled, and one homeless!"

"Give me the name of one person who is saying that!" he snapped.

"No one has to say it. It's obvious. You are letting your greed go to your head."

"I deserve this! I helped Dad out of more pickles and jams than you can imagine," he said.

"As did I. But that's not the point. Look," I said. "Dad named you executor. He signed it over to you with instructions to do with it as he had planned. He trusted you."

"Yes, he did trust me," he said. "That's why he gave it to me."

"So three lots on the Drummond shoreline, and two homes downstate are not enough for you? You have to take mine?"

"Your perception is your reality," he said.

"I should have seen this coming last year when you guys put me out in the street."

"You put yourself in the street." Then he added, "You know, you are the cause of all the problems in this family."

"Oh, I'm the cause?"

"Yes. You."

"You are starting to sound more like an R than a P," I said.

We said a lot of other things that day, none of them nice things, and none of them helpful. I was sick over the idea of never bringing my horses back to the one remaining place my little family of animals knew as home. I couldn't bear the thought of losing this part of myself, this part of my Dad.

"Dad meant this property for you and me, Nancy," Amanda had said earlier that day. We were inside the Lodge looking through some of her things, making last minute decisions on what she would take.

"I know," I said. "But we will give Marcus a chance. Maybe he will do the right thing."

Not holding my breath, I thought bitterly. I was long conditioned to hateful behavior from the R's. I thought nothing they could do would surprise me. But this was, as they say, "The most unkindest cut of all."

I decided to think about something else.

I walked down the hallway of the crooked little house. On the bathroom floor, beneath a pile of plastic bags, paper and other trash, I found Trudy's good English saddle. I carefully picked it up, dusted it off and set it upright. Despite the mistreatment, I was glad at least it was still here. So many of my possessions had gone missing: Clifford's silver bridle and breast collar set. His purple lunge line and cross ties. My favorite knee-high suede boots. My best sandals and dress shoes. My wool coat. All my favorite T-shirts, with Kramer, Zukey Lake Tavern, and others. Nearly everything of mine that was expensive or hip was gone.

I stood by the cupboards Dad had fashioned, now hanging precariously from so many years of overload. I walked into his bedroom, looking through the window at Mom's hollyhocks, bright pink splashes of color waving cheerfully at me by the stone wall. I looked around at the piles of boxes, marked, "Inventory." I realized that there were things I would never see again, things that were meaningful only to me, now probably disposed of: A pencil portrait of Dad that I had drawn on a block of wood when I was seven or eight. Dad had loved to bring it out on occasion and laughingly show it around. I had depicted him with his crooked mouth and strong jaw and eternal upsweep of hair. I didn't know where he had kept the little wooden block. I never went through his things. I knew I would never see these items I had given him, which he had treasured over the years: The sweatshirts with my paintings of Lewis, his dog, and the old Clifford wall calendar from 2007, which he had left on the wall for the rest of his life because he loved the photo.

I realized it would do me no good to pine for these things. It would do me even less good to ask for them back. I had to let them go. But I had the assurance that Dad would live on in my heart forever. I would carry him with me always, and I didn't need objects to remind me of anything. I would think of his wry grin, his big laugh, his pausing to listen when I spoke, his every indication that proved to me that I mattered. My name had been safe in his mouth. No one could ever take that away. Thanks to Dad and Amanda, I knew what real love was.

I also understood now that just because someone was related to me, it didn't mean they loved me or that they even knew how to love. It didn't mean that they had to be part of my life. I realized that Amanda had completely forgiven the R's for their transgressions against her. But forgiveness didn't mean forgetting, or opening oneself up to more abuse or betrayal. It meant freedom from anger. It meant moving on.

The house felt very lonely. It seemed odd that no one here needed me anymore. I had become estranged from all my local siblings, and some other relatives. I was left with no home, no family to walk forward with, no one to mourn with or commiserate with.

Yet I was not alone. Through my head echoed the voices of my friends; Claire, Cindy, Steve and Myrri. "Are you okay? Do you need support right now? We can drive up there. Come and stay with us. There is always a place for you here. Bring your dogs. We miss them! This can be your home base."

These, I realized, were my, "Proud Marys", letting me know that there was a place for me when I was ready.

I knew what Amanda would do.

I walked through the doorway into the living room. On the floor in the corner was a pile of my old sketchbooks. Beneath the pile was a journal with a pink and black striped cover. I recognized it as the one Amanda had taken on our trip to Paradise. I opened it up and read the words, in Amanda's angular, precise cursive handwriting:

"I do the sad moments just for me, but you can do happiness for yourself. I don't want to be sad. How can I sleep that way? How am I supposed to enjoy myself? Tell me how to be happy and proud."

I turned the page.

"I know it's not black or white. Don't let anyone get to you. Treat people the way you want to be treated. I know it is going to be super."

Other Books by Nancy J. Bailey

Clifford of Drummond Island

Return to Manitou

Clifford's Bay

My Best Cat – a Furry Murder Mystery

Holding the Ladder

The Sleeping Lion

25 Ways to Raise a Great Puppy

15 Rules for Clicker Training Your Horse

15 Rules for Clicker Training Your Dog

Made in the USA
Middletown, DE
02 February 2015